BEST HORSE STORIES

First published 1991 by Michael O'Mara Books Limited

This edition published 1992 by
PAN BOOKS LIMITED
a division of Pan Macmillan Publishers Limited
Cavaye Place London SW10 9PG
and Basingstoke
in association with Michael O'Mara Books

Associated companies throughout the world

ISBN 0-330-32375-X

1 3 5 7 9 8 6 4 2

A CIP catalogue record for this book is available from the British Library

Typeset by Florencetype Limited, Kewstoke, Avon
Printed in England by Clays Ltd, St Ives plc

BEST HORSE STORIES

INTRODUCTION BY
JOHN FRANCOME MBE

COMPILED BY
LESLEY O'MARA

PAN BOOKS
in association with
MICHAEL O'MARA BOOKS

ACKNOWLEDGEMENTS

All possible care has been taken to make full acknowledgement in every case where material is still in copyright. If errors have occurred, they will be corrected in subsequent editions if notification is sent to the publisher. Grateful acknowledgement is made for permission to reprint the following:

'The Gymkhana' from *National Velvet* by Enid Bagnold, reproduced by permission of William Heinemann Ltd and the Comtesse d'Harcourt.

'Sugar for the Horse' from *Sugar for the Horse* by H. E. Bates, reproduced by permission of the Estate of H. E. Bates.

'My First Wild Horse' from *Talking to Animals* by Barbara Woodhouse, reproduced by permission of Dr M. C. Woodhouse.

'An Expensive Operation' from *All Things Bright and Beautiful* by James Herriot, reproduced by permission of David Higham Associates Ltd and St Martin's Press, Inc., New York, NY. Copyright © 1974 by James Herriot.

'The 500 Mile Race from Deadwood to Omaha' from *Mavericks* by Jack Schaefer (André Deutsch Ltd, 1967). Reproduced by permission of André Deutsch Ltd and Don Congdon Associates, Inc. Copyright © 1967 by Jack Schaefer.

'The Horse Show' from *Country Matters* by Clare Leighton, reproduced by permission of David Roland Leighton.

'First Money' from *The Drifting Cowboy* by Will James, reprinted by permission of Auguste Dufault.

'Philippa's Fox-Hunt' from *Some Experiences of an Irish R.M.* by E. Somerville and Martin Ross, reproduced by permission of the Macdonald Group.

'Lost in the Moors' by Diana Pullein Thompson, reproduced by permission of the author.

'Ballinasloe Buys and Point-to-Points' from *Breakfast the Night Before* by Marjorie Quarton (André Deutsch Ltd, 1989), reproduced by permission of André Deutsch Ltd.

Illustrations

p. 185 by Gustave Doré, courtesy Mary Evans Picture Library; pp. 37, 103, 112, 205 and 228 © 1991 by William Geldart; pp. 29, 208, 219, 235, 238, 244 and 251 by Lucy Kemp-Welch from a limited edition, courtesy Susan Miles; pp. 130, 133, 136 by Clare Leighton, by kind permission of David Roland Leighton; pp. 89, 92, 143, 193 by Michael Lyne; p. 79 by Joan Martin May; p. 15 by Stuart Tresilian; pp. 60, 146 by Cecil G. Trew.

Contents

Introduction

JOHN FRANCOME MBE

You can take a horse to water but you can't make him drink' is a saying which only tells half the story, because, as anyone who has had anything to do with horses knows, if they don't want to go, you won't even get them to the water.

From the time that I used to walk my first pony up two scaffold planks into the back of my father's transit van to take him hunting, to the time last summer when I had a thoroughbred yearling who would simply lie down whenever it didn't want to do something, horses have never ceased to amaze and amuse me. They can surprise you with their intelligence within moments of being unbelievably stupid, and astonish you with their strength as well as with their gentleness. To really understand them is something few people, including me, are able to do, and as such they have provided generations of authors with an ideal subject on which to loose their imaginations.

Fiction and fact rarely stray far from each other where horses are concerned, as Devon Loch's collapse at the end of the 1956 Grand National proved. I have seen people do just about everything with horses bar getting them to talk. Of all the horses I've been associated with my favourite is still a small black gelding called Osbaldeston, who was responsible for kick-starting my racing career but, more importantly, was an animal of immense character. Peter 'Jumbo' Heaney looked after him while he was at Fred Winter's, and he is still the only horse I have ever known to be actually stable-trained. Apart from getting him to do all his droppings in one corner of his stable, he also trained him to use a bucket like a bed-pan. Even when in full training Jumbo could still leave him loose to pick

grass on the small lawn beside the hostel while he carried on
with his stable duties. He was a truly amazing horse.

This book contains all of my most favourite horse stories,
taken from all branches of the horse world. My own particular
favourite is 'A Stranger to the Wild' by Charles G.D. Roberts,
but whichever type of horse appeals to you most, you will find
a story here to relish.

This is just the sort of book to curl up with by the fire on a
winter's afternoon. I hope you enjoy it as much as I did.

A Stranger to the Wild

CHARLES G. D. ROBERTS

A S THE VESSEL, a big three-masted schooner, struck again and lurched forward, grinding heavily, she cleared the reef by somewhat more than half her length. Then her back broke. The massive swells, pounding upon her from the rear, overwhelmed her stern and crushed it down inescapably upon the rock; and her forward half, hanging in ten fathoms, began to settle sickeningly into the loud hiss and chaos. Around the reef, around the doomed schooner, the lead-coloured fog hung thick, impenetrable at half a ship's length. Her crew, cool, swift, ready,—they were Gaspé and New Brunswick fishermen, for the most part,—kept grim silence, and took the sharp orders that came to them like gunshots through the din. The boats were cleared away forward, where the settling of the bow gave some poor shelter.

At this moment the fog lifted, vanishing swiftly like a breath from the face of a mirror. Straight ahead, not two miles away, loomed a high, black, menacing shore—black, scarred rock, with black woods along its crest and a sharp, white line of surf shuddering along its base. Between that shore and the shattered schooner lay many other reefs, whereon the swells boiled white and broke in dull thunder; but off to the southward was clear water, and safety for the boats. At a glance the captain recognized the land as a cape on the south coast of the Gaspé peninsula, so far from her course had the doomed schooner been driven. Five minutes more, and the loaded boats, hurled up from the seething caldron behind the reef, swung out triumphantly on a long, oil-dark swell, and gained the comparative safety of the open. Hardly had they done so when the broken bow of the schooner, with a final rending of timbers,

9

settled in what seemed like a sudden hurry, pitched nose downward into the smother, and sank with a huge, startling sigh. The rear half of the hull was left lodged upon the reef, a kind of gaping cavern, with the surf plunging over it in cataracts, and a mad mob of boxes, bales, and wine-casks tumbling out from its black depths.

Presently the torrent ceased. Then, in the yawning gloom, appeared the head and fore-quarters of a white horse, mane streaming, eyes starting with frantic terror at the terrific scene that met them. The vision sank back instantly into the darkness. A moment later a vast surge, mightier than any which had gone before, engulfed the reef. Its gigantic front lifted the remnant of the wreck half-way across the barrier, tipping it forward, and letting it down with a final shattering crash; and the white horse, hurled violently forth, sank deep into the tumult behind the reef.

The schooner which had fallen on such sudden doom among the St Lawrence reefs had sailed from Oporto with a cargo, chiefly wine, for Quebec. Driven far south of her course by a terrific north-easter roaring down from Labrador, she had run into a fog as the wind fell, and been swept to her fate in the grip of an unknown tide-drift. On board, as it chanced, travelling as an honoured passenger, was a finely bred, white Spanish stallion of Barb descent, who had been shipped to Canada by one of the heads of the great house of Robin, those fishing-princes of Gaspé. When the vessel struck, and it was seen that her fate was imminent and inevitable, the captain had loosed the beautiful stallion from his stall, that at the last he might at least have a chance to fight his own fight for life. And so it came about that, partly through his own agile alertness, partly by the singular favour of fortune, he had avoided getting his slim legs broken in the hideous upheaval and confusion of the wreck.

When the white stallion came to the surface, snorting with terror and blowing the salt from his wide nostrils, he struck out desperately, and soon cleared the turmoil of the breakers. Over the vast, smooth swells he swam easily, his graceful, high head out of water. But at first, in his bewilderment and panic, he swam straight seaward. In a few moments, however, as he saw that he seemed to be overcoming disaster very well, his wits returned, and the nerve of his breeding came to his aid.

Keeping on the crest of a roller, he surveyed the situation keenly, observed the land, and noted the maze of reefs that tore the leaden surges into tumult. Instead of heading directly shoreward, therefore,—for every boiling whiteness smote him with horror,—he shaped his course in on a long slant, where the way seemed clear.

Once well south of the loud herd of reefs, he swam straight inshore, until the raving and white convulsion of the surf along the base of the cliff again struck terror into his heart; and again he bore away southward, at a distance of about three hundred yards outside the breakers. Strong, tough-sinewed, and endowed with the unfailing wind of his far-off desert ancestors, he was not aware of any fatigue from his long swim. Presently, rounding a point of rock which thrust a low spur out into the surges, he came into a sheltered cove where there was no surf. The long waves rolled on past the point, while in the cove there was only a measured, moderate rise and fall of the grey water, like a quiet breathing, and only a gently back-wash fringed the black-stoned, weedy beach with foam. At the head of the cove a shallow stream, running down through a narrow valley, emptied itself between two little red sand-spits.

Close beside the stream the white stallion came ashore. As soon as his feet were quite clear of the uppermost fringe of foam, as soon as he stood on ground that was not only firm but dry, he shook himself violently, tossed his fine head with a whinny of exultation, and turned a long look of hate and defiance upon the element from which he had just made his escape. Then at a determined trot he set off up the valley, eager to leave all sight and sound of the sea as far as possible behind him.

Reared as he had been on the windy and arid plateau of Northern Spain, the wanderer was filled with great loneliness in these dark woods of fir and spruce. An occasional maple in its blaze of autumn scarlet, or a clump of white birch in shimmering, aerial gold, seen unexpectedly upon the heavy-shadowed green, startled him like a sudden noise. Nevertheless, strange though they were, they were trees, and so not altogether alien to his memory. And the brook, with its eddying pools and brawling, shallow cascades, that seemed to him a familiar, kindly thing. It was only the sea that he really feared and hated. So long as he was sure he was putting the huge surges and loud reefs farther and farther behind him, he felt a certain measure of content as he pushed onward deeper and deeper into the serried gloom and silence of the spruce woods. At last, coming to a little patch of brookside meadow where the grass kept short and sweet and green even at this late season, he stopped his flight, and fell to pasturing.

Late in the afternoon, the even grey mass of cloud which for days had veiled the sky thinned away and scattered, showing the clear blue of the north. The sun, near setting, sent long rays of cheerful light down the narrow valley, bringing out warm, golden bronzes in the massive, dull green of the fir and spruce and hemlock, and striking sharp flame on the surfaces of the smooth pools. Elated by the sudden brightness, the white stallion resumed his journey at a gallop, straight toward the sunset, his long mane and tail, now dry, streaming out on the light afternoon breeze that drew down between the hills. He kept on up the valley till the sun went down, and then, in the swiftly deepening twilight, came to a little grassy point backed by a steep rock. Here where the rippling of the water enclosed him on three sides, and the rock, with a thick mass of hemlocks surmounting it, shut him in the fourth, he felt more secure, less desolate, than when surrounded by the endless corridors of the forest; and close to the foot of the rock he lay down, facing the mysterious gloom of the trees across the stream.

Just as he was settling himself, a strange voice, hollow yet muffled, cried across the open space 'Hoo-hoo, hoo-hoo, woo-hoo-hoo!' and he bounded to his feet, every nerve on the alert. He had never in his life before heard the voice of the great horned owl, and his apprehensive wonder was excusable. Again and yet again came the hollow call out of the deep dark of the banked woods opposite. As he stood listening tensely, eyes and nostrils wide, a bat flitted past his ears, and he jumped half around, with a startled snort. The ominous sound, however, was not repeated, and in a couple of minutes he lay down again, still keeping watchful eyes upon the dark mass across the stream. Then, at last, a broad-winged bird, taking shape softly above the open, as noiseless as a gigantic moth, floated over him, and looked down upon him under his rock with round palely luminous eyes. By some quick intuition he knew that this visitor was the source of the mysterious call. It was only a bird, after all, and no great thing in comparison with the eagles of his own Pyrenean heights. His apprehensions vanished, and he settled himself to sleep.

Worn out with days and nights of strain and terror, the exile slept soundly. Soon, under the crisp autumn starlight, a red fox crept down circumspectly to hunt mice in the tangled dry grasses of the point. At sight of the strange white form sleeping carelessly at the foot of the rock he bounded back into cover, startled quite out of his philosophic composure. He had never before seen any such being as that; and the smell, too, was mysterious and hostile to his wrinkling fastidious nostrils. Having eyed the newcomer for some time from his hiding-place under the branches, he crept around the rock and surveyed him stealthily from the other side. Finding no enlightenment, or immediate prospect of it, he again drew back, and made a careful investigation of the stranger's tracks, which were quite unlike the tracks of any creature he knew. Finally he made up his mind that he must confine his hunting to the immediate neighbourhood, keeping the stranger under surveillance till he could find out more about him.

Soon after the fox's going a tuft-eared lynx came out on the top of the rock, and with round, bright, cruel eyes glared down upon the grassy point, half-hoping to see some rabbits playing there. Instead, she saw the dim white bulk of the sleeping stallion. In her astonishment at this unheard-of apparition, her eyes grew wider and whiter than before, her hair stood up along her back, her absurd little stub of a tail fluffed out to a fussy pompon, and she uttered a hasty, spitting growl as she drew back into the shelter of the hemlocks. In the dreaming ears of the sleeper this angry sound was only a growl of the seas which had for days been clamouring about the gloom of his stall on the ship. It disturbed him not at all.

At about two o'clock in the morning, at that mystic hour when Nature seems to send a message to all her animate children, preparing them for the advent of dawn, the white stallion got up, shook himself, stepped softly down to the brook's edge for a drink, and then fell to cropping the grass wherever it remained green. The forest, though to a careless

ear it might have seemed as silent as before, had in reality stirred to a sudden, ephemeral life. Far off, from some high rock, a she-fox barked sharply. Faint, muffled chirps from the thick bushes told of junkos and chickadees waking up to see if all was well with the world. The mice set up a scurrying in the grass. And presently a high-antlered buck stepped out of the shadows and started across the open toward the brook.

The dark buck, himself a moving shadow, saw the stallion first, and stopped with a loud snort of astonishment and defiance. The stallion wheeled about, eyed the intruder for a moment doubtfully, then trotted up with a whinny of pleased interrogation. He had no dread of the antlered visitor, but rather a hope of companionship in the vast and overpowering loneliness of the alien night.

The buck, however, was in anything but a friendly mood. His veins aflame with the arrogant pugnacity of the rutting season, he saw in the white stranger only a possible rival, and grew hot with rage at his approach. With an impatient stamping of his slim hoofs, he gave challenge. But to the stallion this was an unknown language. Innocently he came up, his nose stretched out in question, till he was within a few feet of the motionless buck. Then, to his astonishment, the latter bounced suddenly aside like a ball, stood straight up on his hind legs, and struck at him like lightning with those keen-edged, slim fore hoofs. It was a savage assault, and two long, red furrows— one longer and deeper than the other—appeared on the stallion's silky, white flank.

In that instant the wanderer's friendliness vanished, and an avenging fury took its place. His confidence had been cruelly betrayed. With a harsh squeal, his mouth wide open and lips drawn back from his formidable teeth, he sprang at his assailant. But the buck had no vain idea of standing up against this whirlwind of wrath which he had evoked. He bounded aside, lightly but hurriedly, and watched for an opportunity to repeat his attack.

The stallion, however, was not to be caught again; and the dashing ferocity of his rushes kept his adversary ceaselessly on the move, bounding into the air and leaping aside to avoid those disastrous teeth. The buck was awaiting what he felt sure would come, the chance to strike again; and his confidence in his own supreme agility kept him from any apprehension as to the outcome of the fight.

But the buck's great weakness lay in his ignorance, his insufficient knowledge of the game he was playing. He had no idea that his rushing white antagonist had any other tactics at command. When he gave way, therefore, he went just far enough to escape the stallion's teeth and battering fore feet. The stallion, on the other hand, soon realized the futility of his present method of attack against so nimble an adversary. On his next rush, therefore, just as the buck bounced aside, he wheeled in a short half-circle, and lashed out high and far with his steel-shod heels. The buck was just within the most deadly range of the blow. He caught the terrific impact on the base of the neck and the forward point of the shoulder, and went down as if an explosive bullet had struck him. Before he could even stir to rise, the stallion was upon him, trampling, battering, squealing, biting madly; and the fight was done. When the wanderer had spent his vengeance, and paused, snorting and wild-eyed, to take breath, he looked down upon a mangled shape that no longer struggled or stirred or even breathed. Then the last of his righteous fury faded out. The sight and smell of the blood sickened him, and in a kind of terror he turned away. For a few hesitating moments he stared about his little retreat and then, finding it had grown hateful to him, he forsook it, and pushed onward up the edge of the stream, between the black, impending walls of the forest.

About daybreak he came out on the flat, marshy shores of a shrunken lake, the unstirred waters of which gleamed violet and pale-gold beneath the twisting coils and drifting plumes of white vapour. All around the lake stood the grim, serried lines of the firs, under a sky of palpitating opal. The marshes, in their autumn colouring of burnt gold and pinky olive, with here and there a little patch of enduring emerald, caught the wanderer's fancy with a faint reminder of home. Here was pasture, here was sweet water, here was room to get away from the oppressive mystery of the woods. He halted to rest and recover himself; and in the clear, tonic air so cold that every morning the edges of the lake were crisped with ice, the aching red gashes on his flank speedily healed.

He had been at the lake about ten days, and was beginning

to grow restlessly impatient of the unchanging solitude, before anything new took place. A vividly conspicuous object in his gleaming whiteness as he roamed the marshes, pasturing or galloping up and down the shore with streaming mane and tail, he had been seen and watched and wondered at by all the wild kindreds who had their habitations in the woods about the lake. But they had all kept carefully out of his sight, regarding him with no less terror than wonder; and he imagined himself utterly alone, except for the fish-hawks, and the southward journeying ducks, which would drop with loud quacking and splashing into the shallows after sunset, and the owls, the sombre hooting of which disturbed him every night. Several times, too, from the extreme head of the lake he heard a discordant call, a great braying bellow, which puzzled him, and brought him instantly to his feet by a note of challenge in it; but the issuer of this hoarse defiance never revealed himself. Sometimes he heard a similar call, with a difference—a longer, less harshly blatant cry, the under note of which was one of appeal rather than of challenge. Over both he puzzled in vain; for the moose, bulls and cows alike, had no wish to try the qualities of the great white stranger who seemed to have usurped the lordship of the lake.

At last, one violet evening in the close of the sunset, as he stood fetlock-deep in the chill water, drinking, a light sound of many feet caught his alert ear. Lifting his head quickly, he saw a herd of strange-looking, heavy-antlered, whitish-brown deer emerging in long line from the woods and crossing the opening toward the foot of the lake. The leader of the caribou herd, a massive bull, nearly white, with antlers almost equal to those of a moose, returned the stallion's inquiring stare with a glance of mild curiosity, but did not halt an instant. It was plain that he considered his business urgent; for the caribou, as a rule, are nothing if not curious when confronted by any strange sight. But at present the whole herd, which journeyed, in the main, in single file, seemed to be in a kind of orderly haste. They turned questioning eyes upon the white stallion as they passed, then looked away indifferently, intent only upon following their leader on his quest. The stallion stood watching, his head high and his nostrils wide, till the very last of the herd had disappeared into the woods across the lake. Then the loneliness of his spacious pasture all at once quite overwhelmed him. He did not want the company of the caribou, by any means, or he might have followed them as they turned their backs toward the sunset; but it was the dwellings of men he wanted, the human hand on his mane, the provendered stall, the voice of kindly command, and the fellowship of his kindred of the uncleft hoof. In some way he had got it into his head that men might be found most readily by travelling toward the southwest. Toward the head of the lake, therefore, and just a little south of the sunset's deepest glow, he now took his way. He was done with the lake and the empty marshes.

From the head of the lake he followed up a narrow still-water for perhaps half a mile, crashing his way through a difficult tangle of fallen, rotting trunks and dense underbrush, till he came out upon another and much smaller lake, very different from the one he had just left. Here were no meadowy margins; but the shores were steep and thick-wooded to the water's edge. Diagonally thrust out across the outlet, and about a hundred yards above it, ran a low, bare spit of white sand, evidently covered at high water. Over the black line of the woods hung a yellow crescent moon, only a few nights old and near setting.

Coming suddenly from the difficult gloom of the woods, where the noise of his own movements kept his senses occupied to the exclusion of all else, the wanderer stopped and stood quite still for a long time under the shadow of a thick hemlock, investigating this new world with ear and eye and nostril. Presently, a few hundred yards around the lake shore, to his left, almost opposite the jutting sand-spit, arose a noisy crashing and thrashing of the bushes. As he listened in wonder, his ears erect and eagerly interrogative, the noise stopped, and again the intense silence settled down upon the forest. A minute or two later a big, high-shouldered, shambling, hornless creature came out upon the sand-spit, stood blackly silhouetted against the moonlight, stretched its ungainly neck, and sent across the water that harsh, bleating cry of appeal which he had been hearing night after night. It was the cow moose calling for her mate. And in almost instant answer arose again that great crashing among the underbrush on the opposite shore.

With a certain nervousness added to his curiosity, the white stallion listened as the crashing noise drew near. At the same time something in his blood began to tingle with the lust of combat. There was menace in the approaching sounds, and his courage arose to meet it. All at once, within about fifty yards of him, and just across the outlet, the noise ceased absolutely. For perhaps ten minutes there was not a sound,—not the snap of a twig or the splash of a ripple,—except that twice again came the call of the solitary cow standing out against the moon. Then, so suddenly that he gave an involuntary snort of amazement at the apparition, the wanderer grew aware of a tall, black bulk with enormous antlers which took shape among the undergrowth not ten paces distant.

The wanderer's mane rose along his arched neck, his lips drew back savagely over his great white teeth, fire flamed into his eyes, and for a score of seconds he stared into the wicked, little, gleaming eyes of the bull moose. He was eager for the fight, but waiting for the enemy to begin. Then, as noiselessly and miraculously as he had come, the great moose disappeared, simply fading into the darkness, and leaving the stallion all a-tremble with apprehension. For some minutes he peered anxiously into every black thicket within reach of his eyes, expecting a rushing assault from some unexpected quarter. Then, glancing out again across the lake, he saw that the cow had vanished from the moonlit point. Bewildered, and in the grasp of an inexplicable trepidation, he waded out into the lake belly-deep, skirted around the south shore, climbed the steep slope, and plunged straight into the dark of the woods. His impulse was to get away at once from the mysteries of that little, lonely lake.

The deep woods, of course, for him were just as lonely as the lake, for his heedless trampling and conspicuous colouring made a solitude all about him as he went. At last, however, he stumbled upon a trail. This he adopted gladly as his path, for it led away from the lake and in a direction which his whim had elected to follow.

Moving now on the deep turf, with little sound save the occasional swish of branches that brushed his flanks, he began to realize that the woods were not as empty as he had thought. On each side, in the soft dark, he heard little squeaks and rustlings and scurryings. Rabbits went bounding across the trail, just under his nose. Once a fox trotted ahead of him, looking back coolly at the great, white stranger. Once a small, stripe-backed animal passed leisurely before him, and a whiff of pungent smell annoyed his sensitive nose. Wide wings winnowed over him now and then, making him jump nervously; and once a pouncing sound, followed by a snarl, a squeal, and a scuffle, moved him to so keen an excitement that he swerved a few steps from the trail in his anxiety to see what it was all about. He failed to see anything, however, and after much stumbling was relieved to get back to the easy trail again. With all these unusual interests the miles and the hours seemed short to him; and when the grey of dawn came filtering down among the trees, he saw before him, a clearing with two low-roofed cabins in the middle of it. Wild with delight at this evidence of man's presence, he neighed shrilly, and tore up to the door of the nearest cabin at full gallop, his hoofs clattering on the old chips which strewed the open.

To his bitter disappointment, he found the cabin, which was simply an old lumber-camp, deserted. The door being ajar, he nosed it open and entered. The damp, cheerless interior, with no furnishing but a rusty stove, a long bench hewn from a log, and a tier of bunks along one side, disheartened him. The smell of human occupation still lingered about the bunks, but all else savoured of desertion and decay. With drooping head he emerged, and crossed over to the log stable. That horses had occupied it once, though not recently, was plain to him through various unmistakable signs; but it was more in the hope of sniffing the scent of his own kind than from any expectation of finding the stable occupied that he poked his nose in through the open doorway.

It was no scent of horses, however, which now greeted his startled nostrils. It was a scent quite unfamiliar to him, but one which, nevertheless, filled him with instinctive apprehension. At the first whiff of it he started back. Then, impelled by his curiosity, he again looked in, peering into the gloom. The next instant he was aware of a huge black shape leaping straight at him. Springing back with a loud snort, he wheeled like lightning and lashed out madly with his heels.

The bear caught the blow full in the ribs, and staggered

against the door-post with a loud, grunting cough, while the stallion trotted off some twenty yards across the chips and paused, wondering. The blow, in all probability, had broken several of the bear's ribs, but without greatly impairing his capacity for a fight; and now, in a blind rage, he rushed again upon the intruder who had dealt him so rude a buffet. The stallion, however, was in no fighting mood. Depressed as he was by the desolation of the cabin, and daunted by the mysterious character of this attack from the dark of the stable, he was now like a child frightened of ghosts. Not the bear alone, but the whole place, terrified him. Away he went at full gallop across the clearing, by good fortune struck the continuation of the loggers' road, and plunged onward into the shadowy forest.

For a couple of miles he ran, then he slowed down to a trot, and at last dropped into a leisurely walk. This trail was much broader and clearer than the one which had led him to the camp, and a short, sweet grass grew along it, so that he pastured comfortably without much loss of time. The spirit of his quest, however, was now so strong upon him that he would not rest after feeding. Mile after mile he pressed on, till the sun was high in the clear, blue heavens, and the shadows of the ancient firs were short and luminous. Then suddenly the woods broke away before him.

Far below he saw the blue sea sparkling. But it was not the beauty of the sea that held his eyes. From his very feet the road dropped down through open, half-cleared burnt lands, a stretch of rough pasture-fields, and a belt of sloping meadow, to a little white village clustering about an inlet. The clutter of roofs was homelike to his eyes, hungry with long loneliness; the little white church, with shining spire and cross, was very homelike. But nearer, in the very first pasture-field, just across the burnt land, was a sight that came yet nearer to his heart. There, in a corner of the crooked snake-fence, stood two bay mares and a foal, their heads over the fence as they gazed up the hill in his direction. Up went the mane and tail, and loud and long he neighed to them his greeting. Their answer was a whinny of welcome, and down across the fields he dashed at a wild gallop that took no heed of fences. When, a little later in the day, a swarthy French-Canadian farmer came up from the village to lead his mares down to water, he was bewildered with delight to find himself the apparent master of a splendid white stallion, which insisted on claiming him, nosing him joyously, and following at his heels like a dog.

Black Horses

LUIGI PIRANDELLO

No sooner had the head groom left, cursing even louder than usual, than Fofo turned to the new arrival —his stable companion, Nero—and remarked with a sigh:

'I've got the hang of it! Velvets, tassels and plumes. You're starting well, old fellow. Today's a first-class job.'

Nero turned his head away. Being a well-bred horse, he did not snort, but he had no wish to become too intimate with that Fofo.

He had come there from a princely stable—a stable where one saw one's reflection in the polished walls, where the stalls were separated by leather-padded partitions, and each had a hay-rack made of beechwood, rings of gun-metal, and posts with bright shining nobs on top of them.

But alas! the young prince was mad on those noisy carriages, foul things which belch out smoke behind and run along of themselves. Three times he had nearly broken his neck in one of them. The old princess—the dear lady—would never have anything to do with those devil-carriages; but, as soon as she was struck down by paralysis, the prince had hastened to dispose of both Nero and Corbino—the last remnants of the stable, hitherto retained to take the mother out for a quiet drive in her landau.

Poor Corbino! Who could tell where he had gone to end his days, after long years of dignified service?

Giuseppe, the good old coachman, had promised them that when he went with the other faithful old retainers to kiss the hand of the princess—now restricted permanently to her armchair— he would intercede for them. But it was of no avail: from the way the old man had stroked their necks and flanks,

23

on his return soon afterwards, they both understood at once that all hope was lost, that their fate was settled—they were to be sold.

And so it had come about and Nero did not yet grasp what kind of a place he had found. Bad?—no, one couldn't say that it was really bad. Of course, it was not like the princess's stable. Yet this stable also was a good one. It had more than a score of horses, all black and all rather old, but fine-looking animals, dignified and quite sedate—for that matter, rather too sedate.

Nero doubted whether his companions had any clear idea as to the work on which they were engaged. They seemed to be constantly pondering over it without ever being able to come to any conclusion: the slow swish of their bushy tails, with an occasional scraping of hoofs showed clearly that they were engaged in thinking deeply over something.

Fofo was the only one who was certain—a good deal too certain—that he knew all about it.

A common, presumptuous animal!

Once a regimental charger, cast out after three years' service, because—according to his own story—a brute of a cavalryman from the Abruzzi had broken his wind, he spent his whole time talking and gossiping. Nero, who was still very sad at the parting from his old friend Corbino, could not stand his new acquaintance, whose confidential manner and habit of making nasty remarks about his stable companions jarred upon him horribly.

Heavens! what a tongue he had! Not one of the twenty escaped from it—there was always some fault to find.

'Look at his tail, do look! Fancy calling that a tail! And what a way to swish it! He thinks that's very dashing, you know. I don't mind betting he's been a doctor's horse.

'And just look over there at that Calabrian nag. D'you see how graceful he pricks up his pig's ears . . . look at his fine mane and his chin! He's a showy beast, too, don't you think?

'Every now and then he forgets that he's a gelding and wants to make love to that mare over there, three stalls to the right— d'you see her?—the one whose face looks so old, who's low in the fore-quarters and has her belly on the ground.

'Is she a mare, that thing? She's a cow, I assure you. If you could only see how she moves—regular riding-school style! You'd think she was walking on hot cinders, the way she puts her hoofs down. And a mouth as hard as iron, my dear fellow!'

* * *

In vain did Nero intimate to Fofo in every possible manner that he did not wish to listen to him. Fofo overwhelmed him with incessant chatter.

'D'you know where we are? We're with a firm of carriers. There are many different sorts of carriers—ours are called undertakers.

'Do you know what it means to be an undertaker's horse? It means that your job is to pull a strange-looking black carriage that has four pillars supporting the roof and is all decked out grand with gilding and a curtain and fringes—in fact a handsome carriage *de luxe*. But it's sheer waste—you'd hardly believe it—sheer waste, 'cause no one ever comes and sits inside it.

'There's only the coachman on the box, looking as solemn as can be.

'And we go slowly, always at a walk. No risk of your ever getting into a muck of sweat and having to be rubbed down on your return, nor of the coachman giving you a cut of the whip or anything else to hurry you up.

'But slowly . . . slowly . . . slowly. . . .

'And the place we go to—our destination—we always seem to be there in time.

'You know the carriage I described to you. Well, I've noticed, by the way, that human beings seem to look upon it as an object of peculiar reverence.

'As I told you before, no one ever dares to sit inside it, and, as soon as people see it stop in front of a house, they all stand still and stare at it with long faces, looking quite frightened; and they all surround it, holding lighted candles, and, as soon as it starts again, they follow after it, walking very quietly.

'Quite often, too, there's a band playing in front of us—a band, my dear fellow, which plays a particular kind of music that makes you feel all funny in your bowels.

'Now you mark my words! You've got a nasty habit of

shaking your head and snorting. Well, you'll have to drop those tricks. If you snort for nothing at all, what d'you think you'll be doing when you have to listen to that music?

'Ours is a soft enough job, I don't deny; but it does call for composure and solemnity. No snorting or jerking your head up and down! The very most we're allowed is to swish our tails, quite, quite gently, because the carriage we pull—I tell you once again—is highly venerated. You'll notice that all the men take off their hats when they see us pass.

'D'you know how I discovered that we're working for a firm of carriers? It was this way:

'About two years ago, I was standing harnessed to one of our canopied carriages, in front of the big gateway leading to the building which is our regular goal.

'You'll see it, that big gateway. Behind the railings are any number of dark trees growing up to a sharp point: they're planted in two rows, forming a long straight avenue. Here and there, between them, there are some fine, green meadows full of good, luscious grass; but that's all sheer waste, too, for one's not allowed to eat it. Woe betide you if you put your lips to it.

'Well—as I was saying—I was standing there, when an old pal of mine from the regimental days came up to me. The poor fellow had come down in the world terribly and was reduced to drawing a waggon—one of those long, low ones, without any springs.

'He said to me:

"Hello, Fofo! D'you see the state I'm in? I'm quite done for!"

"What work are you on?" I asked.

"Transporting boxes!" he replied.—"All day long, from a carrier's office to the custom house."

"Boxes?" I said. "What kind of boxes?"

"Heavy!" he answered. "Frightfully heavy!—full of merchandise to be forwarded."

'Then the light dawned on me, for I may as well tell you that we also transport a kind of very long box. They put it inside our carriage from the back, as gently as can be; while that's being done, with tremendous care, the people standing round all take off their hats and watch, with a sort of frightened look. Why they do that I really can't say, but it's obvious that, as our business also is to take boxes, we must be working for a carrier, don't you think so?

'What the devil can be in those boxes? They're heavy—you can't think how heavy they are. Luckily we only convey one at a time.

'We're carriers employed for the transport of goods, that's certain; but what goods I don't know. They seem to be very valuable, because the transport's always carried out with much pomp and accompanied by a number of persons.

'At a certain point we usually, but not always, stop in front of a splendid office, which may perhaps be the custom house for our line of transport. This building has a great doorway. Out of this doorway there come men dressed in black gowns, with shirts worn outside them—I suppose they're the custom officials. The box is removed from the carriage, all heads being bared again; then those men mark on the box the permit to proceed with it.

'Where all these valuable goods that we transport go to, I really don't know. I must admit that's something I don't understand. But I'm not at all sure that the human beings know much about that—so I console myself with that thought.

'Indeed the magnificence of the boxes and the solemnity of the ceremony might lead one to suppose that men must know something about this transport business of theirs. But I notice they're often filled with doubt and fear; and from the long dealings I've had with them for many years, I have come to this conclusion—that human beings do many things, my dear chap, without any idea at all why they are doing them!'

*   *   *

That morning, as Fofo had already guessed from the head-groom's curses, the preparations included velvets, tassels, and plumes, and four horses to the carriage—evidently a first-class affair.

'You see! What did I tell you?'

Nero found himself harnessed to the shaft, with Fofo as his partner. To his annoyance there was no escape from his companion's ceaseless explanations.

Fofo was also annoyed that morning, on account of the

unfairness of the head-groom, who, when arranging a four-in-hand, always took him as a wheeler, never as one of the leaders.

'The dirty dog! You can see for yourself that pair in front of us is only for show. What are they pulling? Nothing at all! We go so slowly that all the pull falls upon us wheelers. The other pair are merely out for a pleasant walk, to stretch their legs, dressed up to the nines. . . And just look at the kind of animals that are given the preference over me, and I've got to put up with it! D'you recognize them?'

They were the two black horses whom Fofo had described as the doctor's horse and the Calabrian nag.

'That foul Calabrian beast! I'm glad he's in front of you, not of me. You'll get a whiff from him, my dear fellow! You'll soon find that it isn't only in the ears that he's like a pig. Won't you just be grateful to the head-groom for making a pet of him and giving him double rations! . . . If you want to get on in this line of work, don't start snorting. . . Hello! You're beginning it already. Keep your head still. Look here, old chap, if you go on like that, you'll find the reins jerked so hard that your mouth will bleed, I assure you. Because today we're going to have speeches, you know. . . You'll see what a cheery show it's going to be—one speech, two speeches—three speeches. . . I've even had one first-class affair which had five speeches! It was enough to drive one mad—having to stand still for three hours on end, decked out with all this finery so that one could hardly breathe—one's legs shackled, tail imprisoned and ears in two sheaths. . . A jolly fine time, with the flies biting one under the tail! You want to know what speeches are? Oh, just rot! To tell you the truth, I haven't got the hang of it, not altogether. . . These first-class shows must be cases where there's a lot of complication about the transport. Perhaps they have to make those speeches to give the necessary explanations. One isn't enough, so they make a second one. Two aren't enough, so they make a third. They may even run to five, as I told you before. There have been times when I've gone so far as to start kicking to right and left and finished by rolling on the ground like a lunatic . . . Perhaps it'll be the same today. . . It's a swagger affair, I tell you! Have you seen the coachman—doesn't he look grand? There come the servants and the candle-sticks. . . I say, are you apt to shy?'

'I don't understand.'

'Don't you? I mean do you take fright easily? Because, you see, in a short time they'll be shoving their lighted candles almost under your nose. . . Steady! oh, steady! What's come over you? There, you see, you've had a jerk at your mouth. . .

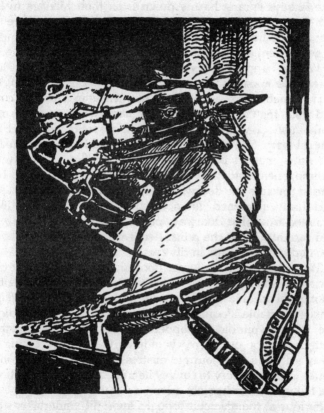

Did it hurt? Well, you'll get many more like it today, I warn you, if. . . What are you up to? What's the matter? Have you gone mad? Don't stretch your neck out like that! (What a funny old chap he is!—does he fancy he's swimming? Or is he start-ing a game of *mora*?) Stand still, I say! . . . There! You've had some more jerks with the reins. . . Here, stop it! You're making him hurt my mouth too. . . (Oh, he's mad! . . . Good God! He's gone clean crazy! He's panting and neighing and snorting and plunging and kicking up a row! My God! what a row! He's mad, quite mad! Fancy doing a kick-up when one's drawing a carriage in a first-class show!)'

Nero did indeed appear to have gone quite mad; he panted and quivered and pawed the ground, neighing and squealing. The lackeys sprang hastily down from their carriage to hold him— they had just reached the door of the palace where they were due to halt, where they were received by a large company of gentlemen, all very trim, in frock-coats and silk hats.

'What's happened?' everyone was asking. 'Oh, look! look! One of the horses is playing up!'

They rushed up, surrounding the hearse in a jostling crowd and watching the proceedings with interest and surprise, some of them shocked and frightened. The servants were unable to control Nero. The coachman stood up and tugged furiously at the reins, but all in vain. The horse continued to paw the ground, neighing and trembling violently, with his head turned towards the doorway of the palace.

He only quietened down when an aged servant in livery emerged from that doorway, pushed the lackeys on one side and caught hold of the reins. Recognizing the animal at once, he cried out with tears in his eyes:

'Why, it's Nero! it's Nero! Poor old Nero! Of course he is excited . . . he was our dear mistress's horse! The horse of the poor princess! He recognizes the palace, you know . . . he smells his stable. Poor Nero! . . . come, be good. Yes, you can see, it's me, your old Giuseppe. . . . Now stand still! . . . that's better. . . Poor old Nero, you have the task of taking her away—d'you see?—your old mistress, whom you still remember . . . it's your duty to convey her. She'll be glad it's you who are to take her for her last drive.'

Furious at the discredit brought upon the undertaker's firm — with all those gentlefolk present, too—the driver was still pulling savagely at the reins and threatening to flog the horse, but Giuseppe called out to him:

'That'll do! That'll do! Stop it! I'll look after him . . . he's as quiet as a lamb. . . Sit down. I'll lead him the whole way. . . We'll go together—eh, Nero?—taking our kind mistress, very quietly, as we always did, eh? You'll be good, so's not to hurt her, won't you? . . . Poor old Nero! You still remember her, don't you? They've shut her up in the big box and now they're just carrying her down. . .'

At this point, Fofo, who had been listening from the other side of the shaft, was so astonished that he broke in with the inquiry:

'Inside the box!—your mistress?'

Nero launched a kick sideways at him. But Fofo was too excited by his new discovery to resent the attack:

'Oh! I see! Now I see! so we . . .' he went on to himself, 'so we . . . I mean to say. . . Yes, of course, I've got it now! . . . That old man's weeping. . . I've often seen lots of others weep on similar occasions . . . so often seen long faces, sad faces . . . and heard sad music . . . just like now. . . . Yes, now I know all about it. . . That's why our job's such a soft one! It's only when men must weep, that we horses can be happy and have a restful time. . .'

He felt strongly tempted to do some kicking and prancing on his own account.

31

The Gymkhana

ENID BAGNOLD

MI RAISED thirty shilling for the gymkhana. He borrowed it from his girl for Velvet's sake. That is to say
he treated love worse than he treated adventure.

'Your girl,' said Velvet, frowning in thought, 'Which girl?
Didn't know you had a girl.'

'Nor I had. Met her at the dance last night,' said Mi. 'Pleased
as Punch, she was. Lent me the money too.' So Mi behaved
badly, and Velvet knew it. But neither she nor Mi cared when
they set their minds firm.

On the day of the gymkhana, about mid-morning, it grew
suddenly very hot and the rain came down in sheets. Inside the
living room, polishing the bits, it was like the tropics. The girls'
faces were wet. Rain came down outside on full leaves, making
a rattle and a sopping sound. Everything dripped. The windows streamed. The glass was like glycerine.

'Oh, Lord,' said Mally, 'oh dear, oh damn!'

'We've only two mackintoshes. Velvet's has stuck to the wall
in the hot cupboard. Won't it rain itself out?'

'The grass'll be slippery. What about their shoes being
roughed?'

'We've no money,' said Velvet, 'for roughing.'

'If Mi had a file . . .' said Mally.

'A file's no good. You want nails in.'

'I'm sweating,' said Edwina, 'can't we have a window open?'

She opened the yard window and the rain came crackling in
over the cactus.

'Hot as pit in here!' said Mi, coming in from the yard, and
taking off his dripping coat. 'The yard's swimming.'

'The gymkhana? No, it'll be over soon. It's a water-spout.
There's a great light coming up the way the wind's coming
from. Your ma going to serve dinner early?'

'Yes, at twelve,' said Edwina. 'We better clear now. Put the bridles and things in the bedroom. Better father doesn't see too much of it!'

'He knows, doesn't he?' said Meredith.

'Yes, he knows, but he doesn't want to think too much about it.'

At dinner they had sardines instead of pudding. Mrs Brown always served sardines for staying power. Dan had dropped them into her mouth from the boat as she crossed the channel.

Donald considered his on his plate.

'I'll take your spines out, Donald,' said Meredith.

'I eat my spines,' said Donald.

'No you don't, Donald. Not the big spine. The little bones but not the big one in the middle. Look how it comes out!'

'I eat my spines I say,' said Donald firmly with rising colour, and held her knife-hand by the wrist.

'But look . . . they come out lovely!' said Merry, fishing with the fork. The spine of the slit sardine dangled in the air and was laid on the edge of the plate. Quick as lightning Donald popped it into his mouth with his fingers and looked at her dangerously.

'I crunch up my spines, I like them,' he said.

'Leave him alone,' said mother.

'D'you eat your tails too?' said Merry vexedly.

'I eat my tails and my spines,' said Donald, and the discussion was finished.

At one the rain stopped and the sun shone. The grass was smouldering with light. The gutters ran long after the rain had stopped.

'Keep up on the hog,' said Velvet, as the horses moved along. 'We don't want 'em splashed. Gutters are all boggy.' They were well on the way to the gymkhana, held in the football field at Pendean.

'We look better in our mackintoshes!' called Mally. 'I'm glad it rained.'

'I'm steamy,' said Edwina. 'Merry, you can wear mine.'

'I'm all right. I don't want it, thank you, Edwina.'

But Edwina was struggling out of her mackintosh. 'You'll look better. You're all untidy . . . Put it on!'

'I don't want it!'

'You're a bully, 'Dwina,' said Mally. 'You jus' want to get rid of it an' not sweat.'

They turned up a chalk road between a cutting and in a few minutes they could see below them the gathering of horse-vans in the corner of Pendean field, the secretary's flagged tent, white-painted jumps dotting the course, and a stream of horses and ponies drawing along the road below.

The soaking land was spread below them, and the flat road of the valley shone like a steel knife. Getting off their horses they led them down the chalk path between blackberry bushes, and in ten minutes of slithering descent they were at the gates of the gymkhana field.

'Competitors' passes,' murmured Edwina and showed their pasteboard tickets.

They picked out a free tree in the field and established themselves.

'Here's someone's programme!' said Mally. 'Squashed and lost. Sixpence saved!'

They crowded round to read it.

After endless waiting the band arrived. Then the local broadcaster rattled up, mounted on its ancient Ford, and settling into its position against the ropes, began to shout in bleak, mechanical tones . . . 'Event Number One! Competitors in the Collecting Ring, please . . . PLEASE.'

Instantly the field was galvanized. Children and ponies appeared from behind trees and hedges and tents. Mally mounted George and rode towards the ring.

In five minutes it was over and Mally was back again. George had had no idea of bending. Nor Mally either. They had broken three poles on the way up and were disqualified.

'We haven't practised!' said Mally, trying to carry it off.

But Velvet, busy saddling Mrs James, made no reply.

'Here's Jacob!' said Edwina suddenly. Jacob sprang lightly against Mrs James's flank and grinned. 'Mi must be here.'

'Event Number Two!' shouted the Voice, and Velvet mounted, and made for the Collecting Ring. Seeing Pendean Lucy waiting at the gate for the first heat, she thrust up beside her. The bar fell and Velvet, Lucy, and three others, two boys and a fat little girl, were let out to the potato posts.

'You know what to do?' shouted the Starter, his flag under

his arm. 'Leave the posts on your right! Take the furthest potato first! . . .'

Velvet tried to take it in but the trembling of Mrs James distracted her attention. Mrs James had broken already into a sweat of hysteria that had turned her grey coat steel-blue.

They were lined up, the flag fell, and Mrs James made a start of such violence that Velvet could not pull her up at the fifth post. Six strides were lost before they could turn. Lucy was cantering down the posts with her potato and Velvet heard the jingle of the bucket as the potato fell neatly into it. The heat was over, and Mrs James, too big, too wild, too excited, too convinced that she was once again playing polo, was left three potatoes behind when the winner had drawn up beside the Starter. Pendean Lucy won the first heat.

'Five shillings gone . . .' muttered Velvet with humiliation as she trotted slowly back to the tree. Mi was there standing beside Sir Pericles.

'Five shillings gone, Mi,' said Velvet aloud to him.

'It's a gamble,' said Mi. 'Keep yer head. Afternoon's young.'

'Jumping . . .' said Mally. 'It's the jumping now. Which you jumping first?'

'Sir Pericles.'

The blazing sun had dried up the burnt grass and the afternoon shone like a diamond as Velvet sat on Sir Pericles in the Collecting Ring. Mi wormed his way between the crowds against the rope. Lucy came on her roan pony, but the pony refused the Gate. Twice and three times, and she trotted back disqualified. A schoolboy in a school cap quartered in purple and white rode out. His almost tailless pony jumped a clear round. Jacob wriggled with excitement between Mi's legs.

'Number Sixteen!' called the Broadcaster.

Sixteen was Lucy's elder sister, a fat girl in a bright blue shirt.

'Blasted girl!' said Mi under his breath, as the blue shirt cleared the first and second jumps. His heart was in his mouth, but he spat whistlingly and joyfully between his teeth as the pony landed astride the wall, and scrambled over in a panic, heaving the wall upon its side.

It seemed they would call every number in the world except Velvet's.

'Break her nerve, waiting!' grumbled Mi. He could see her cotton hair bobbing as she sat.

A small girl came, with pigtails. A little shriek burst from her throat each time her chestnut pony rose at a jump. The plaits flew up and down, the pony jumped like a bird. A clear round.

'Hell!' said Mi. 'Two clear rounds.'

'Number Fifteen!'

Out came Velvet from the black gap between the crowds. Sir Pericles arched his neck, strained on his martingale, and his long eyes shone. He flirted his feet in his delicious doll's canter and came tittupping down over the grass. Velvet in her cotton frock stood slightly in the stirrups, holding him short—then sat down and shortened her reins still more. Mi's stomach ran to soup.

'Got her stirrups in her armpits . . .' sighed Mi approvingly.

There was nothing mean, nothing poor about Sir Pericles. He looked gay as he raced at the first jump.

'Too fast, too fast!' said Mi, praying with his soul.

The horse was over safely and had his eyes fastened on the next jump.

'Haul 'im in, haul 'im in!' begged Mi of the empty air. 'He'll rocket along . . .' He saw Velvet's hands creep further up the reins, and her body straighten itself a little. The horse's pace decreased. It was the double jump, the In-and-Out. Sir Pericles went over it with his little hop—one landing and one take-off. Mi saw Velvet glance behind—but nothing fell. And the Gate. The Gate was twelve paces ahead.

He cleared the Gate with one of his best jumps, an arc in the air, with inches to spare.

'He'll do the wall,' said Mi with relief.

He did the wall, but a lathe fell at the stile. Half a fault. She was out of it then. Mi yawned with fatigue. He had held his breath. His lungs were dry. Jacob was gone from between his legs. He looked round.

'Bitches . . .' he murmured vaguely, then turned again to the ropes to wait for the piebald.

There were no more clear rounds till the piebald came, and when it came a murmur went up from the villagers who stood in the crowd.

'Jumping *that* animal!' said a voice.

'Why that's the one she won at the raffle!'

The piebald strode flashing into the sun. He paused, stood still, and gazed round him. Velvet's knees held him steadily, and she sat behind his raised neck without urging him on.

'I don't expect anything . . .' she whispered. 'Do what you can. Keep steady. You're all right.'

'You next,' said a man at the bar of the Collecting Ring. 'You waiting for anything?'

'I'm going,' said Velvet quietly, 'He just wants to look round.'

Mi saw them come down the grass, the piebald trotting with a sort of hesitation.

'He's in two minds whether he'll bolt,' thought Mi.

'Showy horse . . .' said a spectator.

'Butcher's girl . . .' said another. 'The youngest. Got a seat, an't she?'

The piebald's best eye was towards the crowd, his white eye to the centre of the field.

The trot broke hesitatingly into a canter, but the horse had no concentration in him. He looked childishly from side to side, hardly glancing at the jump ahead.

'He'll refuse,' said Mally, who had arrived at Mi's side. But Mi made no answer.

Sir Pericles had jumped like a trained horse. The piebald's jumping was a joke. Arrived at the jump in another two paces, he appeared to be astonished, planted his forelegs for a second, looked down, trembled, then leapt the little bush and rail with all four legs stiff in the air together. Dropping his hindquarters badly he came down on the rail and broke it in two.

'Two faults,' said Mi.

'Only two for breaking that?'

'Hind feet. Only two.'

Again the piebald trotted, flashing, his grass-fed belly rounded, and his shoulders working under the peculiar colour of his hide.

'Why don't she canter 'im?' said a voice.

Mi turned on the voice. 'First time he's seen anything but his own grazing. It's a miracle if she gets him round.'

'The In-and-Out'll finish him,' said Mally under her breath.

The piebald jumped willingly into the In-and-Out then paused, and remained inside.

A shout of laughter went up from the crowd.

'Oh . . . poor Velvet . . .' murmured Malvolia, agonized.

The piebald attempted to graze, as though he were in a sheep pen, and again the crowd laughed.

'She's handling him gentle,' said Mi. 'She's trying to keep him thinking he's a winner. She's backin' him, see . . . I don't believe he's ever backed a pace before.' The piebald had backed two paces till his quarters lay against the first jump of the In-and-Out. With a light heart he responded to his rider, and with a spring he was out again and cantering on.

'Do they count that as a fault?'

'I don't know,' said Mi. 'Watch out . . . now . . . It's the Gate.'

The piebald broke the gate. He would have liked a stout, stone wall, but this flimsy thing that stood up before him puzzled him and he did his goat jump, all four legs in the air at once, and landed back upon the lathes and broke them.

'That horse is breaking up the field,' said a voice.

Mi glared. 'He's knocked his hock,' said Mi, 'that'll learn him.' For the piebald limped a pace or two. It learnt him. Unlettered as he was he had no thought of refusing. He saw the friendly wall ahead, and taking it to be enduring flint he went for it with a glare of interest, ears pricked and eyes bright. The wall was three foot six. He leapt five. For a second it seemed to the crowd as though the horse had nothing to do with the wall but was away up in the air. A little cheer went up and hands clapped in a burst.

'Don't she ride him!' said the voice. 'It's that Velvet girl. The ugly one.'

'What, that kid with the teeth?'

'That's who it is.'

Mi knew that Mally's beauty stood beside him and he resented it. He half turned his shoulder on her. While Velvet sat the piebald he thought her the loveliest thing on earth. Like Dan, his father, he hardly saw the faces of women.

'Hullo, she's missed the stile!'

'Did he refuse?' asked Mi, keenly.

'I don't think she saw it,' said Mally. 'She simply rode on.'

The judge waved his stick and called to a Starter. Velvet cantered, glowing, radiant, to the exit gate. The man who held the exit spoke to her and pointed. Velvet looked behind her, paused, then shook her head.

'Not coming . . .' shouted the man to the Steward.

After a brief pause.

'The last Competitor,' announced the Broadcaster, 'did not complete the round.'

'Why ever didn't she?' said Mally, as she and Mi left the rope to fight their way round to the tree. They scrambled out from the crowd and ran.

Velvet was standing looking at the piebald as though bemused. Merry, her face happy with pride, was holding the horses.

'Marvellous, Velvet, to get him round!' said Mally, coming up. 'Why didn't you jump the last jump?'

Velvet turned and looked, and Mi could see how her face was shining.

'I thought I'd better not,' she said gently.

'Why?'

'He did the wall so beautifully I thought he'd better end on that.'

In a flash Mi felt again what she was made of. That she could take a decision for her horse's good and throw away her own honours.

'It was the right thing to do,' said Mi.

Edwina arrived. 'What made you miss the Stile?'

Velvet said nothing.

'People near me thought you'd funked it,' said Edwina half indignantly. 'You must have bin asleep to go and miss it.'

'She's no more asleep 'n my eye,' said Mi. And Mi's little eye, like an angry sapphire, raked Edwina till she shuffled her shoulder and itched.

'It's you, Edwina, now!' said Mally looking at the torn programme. 'On Mrs James. Bending.'

'A lot of chance I have!' said Edwina. 'Mrs James'll break every pole.'

'She gets rough and excited,' said Velvet.

'But it's Adults!' said Merry. 'They won't have nippy ponies. It'll be easier.'

But the Adults were seated on the smallest ponies they could ride. They looked like giants on dogs. Every grown-up was riding his sister's pony, and Mrs James, galloping like a wild animal, nostrils blowing and eye rolling, broke all the poles she could break. Edwina led her back without a word, disgusted and shamefaced.

It began to rain. Merry put a sack round her shoulders and pulled out the *Canary Breeder's Annual*. Edwina left them and went towards the tent.

'She got any money?' said Mally, looking after her keenly.

'Can't have,' said Velvet. 'She was broke yesterday.'

'P'raps she's got twopence for an Idris. Wish to God I had a Crunchie,' muttered Mally.

'Kandy Korner's got a stall here,' said Merry, reading. 'What's happening now?'

'It's the tea interval,' said Velvet gloomily. They had won nothing. They had made not a penny. They owed Mi thirty bob.

The rain slid, tapping, through the branches, and swept in windy puffs across the field.

It made a prison for them, it pressed them into a corner of life, a corner of the heart. They were hung up. Velvet was hung up in life. Where was she? A butcher's daughter, without money, in debt, under suzerainty, an amateur at her first trial of skill, destined that night to a bed of disappointment among the sleeping canaries. She did not think like that. But cared only that the piebald had jumped one jump as she had dreamt he might jump, with power, with crashing confidence. He was ignorant but he had no stage nerves. Of her own powers she had no thought.

Staring out into the lines of rain lightly she lifted her hands and placed them together in front of her, as though she held the leathers. So acute was the sensation of the piebald beneath her that she turned with surprise to see him standing under the dripping branches. A look of simplicity and adoration passed into her face, like the look of the mother of a child who has won honours. She had for him a future.

The rain came down in long knitting needles. Backwards and forwards blew the needles, as the wind puffed. Wet horses, wet mackintoshes, wet dogs, wet flapping of tents, and then as the storm was rent a lovely flushing of light in the raindrops. Wind blew the sky into hollows and rents.

'That Violet that Mi met, she's at Kandy Korner,' said Merry. 'Serving with them for a week on appro.'

'We can't borrow from her if she's only on appro. She'll get into trouble.'

'Mi,' said Velvet, looking round the tree, 'you round there? Is it drier there?'

'No.'

'Your Violet's with Kandy Korner. Got a stall down here.'

Silence. Displeasure.

'You couldn't touch her for another twopence?'

'Not till I see daylight with that thirty bob.'

Edwina had gone off with one of the mackintoshes. The saddles were heaped under the other. Merry, Mally, and Velvet flattened themselves, shivering, against the treetrunk.

'There's mother!' said Velvet suddenly.

Across the field, swaying like a ship at sea, came the red and yellow meat van.

'She's brought tea!' said Merry.

'She'll thread my needle!' said Velvet.

Mally ran out into the open and waved. The van nosed and swayed towards them.

'Father's driving! If he stops . . . He'll never let you race, Velvet!'

'Stop him buying the programme if you can! Here, tear ours . . . give him the wrong half! Then he won't buy another.'

Velvet snatched up the programme and tore a little piece out with her thumb-nail. The van drew up under the tree. Mi opened the door and the giant bulk of Mrs Brown descended backwards.

'We've done nothing, mother! Nothing at all!' said Mally.

'That's bad,' said Mrs Brown. 'Here's your tea.'

'I'm not stopping,' said Mr Brown, from the wheel. 'There's a sugar box in the back. Pull it out for your mother to sit on. You're wet through, the lot of you. You ought to come home.'

'Coats is soppy,' said Mrs Brown. 'How's your vests?'

'Dry,' said Velvet, edging away. 'Dry's a bone.'

'You stay for one more race or whatever you call it,' said Mr

Brown, 'an' then you'll take them horses home. I'll be back to fetch Mother.'

'But we've *paid* . . .' began Velvet in horror. The self-starter whirred and he was gone.

'Does he mean it, mother?'

'You're dripping,' said Mrs Brown, cutting up a Madeira cake. 'Mi, come round here an' get some food.'

The cake grew wet even as they ate it.

'What's the next?' said mother. 'Gimme the list.' She studied it for a moment.

'That's next, mother,' said Velvet, pointing.

'Was your name in it?' asked Mrs Brown looking at the hole.

'Yes . . . it was.'Tis.'

There was a long pause and Mrs Brown slowly stroked her chin. Mi looked down on her old felt hat in which a pool of rain was settling. Velvet ran one nail under the other and shot out a piece of earth.

'I'll thread your needle,' said Mrs Brown at last.

Velvet looked into the heavy eyes and smiled. The eyes blinked with the violence and worship of the glance.

The voice of the Broadcaster came roughly through the wind and rain.

'Event Number Five,' said the Voice . . . 'Competitors for Event Number Five . . . go to the Collecting Ring.'

Sir Pericles was saddled and Mrs Brown rose to her feet.

'Where'd I stand?' she asked.

'Mi'll take you. Mi! It's right far up there.'

Mrs Brown walked like a great soldier up the field.

In Velvet's heat she was the only child. She rode out of the gate of the Collecting Ring with four others—two livery-stable-men from Worthing, a grizzled woman with short hair and a hanging underlip, and a young man in checks on a hired horse with poverty streaks.

'I've plenty of chance,' she thought, 'I'm lighter than any of them.' All the horses were dripping and began to steam with excitement.

'Be slippery at the corner there,' said one of the livery-stable-men.

They reached the starting post, and the sodden Starter came down towards them.

The faces, shining in the rain, looked back at him. The young man in the check suit lay up on the inside against the rail. The woman with the hanging lip scowled at him and edged her horse nearer. Velvet came next, and on the outside the two stable-men. The flag was raised. Before it could fall the young man made a false start. While he was getting back into position the grizzled woman took his place.

'Don't shove!' said the young man, but the woman made no reply. Up went the flag again and the bounding of Velvet's heart swept Sir Pericles forward.

'Get back . . . that child!' shouted the Starter.

Velvet swung Sir Pericles back behind the line and brought him up. The flag fell again neatly as she got him square. She drove for the centre of the first hurdle. Out of the corner of her eye she saw the grizzled woman's horse run out. The young man in the checks she never saw again. Perhaps he never started. As she landed she saw a horse and man on the ground beside her. The heat was between Velvet and one livery-stable-man.

Sir Pericles, the little creature, brilliant and honest, never looked to right or left but stayed where Velvet drove him, straight at the middle of each hurdle. He fled along the grass, jumping as neatly as a cat, swung round the sharp, uphill corner towards the table where the sewers stood. Velvet kicking the stirrups free, neck and neck with the livery-man on a blue roan. The roan drew ahead. The sewers' table neared. Velvet flung herself off as they drew up; her feet ran in the air, then met the ground and ran beside the horse.

'What have you got off for? said Mrs Brown calmly, as she began to sew.

Velvet glanced with horror at her rival, leaning from his saddle while a tall girl sewed at his sleeve. 'Oh . . .' she breathed. She had forgotten the instructions. She had no need to dismount.

But Mrs Brown's needle flashed in and out, while the blue roan fidgeted and danced, and the tall girl pivoted on her feet.

It was an easy win for Velvet. She was in the saddle, off, and had time to glance behind, before the roan had started. She heard his galloping feet behind her but he never caught her up

and Sir Pericles went steadily down the grassy slope, jumping
his hurdles with willing care.

A burst of clapping and cheers went up.

'Stay in the field!' said a Steward. 'Wait for the other heats to
be run.' Velvet sat alone in the rain, in a cloud of steam from
the excited horse. One by one the winners of the three heats
joined her.

The first was a boy of about nineteen, with a crooked jaw.
Steaming and shining and smiling he rode up to her on a
brown horse with a hunter-build, long tail and mane.

'You did a good one!' he said to her.

'I'd only one to beat,' she said, 'and even then it was the
button that did it.'

'That's a beautiful little horse,' said the boy. 'He's *neat*.'

They turned to watch the finish of the next heat.

They were joined by a fat little man in a bowler hat, a dark
grey riding coat, and soaking white breeches. He took off his
bowler as he rode towards them and mopped his shining bald
head. His horse was a grey.

'What a horse . . .' he said as he rode up. 'I hired him.
Couldn't hold him fer a minute. Just went slap round as
though he'd got a feed at the winning post. I'll never pull it off
a second time, not unless he chooses to! Lands on his head too,
every time. Not a bit of shoulder.'

'The saddle looks too big for him,' said the boy. 'It's right up
his neck. But he's a grand goer.'

'It's right up his neck, an' so'm I,' said the little man, dis-
mounting. 'It's the way he jumps. Next round I'll be down and
off and rolling out of your light! Here's the last! It's Flora
Banks!'

'Who's she?' said the boy.

'Tough nut from Bognor,' said the little man under his
breath.

Flora Banks wore a yellow waistcoat, had a face like a wet
apple and dripping grey hair. She rode astride on a bay horse
that looked like a racer, lean and powerful and fully sixteen
hands. Velvet's heart sank.

'My poor Flora,' said the little man calmly, bringing out a
match, 'you've got an overreach. You're out of it!'

The Tough Nut was off her bay in a second, flung her

cigarette into the grass, and knelt and took the bleeding fore-foot tenderly in her hands. The big bay hung his head like a disappointed child. He was out of it. She led him, limping, away.

'Makes us three,' said the little man, mopping his head. 'Two really. I can't last another round. You go it, little girl, an' get the fiver. Hi, they're calling us.'

Down went the three horses to the starting post, reins slipping in cold fingers, rain whirling in puffs. Velvet's breath would not sink evenly on the downward stroke. She shuddered as she breathed.

'Lay up against the rails, little girl,' said the bowler hat. 'I'm so fast you can't beat me whatever you do, but I'm coming off. Where's that Starter? Goin' to keep our hearts beating while he drinks his coffee? Hi, where's that Starter? The blighter's drinkin' coffee!'

The Starter burst out of a little tent wiping his mouth and ran through the raindrops, that suddenly grew less. The miraculous sun broke all over the soaking field. The freshness was like a shout. Velvet shaded her eyes, for the start was into the west. Water, filled with light, shone down the grass. The flag was raised and fell.

The boy on the brown horse got a bad start. Velvet and the little man rose together at the first hurdle. Velvet had the inside and the grey lay behind her. At the second hurdle she heard him breathe, then lost him. At the slight curve before the third hurdle he had drawn up on her inside, between her and the rail. She had lost her advantage.

Suddenly the boy on the brown appeared on her left. Both the grey and the brown drew ahead and Velvet strung out a near third. Like hounds over a wall they rose, one, two, three over the fourth hurdle and went sweeping round the uphill curve to the table.

Mrs Brown stood like an oak tree. Velvet galloped and drew up in a stagger beside her, throwing the single rein loose on Sir Pericles' neck. She stooped and hung over him, kicking both feet free from the stirrups to steady him. Trembling, panting, his sides heaving in and out he stood, his four feet still upon the ground, like a bush blown by a gale but rooted. Mrs Brown's needle flashed.

Velvet was off, stirrups flying, down the grass hill, the blazing light no longer in her eyes, going east. First the grey, then the brown, were after her. At the fifth hurdle the grey passed her, but the brown never drew near. The grey was wound up to go. Its hind quarters opened and shut like springs in front of her. She saw it rise at the sixth hurdle just ahead of her, and come down almost upon its head. It slowed. As she drew up she saw the little man was done, stretched up unnaturally on its neck. He took a year falling. She passed him while he was still at it—jumped the seventh and eighth hurdles and whispered to herself as the noise went up behind the ropes, 'A fiver . . .' And the piebald's glistening future spread like a river before her, the gates of the world all open. She pulled up, flung herself off Sir Pericles and glanced down at his feet.

He was all right. And the Steward was examining her button . . . That was all right too! Here came the sisters . . . The little man in the bowler, unhurt, was leading his horse down the track. Mrs Brown . . . Where was mother? Mi was by her side.

'Lead him off! Don't stand there! You look daft,' said Mi lovingly, and his little blue eyes winked and shone. 'Good girl, Velvet!' said Mr Croom as she neared the exit. And hands patted her and voices called.

The ruthless voice of the Broadcaster was gathering competitors for the next event.

*   *   *

'Thirty shilling is yours, Mi.'

'You'll have to give me forty. I want ten to get me teeth out of pawn.'

'You put them in again?'

'I had to. Hadn't nothing.'

'How is it they're so valuable, Mi?'

'Mass o'gold. My old Dad got 'em done. He said, "You always got money on you if you got gold in your mouth." I can raise ten shillings on them most towns.'

'You whistle better without them.'

'Yes, I do,' said Mi. 'Where's that Jacob?'

It was the evening, before supper. They had turned the horses into the field after a good meal, and the piebald in with

47

them. He had shown no sign of kicking. He trotted happily about among the new companions, his tail raised in an arch and his nostrils blown out with excitement. Velvet leaned on the gate and Mi stood beside her. The others had gone home before them down the road, clinking the buckets.

'Sir Pericles was lovely,' said Velvet for the twentieth time. Mi was tired of grunting assent. The reddest sun that ever sank after a wet day went down behind them and sent streams of light through rushes and branches. Mi shaded his eyes to look for Jacob, that thorn in his side.

'Was The Lamb really only fourteen-two?' asked Velvet casually.

'Some say fourteen-two. Some say fifteen.'

'Smallest horse ever won the National, wasn't he?'

'Won it twice.'

'You ever bin round there?'

'The course? Know every stick. Been on it hundreds a times.'

'What's the highest jump?'

Mi gazed into the field. He stuck his chin towards the piebald. 'He jumped as high as any today.'

'I thought he did,' said Velvet, low and happy.

There was a long silence. The fields rolled uphill. The hedge at the top of the field was indigo. Sir Pericles was cropping, like a tawny shadow against it. The piebald, disturbed and excited, cantered the length of the hedge, neighing. Sir Pericles looked up, kicked gaily at the empty air, and cantered too. Mrs James rolled an eye and laid her ears back.

Evenings after triumphs are full of slack and fluid ecstasy. The air swims with motes, visions dip into reach like mild birds willing to be caught. Things are heavenly difficult, but nothing is impossible. Here stood gazing into the field in the sunset the Inspirer, the Inspired, and, within the field, the Medium.

Under his boil of red hair Mi's thoughts were chattering 'Why not?'

And beside him Velvet looked, throbbing with belief, at her horse.

'Pity *you* don't ride,' said Velvet at last.

'The rider's all right,' said Mi mystically.

'What rider?'

'You.'

A pause.

'There's jockeys from Belgium,' said Mi following the insane thread of thought, 'no one's ever seen before. Who's to know?'

'You think he could do it?'

'The two of you could do it.'

'Mi . . . oh, Mi . . .'

Pause.

'Who'd you write to? For entries.'

'Weatherby's.'

'Where are they?'

'Telephone book. London somewhere.'

'Weatherby's.'

There are evenings, full of oxygen and soft air, evenings after rain (and triumph) when mist curls out of the mind, when reason is asleep, stretched out on a low beach at the bottom of the heart, when something sings like a cock at dawn, a long-drawn wild note.

Velvet and Mi dreamed a boldness bordering on madness.

The race was being run in stage light, under the lamps of the mind. The incandescent grass streamed before Velvet's eyes. There was an unearthly light around the horses, their rumps shone. The white of the painted rails was blue-white like ice. The grass snaked in green water under the horses' feet. There was a thunder rolling in the piebald like a drum. His heart, beating for the great day of his life.

'Weatherby's,' said Velvet again. The word was a gateway to a great park. You could touch it, crisp, crested, full of carving . . . *Weatherby's*. Green grass, white rails, silk jackets. Through the arch of Weatherby's.

'Who's to know I'm a girl?' said Velvet, very very far along the road.

Mi was not far behind her.

'Just wants thinking out,' he said. His belly felt hollow with the night air. 'Supper, Velvet.' Slowly they left the gate and walked towards the village.

Sugar for the Horse

H. E. BATES

M Y UNCLE SILAS had a little mare named Jenny, warm, brown and smooth-coated, with a cream arrow on her forehead and flecks of cream on three of her feet. She was a very knowing, friendly creature and she could take sugar off the top of your head. 'Go anywhere and do anything,' my Uncle Silas would say. 'Only got to give her the word. Goo bed wi' me.'

'Upstairs?' I said.

'Upstairs, downstairs,' my Uncle Silas said. 'Anywhere. Where you like. I recollect—'

'Start some more tales,' my grandmother would say. 'Go on. Stuff the child's head with rubbish. Keep on. Some day he'll know the difference between the truth and what he hears from you.'

'Is the truth,' Silas said, 'She comes to bed with me arter the 1897 Jubilee. Over at Kimbolton. I oughta know. There was me and Tig Flawn and Queenie White—'

'That's been a minute,' my grandmother said. She was very small and tart and dry and disbelieving. 'How old's Jenny now? Forty?'

'Well, she's gittin' on.' Silas said. 'I recollect that day Queenie had a big hat on. We got the hat off her and put it on Jenny and she come up to bed with me just like a lamb.'

'Who was Queenie White?' I said. 'Did she come to bed with you too?'

'I'm only tellin' you about the horse,' my Uncle Silas said. 'Queenie was afore your time.'

'Pity she wasn't before yours,' my grandmother said.

'Ah, but she wadn't. 'Course,' he said to me, 'I could tell you a lot about her. Only you wanted to know about the horse. Well, she come to bed in no house of mine.'

Some time later my Uncle Silas came down to Nenweald Fair, on the second Sunday in August, about the time the corn was cut and the first dew-berries were ripe for gathering, with Jenny in a little black trap with yellow wheels and a spray of ash-leaves on her head to keep the flies away. There was always a wonderful dinner for Nenweald Fair and Silas always kept it waiting. There was always roast beef and York-shire pudding and horseradish sauce and chicken to choose from, and little kidney beans and new potatoes and butter, and yellow plum pie and cream with sugar on pastry. There were jugs of beer on the sideboard by the clock with the picture of Philadelphia. The batter of the Yorkshire pudding was as buttery and soft as custard and all over the house there was a wonderful smell of beef burnt at the edges by fire.

But my Uncle Silas was always late and my grandfather, an indulgent, mild-mannered man unaccustomed to revelry and things of that sort, was always full of excuses for him.

'Very like busted a belly-band coming down Longley's Hill or summat,' he would say.

'Start carving,' my grandmother would say. 'I'm having no dinner of mine spoilt for Silas or anybody else.'

'Hold hard a minute. Give him a chance.'

'The meat's on the table,' she would say, 'and if he's not here that's his lookout,' and she would plant the meat before my grandfather and it would sizzle in its gravy.

It was my Uncle Silas's custom, and my grandmother knew it and knew it only too well, not only to arrive late for that dinner but never to arrive alone. He had a habit of arriving with strange men with names like Tig Flawn and Fiddler Bollard and Slop Johnson and Tupman Jarvis. That day he arrived, about two o'clock when most of the meat had gone and the last of the yellow plums were cooling in the dish, with a man named Ponto Pack. I always wanted him to arrive with Queenie White and see what my grandmother thought of that, but he never did and I was always rather disappointed. Whenever he did arrive my grandmother always looked as if she could hit him over the head with the pastry-board, or some other suitable instrument, and that day, when I looked out of the window and saw Silas and the man Ponto, like some gigantic blond sow, falling out of the trap, I felt a carving knife would hardly have been too much.

'Let 'em all come!' my Uncle Silas roared and gave prodigious beery winks from a bloodshot eye that was like a fire in a field of poppies.

'You're late,' my grandmother said. 'Get your dinner and stop shouting as if you were in Yardley Open Fields.'

'Got hung up,' Silas said. 'Belly-band broke.'

My grandmother gave my grandfather such a killing and merciless look that he went out at once to give Jenny a rub down and a drink of water, and Ponto made strange strangled noises with whole potatoes, and said, for the first of several times:

'Onaccountable. Most onaccountable.'

He was such a large man, bulging flesh as tight as bladdered lard into his suit of green-faded Sunday black, that when the rest of us had left the table it still seemed full. His eyes, pink-edged, beery, almost colourless, were uncannily like the eyes of a blond and farrowing sow. He had nothing to say all day but:

'Onaccountable, George,' or 'Onaccountable, Silas. Most onaccountable.'

In the afternoon it was very hot and everyone, including Silas, went to sleep in the front parlour or under the laurel trees, and I played giving Jenny lumps of sugar off the top of my head in the little paddock at the back of the house. I was giving her the seventh or eighth lump of sugar and wondering whether she ever did go to bed with my Uncle Silas or whether it was just another story, when my grandmother rapped on the window sill and said:

'Come you in out of that sun. You'll never stay awake tonight without you get some rest.'

She must have known what was coming. About half-past six my Uncle Silas and my grandfather and Ponto Pack had another jug of beer in the shade of the laurel trees and my Uncle Silas, wet-lipped, bloodshot eye wickedly cocked, began to talk about 'gittin' the belly-band mended while we think on it'. It did not seem to me to be a thing that wanted thinking on at all, and I do not think my grandmother thought so either. She had put on her grey silk dress with the parma violet stitching at the collar and her little high hat with Michaelmas daisies on the brim, and it was time to be thinking of 'walking up street'. To walk up street on the Sunday of Nenweald Fair was a gentle, ponderous, respectable, long-winded custom, and it was something about which neither my Uncle Silas, my grandfather nor Ponto Pack seemed, I thought, very enthusiastic.

'You goo steady on up,' Silas said. 'We'll come on arter we git the belly-band mended.'

'If everything was as right as that belly-band nobody would hurt much,' she said.

'It's too 'nation hot yit for traipsing about,' Silas said.

'Onaccountable hot,' Ponto said. 'Most onaccountable.'

Ten minutes later the trap went jigging past us up the street, my Uncle Silas wearing his black-and-white deer-stalker sideways on, so that the peaks stuck out like ears, and Ponto, bowler hat perched on the top of his head like a cannon ball, looking more than ever like some pink-eyed performing pig. My grandfather pretended not to see us and my grandmother said:

'What one doesn't think of, the other will. The great fool things.'

We seemed to take longer than ever that sultry evening to make the tour under the chestnut trees about the crowded market-place. I always got very bored with the gossiping Sunday-starched crowd of bowler hats and parasols and I kept thinking how nice it would be if my Uncle Silas were to come back with Jenny and I could do my trick of giving her sugar, in full view of everybody, off the top of my head. But Silas never came and by ten o'clock I was yawning and my grandmother had even stopped saying darkly, whenever there was something nice to listen to, 'Little pigs have got big ears', as if I hadn't the vaguest idea of what she meant by that.

I went to bed with a piece of cold Yorkshire pudding to eat and fell asleep with it in my hands. It is hard to say now what time I woke up, but what woke me was like the thunder of one crazy dream colliding with another somewhere at the foot of the stairs. The piece of cold Yorkshire pudding was like a frog crawling on my pillow, and I remember wanting to shriek about it just at the moment I heard my Uncle Silas roaring in the front passage.

'Git up, old gal! Git up there! Pull up, old gal!'

A terrifying sound as of madly-beaten carpets greeted me at the top of the stairs. It was my grandmother beating Ponto Pack across the backside with what I thought was the stick we used for stirring pig swill. She could not get at my Uncle Silas because Silas was leading Jenny up the stairs; and she could not get at my grandfather because he was lying like a sack of oats on Jenny's back. Ponto was pushing Jenny with his round black backside sticking out like a tight balloon and my Uncle Silas kept bawling:

'Git underneath on her, Ponto. You ain't underneath on her.'

Every time Ponto seemed about to git underneath on her my grandmother hit him again with the swill-stick. I thought he did not seem to mind very much. He laughed every time my grandmother hit him and then pushed himself harder than ever against Jenny's hindquarters and called with pig-like fruitiness to my Uncle Silas, tugging at the bridle on the stairs:

'Can't budge the old gal, Silas. Most aggravatin' onaccountable.'

'Get that mare out of my house, you drunken idiots!' my grandmother shrieked.

'Gotta git George to bed fust,' Silas said. 'Must git George to bed.'

'Get that horse off my stair-carpet!'

'Gotta git George to bed. Good gal!' Silas said. 'Come on now, good gal. Tchck, tchck! Up mare! That's a good gal.'

By this time my Uncle Silas had succeeded in tugging Jenny a quarter of the way upstairs when suddenly, down below, sharp and sickening above the pandemonium of voices, there was a crack like a breaking bone. Ponto Pack roared, 'Silas, she's hittin' me on the coconut!' and at the same moment Jenny had something like hysterics, whinnying terribly, and fell down on her front knees on the stairs. My Uncle Silas yelled, 'Why th' Hanover don't you git underneath on her? She'll be down atop on y'!' and for a moment I thought she was. She gave a great lurch backwards and my grandfather let out a groan. My grandmother hit Ponto another crack on the head with the swill-stick and suddenly the whole essence of the situation became, to me at any rate, splendidly clear. My Uncle Silas and Ponto were trying to get my grandfather to bed and my grandmother, in her obstinate way, was trying to stop them.

I remembered in that moment the cold Yorkshire pudding. I fetched it from my bedroom and went half-way down the stairs and held it out to Jenny, most coaxingly, in the flat of my hand.

Whether she thought, at that moment, that I in my white nightshirt was some kind of newly-woken ghost or whether she decided she had had enough of the whole affair, I never knew. Ponto had hardly time to bawl out from the bottom of the stairs, 'It's most onaccountable, Silas, I can't budge her!' and my Uncle Silas from the top of the stairs, 'Hold hard, Pont. The old gal's knockin' off for a mite of pudden!' when my grandmother, aiming another crack at Ponto's head, hit the mare in her fury a blow above the tail.

The frenzy of her hysterical ascent up three steps of stairs and then backwards down the whole flight was something I shall not forget. My grandfather fell off the mare and the mare fell sideways on him, and then my Uncle Silas fell on the mare. The three of them fell on my grandmother and my grandmother fell on Ponto Pack. My Uncle Silas yelled, 'Let 'em all come!' and my grandmother hit Ponto twenty or thirty blows on the top of the head with the swill-stick. My grandfather fell off the horse's back and landed with a terrible crash on the umbrella-stand, and the portrait of Gladstone fell down in the hall. The cold Yorkshire pudding fell down the stairs and I fell after it. My aunt came in the front door with a policeman, and Ponto yelled, 'It's onaccountable, Silas, most onaccountable!' just as the mare broke free and charged the sideboard in the front room.

My Uncle Silas sat on the bottom of the stairs and laughed his head off, and I began to cry because I was sorry for Jenny and thought it was the end of the world.

The Maltese Cat

RUDYARD KIPLING

THEY HAD good reason to be proud, and better reason to be afraid, all twelve of them; for though they had fought their way, game by game, up the teams entered for the polo tournament, they were meeting the Archangels that afternoon in the final match; and the Archangels men were playing with half a dozen ponies apiece. As the game was divided into six quarters of eight minutes each, that meant a fresh pony after every halt. The Skidars' team, even supposing there were no accidents, could only supply one pony for every other change; and two to one is heavy odds. Again as Shiraz, the grey Syrian, pointed out, they were meeting the pink and pick of the polo-ponies of Upper India, ponies that had cost from a thousand rupees each, while they themselves were a cheap lot gathered often from country-carts, by their masters, who belonged to a poor but honest native infantry regiment.

'Money means pace and weight,' said Shiraz, rubbing his black-silk nose dolefully along his neat-fitting boot, 'and by the maxims of the game as I know it—'

'Ah, but we aren't playing the maxims,' said The Maltese Cat. 'We're playing the game; and we've the great advantage of knowing the game. Just think a stride, Shiraz! We've pulled up from bottom to second place in two weeks against all those fellows on the ground here. That's because we play with our heads as well as our feet.'

'It makes me feel undersized and unhappy all the same,' said Kittiwynk, a mouse-coloured mare with a red brow-band and the cleanest pair of legs that ever an aged pony owned. 'They've twice our style, these others.'

Kittiwynk looked at the gathering and sighed. The hard, dusty polo-ground was lined with thousands of soldiers, black and white, not counting hundreds and hundreds of carriages and drags and dog-carts, and ladies with brilliant-coloured parasols, and officers in uniform and out of it and crowds of natives behind them; and orderlies on camels, who had halted to watch the game, instead of carrying letters up and down the station; and native horse-dealers running about on thin-eared Biluchi mares, looking for a chance to sell a few first-class polo-ponies. Then there were the ponies of thirty teams that had entered for the Upper Indian Free-for-All Cup—nearly every pony of worth and dignity, from Mhow to Peshawar, from Allahabad to Multan; prize ponies, Arabs, Syrian, Barb, Country-bred, Deccanee, Waziri, and Kabul ponies of every colour and shape and temper that you could imagine. Some of them were in mat-roofed stables, close to the polo-ground, but most were under saddle, while their masters, who had been defeated in the earlier games, trotted in and out and told the world exactly how the game should be played.

It was a glorious sight, and the come and go of the little, quick hooves, and the incessant salutations of ponies that had met before on other polo-grounds or race-courses were enough to drive a four-footed thing wild.

But the Skidars' team were careful not to know their neigh-bours, though half the ponies on the ground were anxious to scrape acquaintance with the little fellows that had come from the North, and, so far, had swept the board.

'Let's see,' said a soft gold-coloured Arab, who had been playing very badly the day before, to the Maltese Cat; 'didn't we meet in Abdul Rahman's stable in Bombay, four seasons ago? I won the Paikpattan Cup next season, you may remember?'

'Not me,' said The Maltese Cat, politely. 'I was at Malta then, pulling a vegetable-cart. I don't race. I play the game.'

'Oh!' said the Arab, cocking his tail and swaggering off.

'Keep yourselves to yourselves,' said The Maltese Cat to his companions. 'We don't want to rub noses with all those goose-rumped half-breeds of Upper India. When we've won this Cup they'll give their shoes to know *us*.'

'We shan't win the Cup,' said Shirza. 'How do you feel?'

'Stale as last night's feed when a musk-rat has run over it,' said Polaris, a rather heavy-shouldered grey; and the rest of the team agreed with him.

'The sooner you forget that the better,' said The Maltese Cat, cheerfully. 'They've finished tiffin in the big tent. We shall be wanted now. If your saddles are not comfy, kick. If your bits aren't easy, rear, and let the *saises* know whether your boots are tight.'

Each pony had his *sais*, his groom, who lived and ate and slept with the animal, and had betted a good deal more than he could afford on the result of the game. There was no chance of anything going wrong, but to make sure, each *sais* was shampooing the legs of his pony to the last minute. Behind the *saises* sat as many of the Skidars' regiment as had leave to attend the match—about half the native officers, and a hundred or two dark, black-bearded men with the regimental pipers nervously fingering the big, beribboned bagpipes. The Skidars were what they called a Pioneer regiment, and the bagpipes made the national music of half their men. The native officers held bundles of polo sticks, long cane-handled mallets, and as the grandstand filled after lunch they arranged themselves by ones and twos at different points round the ground, so that if a stick were broken the player would not have far to ride for a new one. An impatient British Cavalry Band struck up 'If you want to know the time, ask a p'leeceman!' and the two umpires in light dust-coats danced out on two little excited ponies. The four players of the Archangels' team followed, and the sight of their beautiful mounts made Shiraz groan again.

'Wait till we know,' said The Maltese Cat. 'Two of 'em are playing in blinkers, and that means they can't see to get out of the way of their own side, or they *may* shy at the umpires' ponies. They've *all* got white web-reins that are sure to stretch or slip.'

'And,' said Kittiwynk, dancing to take the stiffness out of her, 'they carry their whips in their hands instead of on their wrists. Hah!'

True enough. No man can manage his stick and his reins and his whip that way,' said The Maltese Cat. 'I've fallen over every square yard of the Malta ground, and I ought to know.'

He quivered his little, flea-bitten withers just to show how satisfied he felt; but his heart was not so light. Ever since he had drifted into India on a troop-ship, taken, with an old rifle, as part payment for a racing debt, The Maltese Cat had played and preached polo to the Skidars' team on the Skidars' stony polo-ground. Now a polo-pony is like a poet. If he is born with a love of the game, he can be made. The Maltese Cat knew that bamboos grew solely in order that polo-balls might be turned from their roots, that grain was given to ponies to keep them in hard condition, and that ponies were shod to prevent them slipping on a turn. But, besides all these things, he knew every trick and device of the finest game in the world, and for two seasons had been teaching the others all he knew or guessed.

'Remember,' he said for the hundredth time, as the riders came up, 'you *must* play together, and you *must* play with your heads. Whatever happens, follow the ball. Who goes out first?'

Kittiwynk, Shiraz, Polaris, and a short high little bay fellow with tremendous hocks and no withers worth speaking of (he was called Corks) were being girthed up, and the soldiers in the background stared with all their eyes.

'I want you men to keep quiet,' said Lutyens, the captain of the team, 'and especially not to blow your pipes.'

'Not if we win, Captain Sahib?' asked the piper.

'If we win you can do what you please,' said Lutyens, with a smile, as he slipped the loop of his stick over his wrist, and wheeled to canter to his place. The Archangels' ponies were a little bit above themselves on account of the many-coloured crowds so close to the ground. Their riders were excellent players, but they were a team of crack players instead of a crack team; and that made all the difference in the world. They honestly meant to play together, but it is very hard for four men, each the best of the team he is picked from, to remember that in polo no brilliancy in hitting or riding makes up for playing alone. Their captain shouted his orders to them by name, and it is a curious thing that if you call his name aloud in public after an Englishman you make him hot and fretty. Lutyens said nothing to his men because it had all been said before. He pulled up Shiraz, for he was playing 'back', to guard the goal. Powell on Polaris was half-back, and Macnamara and Hughes on Corks and Kittiwynk were forwards. The tough, bamboo hall was set in the middle of the ground, 150 yards from the ends, and Hughes crossed sticks, heads up, with the

Captain of the Archangels, who saw fit to play forward; that is a place from which you cannot easily control your team. The little click as the cane-shafts met was heard all over the ground, and then Hughes made some sort of quick wrist-stroke that just dribbled the ball a few yards. Kittiwynk knew that stroke of old, and followed as a cat follows a mouse. While the Captain of the Archangels was wrenching his pony round, Hughes struck with all his strength, and next instant Kittiwynk was away, Corks following close behind her, their little feet pattering like raindrops on glass.

'Pull out to the left,' said Kittiwynk between her teeth; 'it's coming your way, Corks!'

The back and half-back of the Archangels were tearing down on her just as she was within reach of the ball. Hughes leaned forward with a loose rein, and cut it away to the left almost under Kittiwynk's foot, and it hopped and skipped off to Corks, who saw that, if he was not quick enough it would run beyond the boundaries. That long bouncing drive gave the Archangels time to wheel and send three men across the ground to head off Corks. Kittiwynk stayed where she was; for she knew the game. Corks was on the ball half a fraction of a second before the others came up, and Macnamara, with a backhanded stroke sent it back across the ground to Hughes, who saw the way clear to the Archangels' goal, and smacked the ball in before anyone quite knew what had happened.

'That's luck,' said Corks, as they changed ends. 'A goal in three minutes for three hits, and no riding to speak of.'

"Don't know,' said Polaris. 'We've made them angry too soon. Shouldn't wonder if they tried to rush us off our feet next time.'

'Keep the ball hanging, then,' said Shiraz. 'That wears out every pony that is not used to it.'

Next time there was no easy galloping across the ground. All the Archangels closed up as one man, but there they stayed, for Corks, Kittiwynk, and Polaris were somewhere on the top of the ball marking time among the rattling sticks, while Shiraz circled about outside, waiting for a chance.

'We can do this all day,' said Polaris, ramming his quarters into the side of another pony. 'Where do you think you're shoving to?'

'I'll—I'll be driven in an *ekka* if I know,' was the gasping reply, 'and I'd give a week's feed to get my blinkers off. I can't see anything.'

'The dust is rather bad. Whew! That was one for my off-hock. Where's the ball, Corks?'

'Under my tail. At least the man's looking for it there! This is beautiful. They can't use their sticks, and it's driving 'em wild. Give old Blinkers a push and then he'll go over.'

'Here, don't touch me! I can't see. I'll—I'll back out, I think,' said the pony in blinkers, who knew that if you can't see all round your head, you cannot prop yourself against the shock.

Corks was watching the ball where it lay in the dust, close to his near fore-leg, with Macnamara's shortened stick tap-tapping it from time to time. Kittiwynk was edging her way out of the scrimmage, whisking her stump of a tail with nervous excitement.

'Ho! They've got it,' she snorted. 'Let me out!' and she galloped like a rifle-bullet just behind a tall lanky pony of the Archangels, whose rider was swinging up his stick for a stroke.

'Not today, thank you,' said Hughes, as the blow slid off his raised stick, and Kittiwynk laid her shoulder to the tall pony's quarters, and shoved him aside just as Lutyens on Shiraz sent the ball where it had come from, and the tall pony went skating and slipping away to the left. Kittiwynk, seeing that Polaris had joined Corks in the chase for the ball up the ground, dropped into Polaris' place, and then 'time' was called.

The Skidars' ponies wasted no time in kicking or fuming. They knew that each minute's rest meant so much gain, and trotted off to the rails, and their *saises* began to scrape and blanket and rub them at once.

'Whew!' said Corks, stiffening up to get all the tickle of the big vulcanite scraper. 'If we were playing pony for pony, we would bend those Archangels double in half an hour. But they'll bring up fresh ones and fresh ones and fresh ones after that—you see.'

'Who cares?' said Polaris. 'We've drawn first blood. Is my hock swelling?'

'Looks puffy,' said Corks. 'You must have had rather a wipe. Don't let it stiffen. You'll be wanted again in half an hour.'

'What's the game like?' said The Maltese Cat.

'Ground's like your shoe, except where they put too much water on it,' said Kittiwynk. 'Then it's slippery. Don't play in the centre. There's a bog there. I don't know how their next four are going to behave, but we kept the ball hanging, and made 'em lather for nothing. Who goes out? Two Arabs and a couple of country-breds! That's bad. What a comfort it is to wash your mouth out!'

Kitty was talking with a neck of a lather-covered soda-bottle between her teeth, and trying to look over withers at the same time. This gave her a very coquettish air.

'What's bad?' said Grey Dawn, giving to the girth and admiring his well-set shoulders.

'You Arabs can't gallop fast enough to keep yourselves warm —that's what Kitty means,' said Polaris, limping to show that his hock needed attention. 'Are you playing back, Grey Dawn?'

'Looks like it,' said Grey Dawn, as Lutyens swung himself up. Powell mounted The Rabbit, a plain bay country-bred much like Corks, but with mulish ears. Macnamara took Faiz-Ullah, a handy, short-backed little red Arab with a long tail, and Hughes mounted Benami, an old and sullen brown beast, who stood over in front more than a polo-pony should.

'Benami looks like business,' said Shiraz. 'How's your temper, Ben?' The old campaigner hobbled off without answering, and The Maltese Cat looked at the new Archangel ponies prancing about on the ground. They were four beautiful blacks, and they saddled big enough and strong enough to eat the Skidars' team and gallop away with the meal inside them.

'Blinkers again,' said The Maltese Cat. 'Good enough!'

'They're chargers—cavalry chargers!' said Kittiwynk indignantly. '*They'll* never see thirteen-three again.'

'They've all been fairly measured, and they've all got their certificates,' said The Maltese Cat, 'or they wouldn't be here. We must take things as they come along, and keep your eyes on the ball.'

The game began, but this time the Skidars were penned to their own end of the ground, and the watching ponies did not approve of that.

'Faiz-Ullah is shirking—as usual,' said Polaris, with a scornful grunt.

'Faiz-Ullah is eating whip,' said Corks. They could hear the leather-thonged polo-quirt lacing the little fellow's well-rounded barrel. Then The Rabbit's shrill neigh came across the ground.

'I can't do all the work,' he cried, desperately.

'Play the game—don't talk.' The Maltese Cat whickered; and all the ponies wriggled with excitement, and the soldiers and the grooms gripped the railings and shouted. A black pony with blinkers had singled out old Benami, and was interfering with him in every possible way. They could see Benami shaking his head up and down and flapping his under lip.

'There'll be a fall in a minute,' said Polaris. 'Benami is getting stuffy.'

The game flickered up and down between goal-post and goal-post, and the black ponies were getting more confident as they felt they had the legs of the others. The ball was hit out of a little scrimmage, and Benami and The Rabbit followed it, Faiz-Ullah only too glad to be quiet for an instant.

The blinkered black pony came up like a hawk, with two of his own side behind him, and Benami's eye glittered as he raced. The question was which pony should make way for the other, for each rider was perfectly willing to risk a fall in a good cause. The black, who had been driven nearly crazy by his blinkers, trusted to his weight and his temper; but Benami knew how to apply his weight and how to keep his temper. They met, and there was a cloud of dust. The black was lying on his side, all the breath knocked out of his body. The Rabbit was a hundred yards up the ground with the ball, and Benami was sitting down, He had slid nearly ten yards on his tail, but he had had his revenge and sat cracking his nostrils till the black pony rose.

'That's what you get for interfering. Do you want any more?' said Benami, and he plunged into the game. Nothing was done that quarter, because Faiz-Ullah would not gallop, though Macnamara beat him whenever he could spare a second. The fall of the black pony had impressed his companions tremendously, and so the Archangels could not profit by Faiz-Ullah's bad behaviour.

But as The Maltese Cat said when 'time' was called, and the four came back blowing and dripping, Faiz-Ullah ought to have been kicked all round Umballa. If he did not behave better next time The Maltese Cat promised to pull out his Arab tail by the roots and—eat it.

There was no time to talk, for the third four were ordered out.

The third quarter of a game is generally the hottest for each side thinks that the others must be pumped; and most of the winning play in a game is made about that time.

Lutyens took over The Maltese Cat with a pat and a hug, for Lutyens valued him more than anything else in the world; Powell had Shikast, a little grey rat with no pedigree and no manners outside polo; Macnamara mounted Bamboo, the largest of the team; and Hughes Who's Who, alias The Animal. He was supposed to have Australian blood in his veins, but he looked like a clothes-horse and you could whack his legs with an iron crow-bar without hurting him.

They went out to meet the very flower of the Archangels' team; and when Who's Who saw their elegantly booted legs and their beautiful satin skins, he grinned a grin through his light, well-worn bridle.

'My word!' said Who's Who. 'We must give 'em a little football. These gentlemen need a rubbing down.'

'No biting,' said The Maltese Cat, warningly; for once or twice in his career Who's Who had been known to forget himself in that way.

'Who said anything about biting?' I'm not playing tiddly-winks. I'm playing the game.

The Archangels came down like a wolf on the fold, for they were tired of football, and they wanted polo. They got it more and more. Just after the game began, Lutyens hit a ball that was coming towards him rapidly, and it rolled in the air, as a ball sometimes will, with the whirl of a frightened partridge. Shikast heard but could not see it for the minute though he looked everywhere and up into the air as The Maltese Cat had taught him. When he saw it ahead and overhead he went forward with Powell, as fast as he could put foot to ground. It was then that Powell, a quiet and level-headed man as a rule, became inspired, and played a stroke that sometimes comes off successfully after long practice. He took his stick in both hands, and, standing up in his stirrups, swiped at the ball in the air, Munipore fasnion. There was one second of paralysed astonishment, and then all four sides of the ground went up in a yell of applause and delight as the ball flew true (you could see the amazed Archangels ducking in their saddles to dodge the line of flight, and looking at it with open mouths), and the regimental pipes of the Skidars squealed from the railings as long as the pipers had breath.

Shikast heard the stroke; but he heard the head of the stick fly off at the same time. Nine hundred and ninety-nine ponies out of a thousand would have gone tearing on after the ball with a useless player pulling at their heads; but Powell knew him, and he knew Powell; and the instant he felt Powell's right leg shift a trifle on the saddle-flap, he headed to the boundary, where a native officer was frantically waving a new stick. Before the shouts had ended, Powell was armed again.

Once before in his life The Maltese Cat had heard that very same stroke played off his own back, and had profited by the confusion it wrought. This time he acted on experience, and leaving Bamboo to guard the goal in case of accidents, came through the others like a flash, head and tail low—Lutyens standing up to ease him—swept on and on before the other side knew what was the matter, and nearly pitched on his head between the Archangels' goal-post as Lutyens kicked the ball in after a straight scurry of 150 yards. If there was one thing more than another upon which The Maltese Cat prided himself, it was on this quick, streaking kind of run half across the ground. He did not believe in taking balls round the field unless you were clearly overmatched. After this they gave the Archangels five minutes football; and an expensive fast pony hates football because it rumples his temper.

Who's Who showed himself even better than Polaris in this game. He did not permit any wriggling away, but bored joyfully into the scrimmage as if he had his nose in a feed-box and was looking for something nice. Little Shikast jumped on the ball the minute it got clear, and every time an Archangel pony followed it, he found Shikast standing over it, asking what was the matter.

'If we can live through this quarter,' said The Maltese Cat, 'I shan't care. Don't take it out of yourselves. Let them do the lathering.'

So the ponies, as their riders explained afterwards, 'shut-up'.

The Archangels kept them tied fast in front of their goal, but it cost the Archangels' ponies all that was left of their tempers; and ponies began to kick, and men began to repeat compliments, and they chopped at the legs of Who's Who, and he set his teeth and stayed where he was, and the dust stood up like a tree over the scrimmage until that hot quarter ended.

They found the ponies very excited and confident when they went to their *saises*; and The Maltese Cat had to warn them that the worst of the game was coming.

'Now *we* are all going in for the second time,' said he, 'and *they* are trotting out fresh ponies. You think you can gallop, but you'll find you can't; and then you'll be sorry.'

'But two goals to nothing is a halter-long lead,' said Kittiwynk, prancing.

'How long does it take to get a goal?' The Maltese Cat answered. 'For pity's sake, don't run away with a notion that the game is half-won just because we happen to be in luck *now*! They'll ride you into the grandstand, if they can; you must not give 'em a chance. Follow the ball.'

'Football, as usual?' said Polaris. 'My hock's half as big as a nose-bag.'

'Don't let them have a look at the ball, if you can help it. Now leave me alone. I must get all the rest I can before the last quarter.'

He hung down his head and let all his muscles go slack, Shikast, Bamboo, and Who's Who copying his example.

'Better not watch the game,' he said. 'We aren't playing, and we shall only take it out of ourselves if we grow anxious. Look at the ground and pretend it's fly-time.'

They did their best, but it was hard advice to follow. The hooves were drumming and the sticks were rattling all up and down the ground, yells of applause from the English troops told that the Archangels were pressing the Skidars hard. The native soldiers behind the ponies groaned and grunted, and said things in undertones, and presently they heard a long-drawn shout and a clatter of hurrahs.

'One to the Archangels,' said Shikast, without raising his head. 'Time's nearly up. Oh, my sire—and damn!'

'Faiz-Ullah,' said The Maltese Cat, 'if you don't play to the last nail in your shoes this time, I'll kick you on the ground before all the other ponies.'

'I'll do my best when the time comes,' said the little Arab sturdily.

The *saises* looked at each other gravely as they rubbed their ponies' legs. This was the time when long purses began to tell, and everybody knew it. Kittiwynk and the others came back, the sweat dripping over their hooves and their tails were telling sad stories.

'They're better than we are,' said Shiraz. 'I knew how it would be.'

'Shut your big head,' said The Maltese Cat; 'we've one goal to the good yet.'

'Yes; but it's two Arabs and two country-breds to play now,' said Corks. 'Faiz-Ullah, remember!' He spoke in a biting voice.

As Lutyens mounted Grey Dawn he looked at his men, and they did not look pretty. They were covered with dust and sweat in streaks. Their yellow boots were almost black, their wrists were red and lumpy, and their eyes seemed two inches deep in their heads; but the expression in the eyes was satisfactory.

'Did you take anything at tiffin?' said Lutyens; and the team shook their heads. They were too dry to talk.

'All right. The Archangels did. They are worse pumped than we are.'

'They've got the better ponies,' said Powell. 'I shan't be sorry when this business is over.'

That fifth quarter was a painful one in every way. Faiz-Ullah played like a little red demon, and The Rabbit seemed to be everywhere at once, and Benami rode straight at everything, and everything that came in his way; while the umpires on their ponies wheeled like gulls outside the shifting game. But the Archangels had the better mounts,—they had kept their racers till late in the game,—and never allowed the Skidars to play football. They hit the ball up and down the width of the ground till Benami and the rest were outpaced. Then they went forward, and time and again Lutyens and Grey Dawn were just, and only just, able to send the ball away with a long, spitting backhander. Grey Dawn forgot that he was an Arab; and turned from grey to blue as he galloped. Indeed, he forgot too well, for he did not keep his eyes on the ground as an Arab should, but stuck out his nose and scuttled for the dear honour of the game. They had watered the ground once or twice between the quarters, and a careless waterman had emptied the last of his skinful all in one place near the Skidars' goal. It was close to the end of the play, and for the tenth time Grey Dawn was bolting after the ball, when his near hind-foot slipped on the greasy mud, and he rolled over and over, pitching Lutyens just clear of the goal-post; and the triumphant Archangels made their goal. Then 'time' was called—two goals all; but Lutyens had to be helped up, and Grey Dawn rose with his near hind-leg strained somewhere.

'What's the damage?' said Powell, his arm around Lutyens.

'Collar-bone, *of course*,' said Lutyens, between his teeth. It was the third time he had broken it in two years, and it hurt him.

Powell and the others whistled.

'Game's up,' said Hughes.

'Hold on. We've five good minutes yet, and it isn't my right hand. We'll stick it out.'

'I say,' said the captain of the Archangels, trotting up, 'are you hurt, Lutyens? We'll wait if you care to put in a substitute. I wish—I mean—the fact is, you fellows deserve this game if any team does. 'Wish we could give you a man, or some of our ponies—or something.'

'You're awfully good, but we'll play it to a finish, I think.'

The captain of the Archangels stared for a little. 'That's not half bad,' he said, and went back to his own side, while Lutyens borrowed a scarf from one of his native officers and made a sling of it. Then an Archangel galloped up with a big bath-sponge, and advised Lutyens to put it under his armpit to ease his shoulder and between them they tied up his left arm scientifically; and one of the native officers leaped forward with four long glasses that fizzed and bubbled.

The team looked at Lutyens piteously, and he nodded. It was the last quarter, and nothing would matter after that. They drank out the dark golden drink, and wiped their moustaches, and things looked more hopeful.

The Maltese Cat had put his nose into the front of Lutyens' shirt and was trying to say how sorry he was.

'He knows,' said Lutyens, proudly. 'The beggar knows. I've played him without a bridle before now—for fun.'

'It's no fun now,' said Powell, 'But we haven't a decent substitute.'

'No,' said Lutyens. 'It's the last quarter, and we've got to make our goal and win. I'll trust The Cat.'

'If you fall this time, you'll suffer a little,' said Macnamara.

'I'll trust The Cat,' said Lutyens.

'You hear that?' said The Maltese Cat, proudly, to the others. 'It's worth while playing polo for ten years to have that said of you. Now then, my sons, come along. We'll kick up a little bit, just to show the Archangels this team haven't suffered.'

And sure enough, as they went on to the ground, The Maltese Cat, after satisfying himself that Lutyens was home in the saddle, kicked out three or four times, and Lutyens laughed. The reins were caught up anyhow in the tips of his strapped left hand, and he never pretended to rely on them. He knew The Cat would answer to the least pressure of the leg, and by way of showing off—for his shoulder hurt him very much—he bent the little fellow in a close figure-of-eight in and out between the goal-posts. There was a roar from the native officers and men, who dearly loved a piece of *dugabashi* (horse-trick work), as they called it, and the pipes very quietly and scornfully droned out the first bars of a common bazaar tune called 'Freshly Fresh and Newly New,' just as a warning to the other regiments that the Skidars were fit. All the natives laughed.

'And now,' said The Maltese Cat, as they took their place, 'remember that this is the last quarter, and follow the ball!'

'Don't need to be told,' said Who's Who.

'Let me go on. All these people on all four sides will begin to crowd in—just as they did at Malta. You'll hear people calling out, and moving forward and being pushed back; and this is going to make the Archangel ponies very unhappy. But if a ball is struck to the boundary, you go after it, and let the people get out of your way. I went over the pole of a four-in-hand once, and picked a game out of the dust by it. Back me up when I run, and follow the ball.'

There was a sort of an all-round sound of sympathy and

wonder as the last quarter opened, and then there began exactly what The Maltese Cat had foreseen. People crowded in close to the boundaries, and the Archangels' ponies kept looking sideways at the narrowing space. If you know how a man feels to be cramped at tennis—not because he wants to run out of the court, but because he likes to know that he can at a pinch—you will guess how ponies must feel when they are playing in a box of human beings.

'I'll bend some of those men if I can get away,' said Who's Who, as he rocketed behind the ball; and Bamboo nodded without speaking. They were playing the last ounce in them, and The Maltese Cat had left the goal undefended to join them. Lutyens gave him every order that he could to bring him back, but this was the first time in his career that the little wise grey had ever played polo on his own responsibility, and he was going to make the most of it.

'What are you doing here?' said Hughes, as The Cat crossed in front of him and rode off an Archangel.

'The Cat's in charge—mind the goal!' shouted Lutyens, and bowing forward hit the ball full, and followed on, forcing the Archangels towards their own goal.

'No football,' said The Maltese Cat. 'Keep the ball by the boundaries and cramp 'em. Play open order, and drive 'em to the boundaries.'

Across and across the ground in big diagonals flew the ball, and whenever it came to a flying rush and a stroke close to the boundaries the Archangel ponies moved stiffly. They did not care to go headlong at a wall of men and carriages, though if the ground had been open they could have turned on a sixpence.

'Wriggle her up the sides,' said The Cat. 'Keep her close to the crowd. They hate the carriages. Shikast, keep her up this side.'

Shikast and Powell lay left and right behind the uneasy scuffle of an open scrimmage, and every time the ball was hit away Shikast galloped on it at such an angle that Powell was forced to hit it towards the boundary; and when the crowd had been driven away from that side, Lutyens would send the ball over to the other, and Shikast would slide desperately after it till his friends came down to help. It was billiards, and no football, this time—billiards in a corner pocket; and the cues were not well chalked.

'If they get us out in the middle of the ground they'll walk away from us. Dribble her along the sides,' cried The Maltese Cat.

So they dribbled all along the boundary, where a pony could not come in on their right-hand side; and the Archangels were furious and the umpires had to neglect the game to shout at the people to get back, and several blundering mounted policemen tried to restore order, all close to the scrimmage, and the nerves of the Archangels' ponies stretched and broke like cob-webs.

Five or six times an Archangel hit the ball up into the middle of the ground, and each time the watchful Shikast gave Powell his chance to send it back, and after each return, when the dust had settled, men could see that the Skidars had gained a few yards.

Every now and again there were shouts of 'Side! Off side!' from the spectators; but the teams were too busy to care, and the umpires had all they could do to keep their maddened ponies clear of the scuffle.

At last Lutyens missed a short easy stroke, and the Skidars had to fly back helter-skelter to protect their own goal, Shikast leading. Powell stopped the ball with a backhander when it was not fifty yards from the goal-posts, and Shikast spun round with a wrench that nearly hoisted Powell out of his saddle.

'Now's our last chance,' said The Cat, wheeling like a cock-chafer on a pin. 'We've got to ride it out. Come along.'

Lutyens felt the little chap take a deep breath, and, as it were, crouch under his rider. The ball was hopping towards the right-hand boundary, an Archangel riding for it with both spurs and a whip; but neither spur nor whip would make his pony stretch himself as he neared the crowd. The Maltese Cat glided under his very nose, picking up his hind legs sharp, for there was not a foot to spare between his quarters and the other pony's bit. It was as neat an exhibition as fancy figure-skating. Lutyens hit with all the strength he had left, but the stick slipped a little in his hand, and the ball flew off to the left instead of keeping close to the boundary. Who's Who was far across the ground, thinking hard as he galloped. He repeated stride for stride The Cat's manœuvres with another Archangel pony, nipping the ball away from under his bridle, and clearing his opponent by half a fraction of an inch, for Who's Who was clumsy behind. Then he drove away towards the right as The Maltese Cat came up from the left; and Bamboo held a middle course exactly between them. The three were making a sort of Government-broad-arrow-shaped attack; and there was only the Archangels' back to guard the goal; but immediately behind them were three Archangels racing all they knew, and mixed up with them was Powell sending Shikast along on what he felt was their last hope. It takes a very good man to stand up to the rush of seven crazy ponies in the last quarters of a Cup game, when men are riding with their necks for sale, and the ponies are delirious. The Archangels' back missed his stroke and pulled aside just in time to let the rush go by. Bamboo and Who's Who shortened stride to give The Cat room, and Lutyens got the goal with a clean, smooth, smacking stroke that was heard all over the field. But there was no stopping the ponies. They poured through the goal-posts in one mixed mob, winners and losers together, for the pace had been terrific. The Maltese Cat knew by experience what would happen, and, to save Lutyens, turned to the right with one last effort, that strained a back-sinew beyond hope of repair. As he did so he heard the right-hand goal-post crack as a pony cannoned into it—crack, splinter and fall like a mast. It had been sawn three parts through in case of accidents, but it upset the pony nevertheless, and he blundered into another, who blundered into the left-hand post, and then there was confusion and dust and wood. Bamboo was lying on the ground seeing stars; an Archangel pony rolled beside him, breathless and angry; Shikast had sat down dog-fashion to avoid falling over the others, and was sliding along on his little bobtail in a cloud of dust; and Powell was sitting on the ground hammering with his stick and trying to cheer. All the others were shouting at the top of what was left of their voices, and the men who had been spilt were shouting, too. As soon as the people saw no one was hurt, 10,000 natives and English shouted and clapped and yelled, and before any one could stop them the pipers of the Skidars broke on to the ground, with all the native officers and men behind them, and marched up and down, playing a wild

Northern tune called 'Zakhme-Bagán,' and through the inso-
lent blaring of the pipes and the high-pitched native yells you
could hear the Archangels' band hammering, 'For they are all
jolly good fellows,' and then reproachfully to the losing team,
'Ooh, Kafoozalum! Kafoozalum! Kafoozalum!'

Besides all these things, and many more, there was a
Commander-in-chief, and an Inspector-General of Cavalry, .
and the principal veterinary officer of all India standing on the
top of a regimental coach, yelling like school-boys, and briga-
diers and colonels and commissioners, and hundreds of pretty
ladies joined the chorus. But The Maltese Cat stood with his
head down, wondering how many legs were left to him; and
Lutyens watched the men and ponies pick themselves out of
the wreck of the two goal-posts, and he patted The Maltese Cat
very tenderly.

'I say,' said the captain of the Archangels, spitting a pebble
out of his mouth, 'will you take three thousand for that pony —
as he stands?'

'No thank you. I've an idea he's saved my life,' said Lutyens,
getting off and lying down at full length. Both teams were on
the ground, too, waving their boots in the air, and coughing,
and drawing deep breaths, as the *saises* ran up to take away the
ponies, and an officious water-carrier sprinkled the players
with dirty water till they sat up.

'My Aunt!' said Powell, rubbing his back, and looking at the
stumps of the goal-posts. 'That was a game!'

They played it over again, every stroke of it, that night at the
big dinner, when the Free-for-All Cup was filled and passed
down the table, and emptied and filled again, and everybody
made most eloquent speeches. About two in the morning,
when there might have been some singing, a wise little, plain
little, grey little head looked in through the open door.

'Hurrah! Bring him in,' said the Archangels; and his *sais*,
who was very happy indeed, patted The Maltese Cat on the
flank, and he limped in to the blaze of light and the glittering
uniforms looking for Lutyens. He was used to messes, and
men's bedrooms, and places where ponies are not usually
encouraged, and in his youth had jumped on and off a mess-
table for a bet. So he behaved himself very politely, and ate
bread dipped in salt, and was petted all round the table,

moving gingerly; and they drank his health, because he had done more to win the Cup than any man or horse on the ground.

That was glory and honour enough for the rest of his days, and The Maltese Cat did not complain much when the veterinary surgeon said that he would be no good for polo any more. When Lutyens married, his wife did not allow him to play, so he was forced to be an umpire; and his pony on these occasions was a flea-bitten grey with a neat polo-tail, lame all round, but desperately quick on his feet, and, as everyone knew, Past Pluperfect Prestissimo Player of the Game.

My First Wild Horse

BARBARA WOODHOUSE

FOR A LOVER of horses the Argentine is the saddest place to live, for these most intelligent and willing animals and servants of man are never treated as they should be, but are roughly handled from the first. I think I learnt to speak fluent Spanish more quickly than usual because of my rages—as when, for example, I saw a brute of a man knock a horse's eye out with one lash. . . . I learnt to upbraid them in no mild language; but all they said was that horses were worth only a few pesos, and they must be taught quickly. Hence the cruel method of breaking a horse in, by lashing it to make it gallop and then pulling it fiercely back on to its haunches. Three men and horses all putting a concerted pull on its mouth at the same time. I pleaded with them to be kind, but it had no effect, so I decided to show them that I could break horses as quickly and as well as they could and without any cruelty. I begged the manager of the *estancia* to let me have a three year old to start on, but he refused point blank. 'Women don't break horses out here, that is a man's job,' he said, and all my pleading fell on deaf ears.

But I don't believe in being defeated in anything I really wish to do, so I bided my time. Shortly after this the whole of the unit went many miles away out into the camp on a branding job and were away for three days. The only people left were myself, my old Indian cook, and the old native who chopped our logs for us and did all the odd jobs such as butchering. I saw the men off, and then went out to the barn to find old Fernandez. I think he liked me, for I was the only person there who treated him like an ordinary human being and not as a slave. I asked him how long the *capitas* and *patron* would be away, and he said, 'Three sun downs,' so I told him that before they came back I wanted to break in a horse to do everything that their own horses could do. He looked at me as if I were mad, but listened to me when I suggested that we should ride out in the camp together to the wild herd and that he should lasso one of the horses for me. I promised him tobacco and money, and with much wagging of his head he agreed.

I could hardly wait whilst he ponderously saddled his fat old mare and went to fetch a little bay pony for me. Together we rode out and at last came to the herd. At first they paid no attention to us and we quietly rode round them. Then I saw what I wanted, a beautiful golden chestnut with four white socks and a blaze down her face. I pointed her out to Fernandez but he shook his head. 'Don't have her,' he said, 'she has a mala Cara,' which means a bad white face, and in the eyes of the natives suggests a bad bargain even before you start. But I knew this to be nonsense, and told him to catch her. Neatly the rope encircled her neck, and then she flung herself about like a salmon on a line. But eventually she was tied to the ring in the saddle of his own horse, and his old mount played the youngster like an experienced fisherman. Bit by bit she stopped pulling, and in the end we got her tied up near the house on a rawhide halter and a rope. By this time the old man was terrified of what he'd done and begged me to let her go again, for he said the master would kill him when he came home. I told him it was nonsense: that Englishmen didn't behave like that, and that I myself would take full responsibility. And in any case I had heard the *patron* telling him before he left to do all that I wanted. Miserably he slunk off to his barn to continue his routine task of scraping the fat and flesh off the sheep skins to make them ready for the tannery. I could hardly believe my luck. Here was this gorgeous creature for me to tame, and no one to say me nay.

I approached her gently, speaking in a low caressing tone of voice. She flinched at first on my approach and snorted furiously, but did nothing more. I then stroked her nose and her neck and ran my fingers gently down her mane, for I knew that horses loved this, and soon she stood quite dreamily still; so I then ran my hands down her legs and picked up her feet, talking gently and soothingly all the time. Next I went down her body and picked up her back legs; then round the other side and back to her head. Then I got a sack and gently slapped her all over with it. She leapt in the air with the first feel of it, but soon, when she found it did not hurt her, she paid no more attention to it. I whisked it gently over her back and under her tummy. I slapped her legs gently, and down her tail. I then dropped the sack off her back until she no longer flinched, and that ended the first lesson. Next I taught her to eat sugar by putting it between her back teeth. At first she spat it out, so the next time I held it in her mouth until it had nearly melted. That worked wonderfully, and in no time she was crunching up as much as I could give her. But I kept it as a reward for everything new that I wished to teach her. I next fetched my saddle and put it on her back with a very loose girth. Up went her back in a terrific buck, but I talked to her and moved the saddle about, and then tightened the girth one hole and made her move. This time she hunched her back but did not buck, so I tightened it up to make it safe, and then got an old wood block and put it by her side, so that I could stand on it and lean heavily over her, talking all the while. She never stirred, so gently I slung my leg over her and slid on and off about three times like this. I then put reins on the side pieces of her head-collar, since I do not believe in bits, and I sat on her back whilst she was still tied up. Next I urged her forward a pace or two, and then said 'Ssh' and pulled her to a stop on the reins. Encouraged by her docility I slipped off the rope she was tied up with, and leant over to pull gently on the head-collar to urge her forward. She walked on, and after half an hour of this I unsaddled her and took her out into the small paddock by the house and tied the long rope to a moveable tree trunk and let her wander. At first she was terrified of the log moving along after her but soon she got accustomed to it. After lunch I brought her in again and rode her for another half hour. Soon she was trotting and walking well, but I still had the feeling that she might panic at any minute.

By the end of the three days this pony was going extremely well, I opened the gates of the corral, told old Fernandez to follow me at a distance, and off I went on her for my first ride. It was without incident for some time, until something frightened her in the grass, when she put herself into a series of bucks that would have done credit to a buck-jumping contest. I

was ready for it, for all the time she had felt to me as if the slightest error on my part would make her try to get rid of me. However, we came home safely, and I caressed her lovingly and let her free in the small paddock near the house. Next morning I rode along for an hour, and so her breaking continued smoothly.

On the last day before the men came home, I met an old Guarani Indian riding a beautiful little bay mare. We stopped and said polite things to each other, and I told him I was taming the chestnut I was on. He said he thought only his own tribe knew the secret of taming horses without fear, and, when asked what it was, he told me to watch next time I turned strange horses out together and to see what they did. I asked what he meant, and he told me that horses always go up to each other and sniff each other's noses, which is their way of saying 'How do you do?' in their language, and that he always did the same thing when he wished to tame a horse himself. He said: 'Stand with your hands behind your back and blow gently down through your nostrils. Keep quite still, and the horse will come up to you and sniff and will blow up your own nose after which all fear will have left him. That horse, providing that you don't give it reason to turn vicious will always be your friend and the friend of man.' And with that he cantered off at the easy gallop of the perfectly matched horse and rider, with his reins hanging loosely and without a saddle, just a blanket on the horse's back.

That evening the men came home and I told them what I had been up to, and of course got the most severe scolding possible. Fernandez was threatened with the sack, but I pointed out that it was my fault entirely and that he had been ordered to do what I wanted. No more was said until I gave a little show with my mare Cara, who behaved like a lamb, and the manager said he supposed I could break a horse. I felt this was the moment to ask for another, for I was dying to try out the Guarani's trick. So another was caught up for me. I sniffed up her nose and immediately stroked her and saddled her up. From her behaviour she might have been any old horse, for she never flinched or snorted or showed any sign of fear. I cut out the preliminary sack flapping and fondling and gently mounted her, loosed the rope, and with my heels urged her on. She went smoothly with me, and I never for a second had that feeling that I had had with the other horse, that at any minute she and I might part company. In twenty minutes in the corral I taught her to stop, and to turn, and to trot, and then I asked the men watching me to open the gate and away we went. In an hour she was cantering, turning, stopping, and allowing me to mount and dismount without any protest or signs of fear.

I knew the Indian was right, for that horse never put a foot wrong and in three days was a completely trained pony. I could safely round up cattle with her, open and shut gates, and so on; and all this on a head-collar only. I have won many a bet in England that I would do anything normal on a horse without saddle or bridle, winning simply because I knew that my horse knew every command of voice. For a bet, I have played fast polo on reins of one strand of '50' cotton. My success with the Guarani's trick gave me the chance in life I had always wanted, for from now on, instead of the *peons* being paid to tame the horses, they were given more useful jobs, like fencing, to do, and I was promoted to be horse-breaker at ten shillings per horse. The Inspector of the cattle company was told about me and came out later to see why a woman was allowed to do this. He rode one of my horses that had been completely untouched two hours before and could find no fault in it except lack of experience. It was thus that I became the happiest woman on earth in my self-chosen job.

Mr Carteret and His Fellow Americans Abroad

DAVID GRAY

I T MUST have been highly interesting,' observed Mrs Archie Brawle; 'so much pleasanter than a concert.'

'Rather!' replied Lord Frederic. 'It was ripping!'

Mrs Ascott-Smith turned to Mr Carteret. She had been listening to Lord Frederic Westcote, who had just come down from town where he had seen the Wild West Show. 'Is it so?' she asked. 'Have you ever seen them?' By 'them' she meant the Indians.

Mr Carteret nodded.

'It seems odd,' continued Mrs Archie Brawle, 'that they should ride without saddles, is it a pose?'

'No, I fancy not,' replied Lord Frederic.

'They must get very tired without stirrups,' insisted Mrs Archie. 'But perhaps they never ride very long at a time.'

'That is possible,' said Lord Frederic doubtfully, 'They are only on about twenty minutes in the show.'

Mr Pringle, the curate, who had happened in to pay his monthly call upon Mrs Ascott-Smith, took advantage of the pause. 'Of course, I am no horse-man,' he began apprehensively, 'and I have never seen the Red Indians, either in their native wilds or in a show, but I have read not a little about them, and I have gathered that they almost live on horseback.'

Major Hammerslea reached towards the tea table for another muffin and hemmed. 'It is a very different thing,' he said, with heavy impressiveness. 'It is a very different thing.'

The curate looked expectant, as if believing that his remarks were going to be noticed. But nothing was farther from the Major's mind.

'What is so very different?' inquired Mrs Ascott-Smith, after a pause had made it clear that the Major had ignored Pringle.

'It is one thing, my dear Madame, to ride a stunted, half-starved pony, as you say, "bareback" and another to ride a conditioned British hunter (he pronounced it huntaw) without a saddle. I must say that the latter is an impossibility.' The oracle came to an end and the material Major began on a muffin.

There was an approving murmur of assent. The Major was the author of 'Schooling and Riding British Hunters'; however, it was not only his authority which swayed the company, but individual conviction. Of the dozen people in the room, excepting Pringle, all rode to hounds with more or less enthusiasm, and no one had ever seen anyone hunting without a saddle, and no one had ever experienced any desire to try the experiment.

'Nevertheless,' observed Lord Frederic, 'I must say their riding is very creditable—quite as good as one sees on any polo field in England.'

Major Hammerslea looked at him severely, as if his youth were not wholly an excuse. 'It is, as I said,' he observed. 'It is one thing to ride an American pony and another to ride a British hunter. One requires horsemanship, the other does not. And horsemanship,' he continued, 'which properly is the guiding of a horse across country, requires years of study and experience.'

Lord Frederic looked somewhat unconvinced, but he said nothing.

'Of course the dear Major (she called him deah Majaw) is quite right,' said Mrs Ascott-Smith.

'Undoubtedly,' said Mr Carteret. 'I suppose that he has often seen these Indians ride?'

'Have you often seen these Indians ride?' inquired Mrs Ascott-Smith of the Major.

'Do you mean Indians or the Red Men of North America?' replied the Major. 'And do you mean ride upon ponies in a show or ride upon British hunters?'

'Which do you mean?' asked Mrs Ascott-Smith.

'I suppose that I mean American Indians,' said Mr Carteret, 'and either upon ponies or upon British hunters.'

'No,' said the Major. 'I have not. Have you?'

'Not upon British hunters,' said Mr Carteret.

'But do you think that they could?' inquired Lord Frederic.

'It would be foolish of me to express an opinion,' replied Mr Carteret, 'because, in the first place, I have never seen them ride British hunters over fences—'

'They would come off at the first obstacle,' observed the Major, more in sorrow than anger.

'And in the second place,' continued Mr Carteret, 'I am perhaps naturally prejudiced on behalf of my fellow-countrymen.'

Mrs Ascott-Smith looked at him anxiously. His sister had married a British peer. 'But you Americans are quite distinct from the Red Indians,' she said. 'We quite understand that nowadays. To be sure, my dear Aunt—' she stopped.

'Rather!' said Mrs Archie Brawle. 'You don't even intermarry with them, do you?'

'That is a matter of personal taste,' said Mr Carteret. 'There is no law against it.'

'But nobody that one knows—' began Mrs Ascott-Smith.

'There was John Rolfe,' said Mr Carteret; 'he was a very well-known chap.'

'Do you know him?' asked Mrs Brawle.

The curate sniggered. His hour of triumph had come. 'Rolfe is dead,' he said.

'Really!' said Mrs Brawle coldly. 'It had quite slipped my mind. You see I never read the papers during hunting. But is his wife received?'

'I believe that she was,' said Mr Carteret.

The curate was still sniggering, and Mrs Brawle put her glass in her eye and looked at him. Then she turned to Mr Carteret. 'But all this,' she said, 'of course has nothing to do with the question. Do you think that these red Indians could ride bare-back across our country?'

'As I said before,' replied Mr Carteret. 'It would be silly of me to express an opinion, but I should be interested in seeing them try it.'

'I have a topping idea!' cried Lord Frederic. He was an enthusiastic, simple-minded fellow.

'You must tell us,' exclaimed Mrs Ascott-Smith.

'Let us have them down, and take them hunting!'

'How exciting!' exclaimed Mrs Ascott-Smith. 'What sport!'

The Major looked at her reprovingly. 'It would be as I said,' he observed.

'But it would be rather interesting,' said Mrs Brawle.

'It might,' said the Major, 'it might be interesting.'

'It would be ripping!' said Lord Frederic. 'But how can we manage it?'

'I'll mount them,' said the Major with a grim smile. 'My word! They shall have the pick of my stable though I have to spend a month rebreaking horses that have run away.'

'But it isn't the difficulty of mounting them,' said Lord Frederic. 'You see I've never met any of these chaps.' He turned to Mr Carteret with a sudden inspiration. 'Are any of them friends of yours?' he asked.

Mrs Ascott-Smith looked anxiously at Mr Carteret as if she feared that it would develop that some of the people in the show were his cousins.

'No,' he replied, 'I don't think so, although I may have met some of them in crossing reservations. But I once went shooting with Grady, one of the managers of the show.'

'Better yet!' said Lord Frederic. 'Do you think that he would come and bring some of them down?' he asked.

'I think he would,' said Mr Carteret. He knew that the showman was strong in Grady—as well as the sportsman.

The Major rose to go to the billiard room. 'I have one piece of advice to give you,' he said. 'This prank is harmless enough, but establish a definite understanding with this fellow that you are not to be liable in damages for personal injuries which his Indians may receive. Explain to him that it is not child's play and have him put it in writing.'

'You mean have him execute a kind of release?'

'Precisely that,' said the Major. 'I was once sued for twenty pounds by a groom that fell off my best horse, and let him run away, and damme, the fellow recovered.' He bowed to the ladies and left the room.

'Of course we can fix all that up,' said Lord Frederic. 'The old chap is a bit overcautious nowadays, but how can we get hold of this fellow Grady?'

'I'll wire him at once, if you wish,' said Mr Carteret, and he went to the writing table. 'When do you want him to come down?' he asked as he began to write.

'We might take them out with the Quorn on Saturday,' said Lord Frederic, 'but the meet is rather far for us. Perhaps it would be better to have them on Thursday with Charley Ploversdale's hounds.'

Mr Carteret hesitated a moment. 'Wouldn't Ploversdale be apt to be fussy about experiments? He's rather conservative, you know, about the way people are turned out. I saw him send a man home one day who was out without a hat. It was an American who was afraid that hats made his hair come out.'

'Pish,' said Lord Frederic. 'Charley Ploversdale is as mild as a dove.'

'Suit yourself,' said Mr Carteret. 'I'll make it Thursday. One more question,' he added. 'How many shall I ask him to bring down?' At this moment the Major came into the room again. He had mislaid his spectacles.

'I should think that a dozen would be about the right number,' said Lord Frederic, replying to Mr Carteret. 'It would be very imposing.'

'Too many!' said the Major. 'We must mount them on good horses and I don't want my entire stable ruined by men who have never leapt a fence.'

'I think the Major is right about the matter of numbers,' said Mr Carteret, 'how would three do?'

'Make it three,' said the Major.

Before dinner was over a reply came from Grady saying that he and three bucks would be pleased to arrive Thursday morning prepared for a hunting party.

This took place on Monday, and at various times during Tuesday and Wednesday Mr Carteret gave the subject thought. By Thursday morning his views had ripened. He ordered his tea and eggs to be served in his room and came down a little past ten dressed in knickerbockers and an old shooting coat. He wandered into the dining-room and found Mrs Ascott-Smith sitting by the fire entertaining Lord Frederic, as he went to and from the sideboard in search of things to eat.

'Good morning,' said Mr Carteret, hoarsely.

Lord Frederic looked around and as he noticed Mr Carteret's clothes his face showed surprise.

'Hello!' he said. 'You had better hurry and change, or you'll be late. We have to start in half an hour to meet Grady.'

Mr Carteret coughed. 'I don't think that I can go out today. It is a great disappointment.'

'Not going hunting?' exclaimed Mrs Ascott-Smith. 'What is the matter?'

'I have a bad cold,' said Mr Carteret miserably.

'But, my dear fellow,' exclaimed Lord Frederic, 'it will do your cold a world of good!'

'Not a cold like mine,' said Mr Carteret.

'But this day, don't you know?' said Lord Frederic. 'How am I going to manage things without you?'

'All that you have to do is to meet them at the station and take them to the meet,' said Mr Carteret. 'Everything else has been arranged.'

'But I'm awfully disappointed,' said Lord Frederic. 'I had counted on you to help, don't you see, and introduce them to Ploversdale. It would be more graceful for an American to do it than for me. You understand?'

'Yes,' said Mr Carteret, 'I understand. It's a great disappointment, but I must bear it philosophically.'

Mrs Ascott-Smith looked at him sympathetically, and he coughed twice. 'You must be suffering,' she said. 'Freddy, you really must not urge him to expose himself. Have you a pain here?' she inquired, touching herself in the region of the pleura.

'Yes,' said Mr Carteret, 'it is just there, but I dare say it will soon be better.'

'I am afraid not,' said his hostess. 'This is the way pneumonia begins. You must take a medicine that I have. They say it is quite wonderful for inflammatory colds. I'll send Hodgson for it,' and she touched the bell.

'Please, please don't take that trouble,' entreated Mr Carteret.

'But you must take it,' said Mrs Ascott-Smith. 'They call it Broncholine. You pour it in a tin and inhale it or swallow it, I forget which, but it's very efficacious. They used it on Teddy's pony when it was sick. The little creature died, but that was because they gave it too much, or not enough, I forget which.'

Hodgson appeared and Mrs Ascott-Smith gave directions about the Broncholine.

'I thank you very much,' said Mr Carteret humbly, 'I'll go to my room and try it at once.'

'That's a good chap!' said Lord Frederic, 'Perhaps you will feel so much better that you can join us.'

'Perhaps,' said Mr Carteret gloomily, 'or it may work as it did on the pony,' and he left the room.

After Hodgson had departed from his chamber leaving explicit directions as to how and how not to use the excellent Broncholine, Mr Carteret poured a quantity of it from the bottle and threw it out of the window, resolving to be on the safe side. Then he looked at his boots and his pink coat and his white leathers, which were laid out upon the bed. 'I don't think there can be any danger,' he thought, 'if I turn up after they have started. I loathe stopping in all day.' He dressed leisurely, ordered his second best horse to be sent on, and some time after the rest of the household had gone to the meet he sallied forth. As he knew the country and the coverts which Lord Ploversdale would draw, he counted on joining the tail of the hunt, thus keeping out of sight. He inquired of a rustic if he had seen hounds pass and receiving a 'no' for an answer, he jogged on at a faster trot, fearing that the hunt might have gone away in some other direction.

As he came round a bend in the road, he saw four women riding towards him, and as they drew near he saw that they were Lady Violet Weatherbone and her three daughters. These young ladies were known as the Three Guardsmen, a sobriquet not wholly inappropriate; for, as Lord Frederic described them, they were 'big-boned, up-standing fillies,' between twenty-five and thirty, and very hard goers across any country, and always together.

'Good morning,' said Mr Carteret, bowing. 'I suppose the hounds are close by?' It was a natural assumption, as Lady Violet, on hunting days, was never very far from hounds.

'I do not know,' she responded, and her tone implied that she did not care.

Mr Carteret hesitated a moment. 'Is anything the matter?' he asked. 'Has anything happened?'

'Yes,' said Lady Violet frankly, 'something has happened.'

Here the daughters modestly turned their horses away.

'Someone,' continued Lady Violet, 'brought savages to the meet.' She paused impressively.

'Not really!' said Mr Carteret. It was all that he could think of to say.

'Yes,' said Lady Violet, 'and while it would have mattered little to me, it was impossible—' she motioned her head towards the three maidens, and paused.

'Forgive me,' said Mr Carteret, 'but do I quite understand?'

'At the first I thought,' said Lady Violet, 'that they were attired in painted fleshings, but upon using my glasses, it was clear that I was mistaken. Otherwise, I should have brought them away at the first moment.'

'I see,' said Mr Carteret. 'It is most unfortunate!'

'It is indeed!' said Lady Violet; 'but the matter will not be allowed to drop. They were brought to the meet by that young profligate, Lord Frederic Westcote.'

'You amaze me,' said Mr Carteret. He bowed, started his horse, and jogged along for five minutes, then he turned to the right upon a crossroad and suddenly found himself with hounds. They were feathering excitedly about the mouth of a tile drain into which the fox had evidently gone. No master, huntsmen or whips were in sight, but sitting wet and mud-daubed upon horses dripping with muddy water were Grady dressed in cowboy costume and three naked Indians. Mr Carteret glanced about over the country and understood. They had swum the brook at the place where it ran between steep clay banks and the rest of the field had gone around to the bridge. As he looked towards the south, he saw Lord Ploversdale riding furiously towards him followed by Smith, the huntsman. Grady had not recognized Mr Carteret turned out in pink as he was, and for the moment the latter decided to remain incognito.

Before Lord Ploversdale, Master of Foxhounds, reached the road, he began waving his whip. He appeared excited. 'What do you mean by riding upon my hounds?' he shouted. He said this in several ways with various accompanying phrases, but neither the Indians nor Grady seemed to notice him. It occurred to Mr Carteret that, although Lord Ploversdale's power of expression was wonderful for England, it neverthe-less fell short of Arizona standards. Then, however, he noticed that Grady was absorbed in adjusting a Kodak camera, with which he was evidently about to take a picture of the Indians alone with the hounds. He drew back in order both to avoid being in the field of the picture and to avoid too close proximity with Lord Ploversdale as he came over the fence on to the road.

'What do you mean, sir!' shouted the enraged Master of Foxhounds, as he pulled up his horse.

'A little more in the middle,' replied Grady, still absorbed in taking the picture.

Lord Ploversdale hesitated. He was speechless with surprise for the moment.

Grady pressed the button and began putting up the machine.

'What do you mean by riding on my hounds, you and these persons?' demanded Lord Ploversdale.

'We didn't,' said Grady amicably, 'but if your bunch of dogs don't know enough to keep out of the way of a horse, they ought to learn.'

Lord Ploversdale looked aghast and Smith, the huntsman, pinched himself to make sure that he was not dreaming.

'Many thanks for your advice,' said Lord Ploversdale. 'May I inquire who you and your friends may be?'

'I'm James Grady,' said that gentleman. 'This,' he said pointing to the Indian nearest, 'is Chief Hole-in-the-Ground of the Ogallala Sioux. Him in the middle is Mr Jim Snake, and the one beyond is Chief Skytail, a Pawnee.'

'Thank you, that is very interesting,' said Lord Ploversdale, with polite irony. 'Now will you kindly take them home?'

'See here,' said Grundy, strapping the camera to his saddle. 'I was invited to this hunt, regular, and if you hand me out any more hostile talk—' he paused.

'Who invited you?' inquired Lord Ploversdale.

'One of your own bunch,' said Grady, 'Lord Frederic Westcote, I'm no butter-in.'

'Your language is difficult to understand,' said Lord Ploversdale. 'Where is Lord Frederic Westcote?'

Mr Carteret had watched the field approaching as fast as whip and spur could drive them, and in the first flight he noticed Lord Frederic and the Major. For this reason he still hesitated about thrusting himself into the discussion. It seemed that the interference of a third party could only complicate matters, inasmuch as Lord Frederic would so soon be upon the spot.

Lord Ploversdale looked across the field impatiently. 'I've no doubt, my good fellow, that Lord Frederic Westcote brought you here, and I'll see him about it, but kindly take these fellows home. They'll kill all my hounds.'

'Now you're beginning to talk reasonable,' said Grady, 'I'll discuss with you.'

The words were hardly out of his mouth before hounds gave tongue riotously and went off. The fox had slipped out of the other end of the drain, and old Archer had found the line.

As if shot out of a gun the three Indians dashed at the stake-and-bound fence on the farther side of the road, joyously using their heavy quirts on the Major's thoroughbreds. Skytail's horse, being hurried too much, blundered his take-off, hit above the knees and rolled over on the Chief who was sitting tight. There was a stifled grunt and then the Pawnee word, 'Go-dam!'

Hole-in-the-Ground looked back and laughed one of the few

laughs of his life. It was a joke which he could understand. Then he used the quirt again to make the most of his advantage.

'That one is finished,' said Lord Ploversdale gratefully. But as the words were in his mouth, Skytail rose with his horse, vaulted up and was away.

The M.F.H. followed over the fence shouting at Smith to whip off the hounds. But the hounds were going too fast. They had got a view of the fox and three whooping horsemen were behind them driving them on.

The first flight of the field followed the M.F.H. out of the road and so did Mr Carteret, and presently he found himself riding between Lord Frederic and the Major. They were both a bit winded and had evidently come fast.

'I say,' exclaimed Lord Frederic, 'where did you come from?'

'I was cured by the Broncholine,' said Mr Carteret, 'amazing stuff!'

'Is your horse fresh?' asked Lord Frederic.

'Yes,' replied Mr Carteret, 'I happened upon them at the road.'

'Then go after that man Grady,' said Lord Frederic, 'and beg him to take those beggars home. They have been riding on hounds for twenty minutes.'

'Were they able,' asked Mr Carteret, 'to stay with their horses at the fences?'

'Stay with their horses!' puffed the Major.

'Go on, like a good chap,' said Lord Frederic, 'stop that fellow or I shall be expelled from the hunt; perhaps put in jail. Was Ploversdale vexed?' he added.

'I should judge by his language,' said Mr Carteret, 'that he was vexed.'

'Hurry on,' said Lord Frederic. 'Put your spurs in.'

Mr Carteret gave his horse its head and he shot to the front, but Grady was nearly a field in the lead and it promised to be a long chase as he was on the Major's black thoroughbred. The cowboy rode along with a loose rein and an easy balance seat. At his fences he swung his hat and cheered. He seemed to be enjoying himself and Mr Carteret was anxious lest he might begin to shoot from pure delight. Such a demonstration would have been misconstrued. Nearly two hundred yards ahead at the heels of the pack galloped the Indians, and in the middle distance between them and Grady rode Lord Ploversdale and Smith vainly trying to overtake the hounds and whip them off. Behind and trailing over a mile or more came the field and the rest of the hunt servants in little groups, all awestruck at what had happened. It was unspeakable that Lord Ploversdale's hounds which had been hunted by his father and his grand-father should be so scandalized.

Mr Carteret finally got within a length of Grady and hailed him.

'Hello, Carty,' said Grady, 'glad to see you. I thought you were sick. What can I do? They've stampeded. But it's a great ad. for the show isn't it? I've got four reporters in a hack on the road.'

'Forget about the show,' said Mr Carteret. 'This isn't any laughing matter. Ploversdale's hounds are one of the smartest packs in England. You don't understand.'

'It will make all the better story in the papers,' said Grady.

'No, it won't,' said Mr Carteret. 'They won't print it. It's like blasphemy upon the Church.'

'Whoop!' yelled Grady, as they tore through a bullfinch.

'Call them off,' said Mr Carteret, straightening his hat.

'But I can't catch 'em,' said Grady, and that was the truth.

Lord Ploversdale, however, had been gaining on the Indians, and by the way in which he clubbed his heavy crop, loaded at the butt, it was apparent that he meant to put an end to the proceedings if he could.

Just then the hounds swept over the crest of a green hill and as they went down the other side, they viewed the fox in the field beyond. He was in distress, and it looked as if the pack would kill in the open. They were running wonderfully together, the traditional blanket would have covered them, and in the natural glow of pride which came over the M.F.H., he loosened his grip upon the crop. But as the hounds viewed the fox so did the three sons of the wilderness who were following close behind. From the hill-top fifty of the hardest going men in England saw Hole-in-the-Ground flogging his horse with the heavy quirt which hung from his wrist. The outraged British hunter shot forward scattering hounds to right and left, flew a ditch, and hedge and was close on the fox who had stopped to make a last stand. Without drawing rein, the astonished onlookers saw the lean Indian suddenly disappear under the neck of his horse and almost instantly swing back into his seat swinging a brown thing above his head. *Hole-in-the-Ground had caught the fox!*

'Most unprecedented!' Mr Carteret heard the Major exclaim. He pulled up his horse, as the field did theirs, and waited apprehensively. He saw Hole-in-the-Ground circle round, jerk the Major's five hundred guinea hunter to a standstill close to Lord Ploversdale and address him. He was speaking in his own language.

As the Chief went on, he saw Grady smile.

'He says,' said Grady translating, 'that the white chief can eat the fox if he wants him. He's proud himself bein' packed with store grub.'

The English onlookers heard and beheld with blank faces. It was beyond them.

The M.F.H. bowed stiffly as Hole-in-the-Ground's offer was made known to him. He regarded them a moment in thought. A vague light was breaking in upon him. 'Aw, thank you,' he said, 'thanks awfully. Smith, take the fox. Good afternoon!'

Then he wheeled his horse, called the hounds in with his horn and trotted out to the road that led to the kennels. Lord Ploversdale, though he had never been out of England, was cast in a large mould.

The three Indians sat on their panting horses, motionless, stolidly facing the curious gaze of the crowd; or rather they looked through the crowd, as the lion with the high breeding of the desert looks through and beyond the faces that stare and gape before the bars of his cage.

'Most amazing! Most amazing!' muttered the Major.

'It is,' said Mr Carteret, 'if you have never been away from this.' He made a sweeping gesture over the restricted English scenery, pampered and brought up by hand.

'Been away from this?' repeated the Major. 'I don't understand.'

Mr Carteret turned to him. How could he explain it?

'With us,' he began, laying emphasis on the 'us'. Then he stopped. 'Look into their eyes,' he said hopelessly.

The Major looked at him blankly. How could he, Major

Hammerslea of 'The Blues', tell what those inexplicable dark eyes saw beyond the fenced tillage! What did he know of the brown, bare, illimitable range under the noonday sun, the evening light on far, silent mountains, the starlit desert!

An Expensive Operation

JAMES HERRIOT

WELL, do you want t'job or don't you?'

Walt Barnett towered over me in the surgery doorway and his eyes flickered from my head to my feet and up again without expression. The cigarette dangling from his lower lip semed to be a part of him as did the brown trilby hat and the shining navy blue serge suit stretched tightly over his bulky form. He must have weighed nearly twenty stones and with his red beefy brutal mouth and overbearing manner he was undeniably formidable.

'Well, er . . . yes. Of course we want the job,' I replied. 'I was just wondering when we could fit it in.' I went over to the desk and began to look through the appointment book. 'We're pretty full this week and I don't know what Mr Farnon has fixed for the week after. Maybe we'd better give you a ring.'

The big man had burst in on me without warning or greeting and barked, 'I 'ave a fine big blood 'oss to geld. When can you do 'im?'

I had looked at him hesitantly for a few moments, taken aback partly by the arrogance of his approach, partly by his request. This wasn't good news to me; I didn't like castrating fine big blood 'osses—I much preferred the ordinary cart colts and if you came right down to it I had a particular preference for Shetland ponies. But it was all part of living and if it had to be done it had to be done.

'You can give me a ring if you like, but don't be ower long about it.' The hard unsmiling stare still held me. 'And I want a good job doin', think on!'

'We always try to do a good job, Mr Barnett,' I said, fighting a rising prickle of resentment at his attitude.

'Aye well I've heard that afore and I've had some bloody

97

balls-ups,' he said. He gave me a final truculent nod, turned and walked out, leaving the door open.

I was still standing in the middle of the room seething and muttering to myself when Siegfried walked in. I hardly saw him at first and when he finally came into focus I found I was glowering into his face.

'What's the trouble, James?' he asked. 'A little touch of indigestion, perhaps?'

'Indigestion? No . . . no . . . Why do you say that?'

'Well you seemed to be in some sort of pain, standing there on one leg with your face screwed up.'

'Did I look like that? Oh it was just our old friend Walt Barnett. He wants us to cut a horse for him and he made the request in his usual charming way—he really gets under my skin, that man.'

Tristan came in from the passage. 'Yes, I was out there and I heard him. He's a bloody big lout.'

Siegfried rounded on him. 'That's enough! I don't want to hear that kind of talk in here.' Then he turned back to me. 'And really, James, even if you were upset I don't think it's an excuse for profanity.'

'What do you mean?'

'Well, some of the expletives I heard you muttering there were unworthy of you.' He spread his hands in a gesture of disarming frankness. 'Heaven knows I'm no prude but I don't like to hear such language within these walls.' He paused and his features assumed an expression of deep gravity. 'After all, the people who come in here provide us with our bread and butter and they should be referred to with respect.'

'Yes, but . . .'

'Oh I know some are not as nice as others but you must never let them irritate you. You've heard the old saying, "The customer is always right." Well, I think it's a good working axiom and I always abide by it myself.' He gazed solemnly at Tristan and me in turn. 'So I hope I make myself clear. No swearing in the surgery—particularly when it concerns the clients.'

'It's all right for you!' I burst out heatedly. 'But you didn't hear Barnett. I'll stand so much, but . . .'

Siegfried put his head on one side and a smile of ethereal

beauty crept over his face. 'My dear old chap, there you go again, letting little things disturb you. I've had to speak to you about this before, haven't I? I wish I could help you, I wish I could pass on my own gift of remaining calm at all times.'

'What's that you said?'

'I said I wanted to help you, James, and I will.' He held up a forefinger. 'You've probably often wondered why I never get angry or excited.'

'Eh?'

'Oh I know you have—you must have. Well I'll let you into a little secret.' His smile took on a roguish quality. 'If a client is rude to me I simply charge him a little more. Instead of getting all steamed up like you do I tell myself that I'm putting ten bob extra on the bill and it works like magic.'

'Is that so?'

'Yes indeed, my boy.' He thumped my shoulder then became very serious. 'Of course I realise that I have an advantage right at the start—I have been blessed with a naturally even temperament while you are blown about in all directions by every little wind of circumstance. But I do think that this is something you could cultivate, so work at it, James, work at it. All this fretting and fuming is bad for you—your whole life would change if you could just acquire my own tranquil outlook.'

I swallowed hard. 'Well thank you, Siegfried,' I said. 'I'll try.'

* * *

Walt Barnett was a bit of a mystery man in Darrowby. He wasn't a farmer, he was a scrap merchant, a haulier, a dealer in everything from linoleum to second hand cars, and there was only one thing the local people could say for certain about him—he had brass, lots of brass. They said everything he touched turned to money.

He had bought a decaying mansion a few miles outside the town where he lived with a downtrodden little wife and where he kept a floating population of livestock; a few bullocks, some pigs and always a horse or two. He employed all the vets in the district in turn, probably because he didn't think much of any of us; a feeling which I may say, was mutual. He never seemed to do any physical work and could be seen most days of the week shambling around the streets of Darrowby, hands in pockets, cigarette dangling, his brown trilby on the back of his head, his huge body threatening to burst through that shiny navy suit.

After my meeting with him we had a busy few days and it was on the following Thursday that the phone rang in the surgery. Siegfried lifted it and immediately his expression changed. From across the floor I could clearly hear the loud hectoring tones coming through the receiver and as my colleague listened a slow flush spread over his cheeks and his mouth hardened. Several times he tried to put in a word but the torrent of sound from the far end was unceasing. Finally he raised his voice and broke in but instantly there was a click and he found himself speaking to a dead line.

Siegfried crashed the receiver into its rest and swung round. 'That was Barnett—playing hell because we haven't rung him.' He stood staring at me for a few moments, his face dark with anger.

'The bloody bastard!' he shouted. 'Who the hell does he think he is? Abusing me like that, then hanging up on me when I try to speak!'

For a moment he was silent then he turned to me. 'I'll tell you this, James, he wouldn't have spoken to me like that if he'd been in this room with me.' He came over to me and held out his hands, fingers crooked menacingly. 'I'd have wrung his bloody neck, big as he is! I would have, I tell you, I'd have strangled the bugger!'

'But Siegfried,' I said. 'What about your system?'

'System? What system?'

'Well, you know the trick you have when people are unpleasant—you put something on the bill, don't you?'

Siegfried let his hands fall to his sides and stared at me for some time, his chest rising and falling with his emotion. Then he patted me on the shoulder and turned away towards the window where he stood looking out at the quiet street.

When he turned back to me he looked grim but calmer. 'By God, James, you're right. That's the answer. I'll cut Barnett's horse for him but I'll charge him a tenner.'

I laughed heartily. In those days the average charge for

castrating a horse was a pound, or if you wanted to be more professional, a guinea.

'What are you laughing at?' my colleague enquired sourly.

'Well . . . at your joke. I mean, ten pounds . . . ha-ha-ha!'

'I'm not joking, I'm going to charge him a tenner.'

'Oh come on, Siegfried, you can't do that.'

'You just watch me,' he said. 'I'm going to sort that bugger.'

* * *

Two mornings later I was going through the familiar motions of preparing for a castration; boiling up the emasculator and laying it on the enamel tray along with the scalpel, the roll of cotton wool, the artery forceps, the tincture of iodine, the suture materials, the tetanus antitoxin and syringes. For the last five minutes Siegfried had been shouting at me to hurry.

'What the hell are you doing through there, James? Don't forget to put in an extra bottle of chloroform. And bring the sidelines in case he doesn't go down. Where have you hidden those spare scalpel blades, James?'

The sunshine streamed across the laden tray, filtering through the green tangle of the wisteria which fell untidily across the surgery window. Reminding me that it was May and that there was nowhere a May morning came with such golden magic as to the long garden at Skeldale House; the high brick walls with their crumbling mortar and ancient stone copings enfolding the sunlight in a warm clasp and spilling it over the untrimmed lawns, the banks of lupins and bluebells, the masses of fruit blossom. And right at the top the rooks cawing in the highest branches of the elms.

Siegfried, chloroform muzzle looped over one shoulder, made a final check of the items on the tray then we set off. In less than half an hour we were driving through the lodge gates of the old mansion then along a mossy avenue which wandered among pine and birch trees up to the house which looked out from its wooded background over the rolling miles of fell and moor.

Nobody could have asked for a more perfect place for the operation; a high-walled paddock deep in lush grass. The two-year-old, a magnificent chestnut, was led in by two characters who struck me as typical henchmen for Mr Barnett. I don't know where he had dug them up but you didn't see faces like that among the citizens of Darrowby. One was a brown goblin who, as he conversed with his companion, repeatedly jerked his head and winked one eye as though they were sharing some disreputable secret. The other had a head covered with ginger stubble surmounting a countenance of a bright scrofulous red which looked as though a piece would fall off if you touched it; and deep in the livid flesh two tiny eyes darted.

The two of them regarded us unsmilingly and the dark one spat luxuriously as we approached.

'It's a nice morning,' I said.

Ginger just stared at me while Winker nodded knowingly and closed one eye as if I had uttered some craftiness which appealed to him.

The vast hunching figure of Mr Barnett hovered in the background, cigarette drooping, the bright sunshine striking brilliant shafts of light from the tight sheen of the navy suit.

I couldn't help comparing the aspect of the trio of humans with the natural beauty and dignity of the horse. The big chestnut tossed his head then stood looking calmly across the paddock, the large fine eyes alight with intelligence, the noble lines of the face and neck blending gently into the grace and power of the body. Observations I had heard about the higher and lower animals floated about in my mind.

Siegfried walked around the horse, patting him and talking to him, his eyes shining with the delight of the fanatic.

'He's a grand sort, Mr Barnett,' he said.

The big man glowered at him. 'Aye well, don't spoil 'im, that's all. I've paid a lot o' money for that 'oss.'

Siegfried gave a thoughtful look then turned to me.

'Well, let's get on. We'll drop him over there on that long grass. Are you ready, James?'

I was ready, but I'd be a lot more at ease if Siegfried would just leave me alone. In horse work I was the anaesthetist and my colleague was the surgeon. And he was good; quick, deft, successful. I had no quarrel with the arrangement; he could get on with his job and let me do mine. But there was the rub; he would keep butting into my territory and I found it wearing.

Anaesthesia in the large animals has a dual purpose; it

abolishes pain and acts as a means of restraint. It is obvious that you can't do much with these potentially dangerous creatures unless they are controlled.

That was my job. I had to produce a sleeping patient ready for the knife and very often I thought it was the most difficult part. Until the animal was properly under I always felt a certain tension and Siegfried didn't help in this respect. He would hover at my elbow, offering advice as to the quantity of chloroform and he could never bear to wait until the anaesthetic had taken effect. He invariably said,

'He isn't going to go down, James.' Then, 'Don't you think you should strap a fore leg up?'

Even now, thirty years later, when I am using such intravenous drugs as thiopentone he is still at it. Stamping around impatiently as I fill my syringe, poking over my shoulder with a long forefinger into the jugular furrow. 'I'd shove it in just there, James.'

I stood there irresolute, my partner by my side, the chloroform bottle in my pocket, the muzzle dangling from my hand. It would be wonderful, I thought, if just once I could be on my own to get on with it. And, after all, I had worked for him for nearly three years—surely I knew him well enough to be able to put it to him.

I cleared my throat. 'Siegfried, I was just wondering. Would you care to go and sit down over there for a few minutes till I get him down?'

'What's that?'

'Well I thought it would be a good idea if you left me to it. There's a bit of a crowd round the horse's head—I don't want him excited. So why don't you relax for a while. I'll give you a shout when he's down.'

Siegfried raised a hand. 'My dear chap, anything you say. I don't know what I'm hanging around here for anyway. I never interfere with your end as you well know.' He turned about and, tray under arm, marched off to where he had parked his car on the grass about fifty yards away. He strode round behind the Rover and sat down on the turf, his back against the metal. He was out of sight.

Peace descended. I became suddenly aware of the soft warmth of the sun on my forehead, of the bird song echoing among the nearby trees. Unhurriedly I fastened on the muzzle under the head collar and produced my little glass measure.

This once I had plenty of time. I'd start him off with just a couple of drachms to get him used to the smell of it without frightening him. I poured the clear fluid on to the sponge.

'Walk him slowly round in a circle,' I said to Ginger and Winker. 'I'm going to give him a little bit at a time, there's no hurry. But keep a good hold of that halter shank in case he plays up.'

There was no need for my warning. The two-year-old paced round calmly and fearlessly and every minute or so I trickled a little extra on to the sponge. After a while his steps became laboured and he began to sway drunkenly as he walked. I watched him happily; this was the way I liked to do it. Another little dollop would just about do the trick. I measured out another half ounce and walked over to the big animal.

His head nodded sleepily as I gave it to him. 'You're just about ready aren't you, old lad,' I was murmuring when the peace was suddenly shattered.

'He isn't going to go down, you know, James!' It was a booming roar from the direction of the car and as I whipped round in consternation I saw a head just showing over the bonnet. There was another cry.

'Why don't you strap up a . . .?'

At that moment the horse lurched and collapsed quietly on the grass and Siegfried came bounding knife in hand from his hiding place like a greyhound.

'Sit on his head!' he yelled. 'What are you waiting for, he'll be up in a minute! And get that rope round that hind leg! And bring my tray! And fetch the hot water!' He panted up to the horse then turned and bawled into Ginger's face, 'Come on, I'm talking to you. MOVE!'

Ginger went off at a bow-legged gallop and cannoned into Winker who was rushing forward with the bucket. Then they had a brief but frenzied tug of war with the rope before they got it round the pastern.

'Pull the leg forward,' cried my partner, bending over the operation site, then a full blooded bellow, 'Get the bloody foot out of my eye, will you! What's the matter with you, you wouldn't pull a hen off its nest the way you're going.'

I knelt quietly at the head, my knee on the neck. There was no need to hold him down; he was beautifully out, his eyes blissfully closed as Siegfried worked with his usual lightning expertise. There was a mere few seconds of silence broken only by the tinkling of instruments as they fell back on the tray, then my colleague glanced along the horse's back. 'Open the muzzle, James.'

The operation was over.

I don't think I've ever seen an easier job. By the time we had washed our instruments in the bucket the two-year-old was on his feet, cropping gently at the grass.

'Splendid anaesthetic, James,' said Siegfried, drying off the emasculator. 'Just right. And what a grand sort of horse.'

We had put our gear back in the boot and were ready to leave when Walt Barnett heaved his massive bulk over towards us. He faced Siegfried across the bonnet of the car.

'Well that were nowt of a job,' he grunted, slapping a cheque book down on the shining metal, 'How much do you want?'

There was an arrogant challenge in the words and, faced with the dynamic force, the sheer brutal presence of the man, most people who were about to charge a guinea would have changed their minds and said a pound.

'Well, I'm askin' yer,' he repeated. 'How much do you want?'

'Ah yes,' said Siegfried lightly. 'That'll be a tenner.'

The big man put a meaty hand on the cheque book and stared at my colleague. 'What?'

'That'll be a tenner,' Siegfried said again.

'Ten pounds?' Mr Barnett's eyes opened wider.

'Yes,' said Siegfried, smiling pleasantly. 'That's right. Ten pounds.'

There was a silence as the two men faced each other across the bonnet. The bird song and the noises from the wood seemed abnormally loud as the seconds ticked away and nobody moved. Mr Barnett was glaring furiously and I looked from the huge fleshy face which seemed to have swollen even larger across to the lean, strong-jawed, high-cheekboned profile of my partner. Siegfried still wore the remains of a lazy smile but down in the grey depths of his eye a dangerous light glinted.

Just when I was at screaming point the big man dropped his head suddenly and began to write. When he handed the cheque over he was shaking so much that the slip of paper fluttered as though in a high wind.

'Here y'are, then,' he said hoarsely.

'Thank you so much.' Siegfried read the cheque briefly then stuffed it carelessly into a side pocket. 'Isn't it grand to have some real May weather, Mr Barnett. Does us all good. I'm sure.'

Walt Barnett mumbled something and turned away. As I got into the car I could see the great expanse of navy blue back moving ponderously towards the house.

'He won't have us back, anyway,' I said.

Siegfried started the engine and we moved away. 'No, James, I should think he'd get his twelve bore out if we ventured down this drive again. But that suits me—I think I can manage to get through the rest of my life without Mr Barnett.'

Our road took us through the little village of Baldon and Siegfried slowed down outside the pub, a yellow-washed building standing a few yards back from the road with a wooden sign reading The Cross Keys and a large black dog sleeping on the sunny front step.

My partner looked at his watch. 'Twelve fifteen—they'll just have opened. A cool beer would be rather nice, wouldn't it? I don't think I've been in this place before.'

After the brightness outside, the shaded interior was restful, with only stray splinters of sunshine filtering through the curtains on to the flagged floor, the fissured oak tables, the big fireplace with its high settle.

'Good morning to you, landlord,' boomed my partner, striding over to the bar. He was in his most ducal mood and I felt it was a pity he didn't have a silver-knobbed stick to rap on the counter.

The man behind the counter smiled and knuckled a forelock in the approved manner. 'Good morning to you, sir, and what can I get for you gentlemen?'

I half expected Siegfried to say, 'Two stoups of your choicest brew, honest fellow,' but instead he just turned to me and murmured 'I think two halves of bitter, eh James?'

The man began to draw the beer.

'Won't you join us?' Siegfried enquired.

'Thank ye sir, I'll 'ave a brown ale with you.'

'And possibly your good lady, too?' Siegfried smiled over at the landlord's wife who was stacking glasses at the end of the counter.

'That's very kind of you, I will.' She looked up, gulped, and an expression of wonder crept over her face. Siegfried hadn't stared at her—it had only been a five second burst from the grey eyes—but the bottle rattled against the glass as she poured her small port and she spent the rest of the time gazing at him dreamily.

'That'll be five and sixpence,' the landlord said.

'Right.' My partner plunged a hand into his bulging side pocket and crashed down on the counter an extraordinary mixture of crumpled bank notes, coins, veterinary instruments, thermometers, bits of string. He stirred the mass with a forefinger, flicking out a half crown and two florins across the woodwork.

'Wait a minute!' I exclaimed. 'Aren't those my curved scissors? I lost them a few days . . .'

Siegfried swept the pile out of sight into his pocket.

'Nonsense! What makes you think that?'

'Well, they look exactly like mine. Unusual shape—lovely long, flat blades. I've been looking everywhere . . .'

'James!' He drew himself up and faced me with frozen hauteur. 'I think you've said enough. I may be capable of stooping to some pretty low actions but I'd like to believe that certain things are beneath me. And stealing a colleague's curved scissors is one of them.'

I relapsed into silence. I'd have to bide my time and take my chance later. I was fairly sure I'd recognized a pair of my dressing forceps in there too.

In any case, something else was occupying Siegfried's mind. He narrowed his eyes in intense thought then delved into his other pocket and produced a similar collection which he proceeded to push around the counter anxiously.

'What's the matter?' I asked.

'That cheque I've just taken. Did I give it to you?'

'No, you put it in that pocket. I saw you.'

'That's what I thought. Well it's gone.'

'Gone?'

'I've lost the bloody thing!'

I laughed. 'Oh you can't have. Go through your other pockets—it must be on you somewhere.'

Siegfried made a systematic search but it was in vain.

'Well James,' he said at length. 'I really have lost it, but I've just thought of a simple solution. I will stay here and have one more beer while you slip back to Walt Barnett and ask him for another cheque.'

The 500 Mile Race from Deadwood to Omaha

JACK SCHAEFER

YOUNG JAKE HANLON, point man of the Triple X trail crew, has delivered a herd of rough and rangy steers to a ranch near Deadwood in the Black Hills of Dakota just ten days ago. He is tall in a plain tough working saddle on a smallish dun-coloured mustang and he is ramming steadily forward along an excuse for a road through the sandhills of Nebraska.

Many people think he has played the fool, talking big about a little mustang. Saying it could make a good showing in the 530-mile race from Deadwood to Omaha scheduled to start in a few days. What? That scrubby misfit piece of wolf-bait that must already be worn out from a thousand miles of bringing a trail herd out of the southwest all the way to Dakota? Why, a scrawny little half-dead horse like that won't even be in the running against those fine big horses, bred right and fed right, that have been in training several months and more for this race.

There is plenty of money riding the route. Bets are high on the other horses. All that has been put on the little mustang is what the others of the Triple X trail crew have been able to scrape together. Perhaps it is only loyalty to the outfit that has prompted them to empty their pockets. Perhaps not. They have been given odds of five to one and they know a thing or two of their own. On the long trail north they have seen that little dun, after the cavvy was thinned by drownings at a river-crossing, do the work of two horses and never turn a hair. They have run mustangs themselves and they have a few in their strings and they know the feel of them under saddles and that when it appears to be done, worn out, finished, a little south-western mustang has just begun to fight . . .

They pushed on. Young Jake and Jimmie Dun, a lanky cowhand and a smallish mustang, two working partners from the far desert distances of New Mexico, following now the rutted traces of a road through the unfamiliar distances of Nebraska. They moved steadily, not fast, not slow, at a jogging foxtrot that gnawed away at the miles.

Young Jake had this race planned in his mind. He knew no long-distance race was ever won by speed at the start, by burning up reserve energy in the early days of the running. This was the morning of the fifth day and almost 300 miles were behind him and still he held to his strict routine: an easy trot for an hour, an easier flat-footed walk for the next hour, then the trot again and repeat. Out of blanket at daybreak each morning and trot-walk-trot till noon. Stop by water, a stream or ranch or farmhouse pump, and strip down Jimmie Dun and let him drink sparingly and rub him thoroughly and give him the small bait of mixed feed carried in a bag behind the saddle cantle and chomp hungrily himself on the two sandwiches from the one saddlebag and lie down in a spot of shade for several hours' rest. Up again and trot-walk-trot through the afternoon until dusk and stop at the quick camp made by his advance man, Peter Corle, who was travelling ahead with a light supply wagon drawn by the two long-legged mules that had brought the Triple X chuck wagon to Deadwood. Another rubdown and rations of water and feed for Jimmie Dun and a meal of Petey's campfire cooking for himself and an hour of rest for them both. In saddle again and trot-walk-trot until about midnight. Then pull off the road a bit and unsaddle and picket Jimmie Dun by good grass on a good length of rope and roll himself in the one thin blanket carried with the bag behind the cantle and sleep until the familiar summons of dawn.

They pushed on, Young Jake and Jimmie Dun, and heard hoofbeats coming up behind and alongside. The thin-faced man on the big black Thoroughbred called Cannonball. He was frowning, annoyed. 'So you're still with us,' he said.

'Why, sure,' said Young Jake. 'Ain't you heard? We're headed for Omaha.'

The thin faced man kept the frown, glancing down sidewise at Jimmie Dun. 'That thing won't last the day,' he said. Contemptuous, impatient, he used his spurs and the big black leaped into a canter, dwindling into the distance ahead.

Young Jake grinned to himself. He had seen the sweat streaks starting already on the big black in the cool of the morning before the heat of the day. He rubbed a hand along Jimmie Dun's neck. He felt along the hard flanks. No moisture. Only an even warmth. Jimmie Dun could do what he was doing all day without working up a real sweat. No overdoses of rich food in him and no consequent overweight of hot flesh on him. And generations of stubborn desert endurance behind him. Young Jake grinned again. Then he shook his head slightly. 'All the same,' he muttered, 'that'll be one to beat. Thoroughbred. Never know just what they've got left when the finish line's in sight.'

They pushed on and they heard hoofbeats again coming up and alongside. The black-bearded man on the tall big-boned half-bred bay called Jay Bird. He was moving at a fast pace and he glared once at Young Jake as he went past and then he and the big bay were diminishing into distance ahead.

'Two,' said Young Jake. 'Wonder how many it'll be this time.'

Each morning it was the same. Others came up and passed him, impatient, hurrying, hammering on ahead of him as they all had done at the start on the first day. They rode too hard when they rode and had to stop too often to breathe their horses and were taking too much out of them too early and they themselves were too soft, too civilized, insisting on three meals a day and plenty of sleep. His own routine wore away at the miles more slowly but more steadily and for longer hours. Each evening, when he stopped at Petey Corle's quick camp, he would not be far behind them.

They pushed on. Young Jake and Jimmie Dun, not fast, not slow, and heard hoofbeats again and these came alongside and slowed to the same pace. The red-haired man with jutting chin on the big reddish-brown high-shouldered Thoroughbred and Hambletonian cross called Sorrel Clipper. 'So you did it again,' he said, stating a fact. He stared down at Jimmie Dun trotting quietly, lazy-eyed and relaxed. 'Must be related to a turtle,' he said. 'Looks half-starved and half-dead to me. But I thought the same at the start. Maybe he'll last after all.'

'Why, sure,' said Young Jake. 'He'll last.'

'Lasting ain't winning,' said the man. He jabbed with spurs and the big sorrel picked up speed and moved out ahead.

The time clock in his mind gave its signal and he relayed the message along the reins. Jimmie Dun slowed to a walk, the flat-footed walk that was almost a resting for him. And again hoofbeats sounded and came up. The thin-lipped eye-twitching man on the big long-bodied grey Morgan and Standard cross called Thunderbolt. His thin lips twisted as if he would say something and what he would say would be mean and nasty and he thought better of it and said nothing and spurred on and Young Jake saw the flecks of foam dropping from the bit in the big grey's mouth and its energy-wasting head tossing under the impact of the spurs.

Time passed and the clock in Young Jake's mind nudged and Jimmie Dun knew and leaned forward into a trot, the jogging foxtrot that gnawed away at the miles. Young Jake looked back. He could see along the road at least a mile. Not another rider in sight. 'Four,' he said.

There had been nine others the first day, all of them joking and jeering at Jimmie Dun and hurrying on ahead in the excitement of the start. Eight had passed him on the morning of the second day, one man already out with his horse lamed by a stone in a hoof not noticed and removed in time. Seven on the morning of the third day, another man out with a horse that had suffered from colic and cramps all night, probably caused by too quick a watering after a bucket of oats. Five on the morning of the fourth day, two more men out, one with a horse limping badly from a sprained ankle, the other frankly admitting he was out-classed and voluntarily withdrawing.

'Four today,' said Young Jake. 'With Jimmie'n me that makes five left.'

In the hush of dusk dropping towards dark Young Jake sat on a flat-topped rock by Petey Corle's campfire eating Petey Corle's short-order specialty, singed beef and refried beans. Twenty feet away the skimpy supply wagon was a squat shape in the dimness. Forty feet beyond, Jimmie Dun cropped grass in companionable competition with two long-legged mules. A third of a mile further along the road and closer to it several other fires made their own small circles of flickering light.

'All of 'em over there,' said Petey Corle. 'They stopped early today. Saw me here an' stopped till they was gathered like they wanted to be somewheres near.'

Young Jake grunted. He was too busy eating to say anything.

'Them mules,' said Petey. 'They're almighty tired.'

Young Jake scraped his tin plate and lifted it to lick away the last traces of the beans. 'Better'n three hunnerd fifty miles by now,' he said. 'Make it a hunnerd sixty-seventy to go. Them mules now. They last through tomorrow, that'll do it. Me'n Jimmie'll be in the homestretch after that.'

The darkness deepened and Young Jake was sitting on the ground, back against the flat-topped rock, and Petey was at the wagon, measuring feed into the bag, when they heard footsteps approaching from the direction of the other fires. Young Jake sat up straighter, peering into the dark, and Petey reached further into the wagon and took his gunbelt and buckled it on and eased around by the edge of firelight, between it and Jimmie Dun.

There were three of them, the thin-faced man and the black-bearded man and the eye-twitching man.

'You got time for a little conversation?' said the thin-faced man.

'Mebbe so,' said Young Jake.

'Short an' sweet,' said Petey Corle.

'You don't know it yet,' said the thin-faced man, 'but Henderson's out. That Sorrel Clipper horse of his has been took sick. He's leading it on to the next town. But it's out. That leaves four of us.'

'Wasn't sick back at the river,' said Young Jake. 'Wore down some. An' skittish. But a good hoss. A lot left in 'im.'

'Not now.' said the thin-faced man. 'Things happen. Like I say, that leaves four of us. And there's four prizes. A thousand, five hundred, three hundred, two hundred. Add those and you get two thousand. Divide that by four and you get five hundred.'

'I can figger,' said Young Jake. 'Where you headin'?'

'Well, now,' said the thin-faced man. 'Suppose we just agree among ourselves, nobody else knowing, that no matter how we come in, we pool those prizes. Then we split even, five hundred apiece. No sense killing ourselves and the horses on these last miles. Just make it look good at the finish. We cut cards to see who's to come in first, but no matter what the cards say, we pool it and split even.'

Young Jake stared down at his fingernail, remembering many things. He remembered that even though he was still called Young Jake, he was not as young as he used to be and this last long drive out of New Mexico had tightened his belt and put an ache of tiredness in his bones that was already renewed by the riding of the past five days. He remembered that he was still just an often overworked cowhand at thirty and found a month who had never had anything like five hundred dollars jingling in his pocket. And then he remembered something else. A smallish dun mustang cropping grass about sixty-five feet away.

That horse never asked odds of anything life threw at it. He had talked big and that horse was ready to give the last ounce of stubborn endurance in it to back up his talk. This was Jimmie Dun's race too.

Young Jake raised his head. 'No,' he said, 'I started this thing as a hoss race an' I'll just finish it the same.'

'Is that final?' said the thin-faced man.

'Final,' said Young Jake.

'Double-cinched,' said Petey Corle.

'You'll regret it,' said the thin-faced man. 'Like I told you, things happen.' He turned away.

'You'll never even finish,' said the eye-twitching man, turning to follow.

'Right,' said the black-bearded man. 'We'll run that jug-headed mutt of yours off its legs tomorrow.' And he too turned and followed.

The footsteps died away. Young Jake and Petey Corle looked at each other.

'Took sick,' said Young Jake. 'Mighty sudden.'

'Yeah,' said Petey Corle. 'An' neither of us is doing any moving on tonight. Not past that bunch in the dark. They'll keep till morning anyway. You need the rest too. I don't count. You bed down an' I'll keep an eye on Jimmy.'

Sounds of hurried doings tapped at Young Jake's eardrums,

penetrating at last to awareness. He came out of sleep still tired and with a stiffness in his backbone. the darkness of sky overhead had shifted to a dull grey and a few stars still fought against the seeping glimmer of the false dawn. He raised one elbow and looked around. Petey was by the wagon with the two mules, slapping harness on them.

Young Jake pushed up and stretched. He took the bucket half full of water which Petey had placed near him and walked a short distance away for a wash-up and other necessary activities. Five minutes later he was back by the dead campfire, setting down the empty bucket to stretch again, and Petey was hurrying towards him with a tin cup of cold coffee in one hand, a bulky sandwich in the other.

'Gobble these,' said Petey. 'Fast. An' kick me. Hard.'

'Loco,' said Young Jake.

'I must of dozed some,' said Petey. 'Take a look over there.'

Young Jake looked. On ahead, near the road, where the other camps had been, was only a blank emptiness in the dingy greyness of dawn.

'Yeah,' said Petey. 'They slipped out in the dark. Could have fifteen-twenty miles on you by now. I'd of saddled Jimmie but you know how he fights anyone but you.' Petey grabbed the bucket and ran to the wagon and threw the bucket in and jumped to the driving seat. He slapped with reins and was moving past towards the road. 'I'll push ahead fast as I can. See what I can find out.'

Young Jake drained the cup in two gulps and let it fall. He crunched a bite out of the sandwich and chewed rapidly and crammed the rest into his mouth. He scooped up his blanket and the small bag of feed with one hand, the saddle and trailing bridle with the other, and ran towards Jimmie Dun.

He was pulling on the cinch when he heard, faintly, somewhere off by the road, a sharp crack and a clatter. He hesitated briefly, listening, and heard nothing more. Swiftly he finished saddling and swung up and Jimmie Dun rose in the air, head down and back arched, bucking once, twice, three times, to get the kinks our of his backbone, and levelled into a fast lope towards the road.

There they were, Petey and the mules and the wagon, Petey standing in the road with a hatchet in one hand, the mules motionless except for twitching tails, the wagon tip-tilted with some of its contents spilled and the remainder a crazy jumble. The right rear wheel had hit a boulder and the spokes had shattered.

'I got two kicks coming,' said Petey. 'But don't you worry none about me. I'll cut me a tree limb an' brace it under for a drag. Make it to the next town an' get a wheel. Drive like hell an' catch up later today.'

Young Jake looked forward along the road that stretched to far hill horizon where the first faint flush of colour was creeping up the sky. Somewhere beyond three riders on three big strong horses were knocking off more miles. 'Take your time,' he said. 'You ain't agoin' to do no catchin' up. Not the way me'n Jimmie'll be movin' from here on in.'

The little crossroads settlement seemed to be deserted in the early morning sunlight. No. A man who had been sitting on a bench by the blacksmith shop was walking out into the roadway. A red-haired man with a jutting chin. He had a hand up signalling. Young Jake reined in.

'I figure they've got about fifteen miles on you,' said the man. 'They're moving right along. You going to try to nail them?'

'Not try,' said Young Jake. 'Jimmie here's agoin' to do it.'

'I hope he does,' said the man. 'I'll be hoping mighty hard he does. But watch yourself. I know better'n to say anything else. Just keep a sharp eye out. Watch yourself.'

Jimmie Dun moved strong and steady under him. Lope-trot-lope. Lope for half an hour in the smooth undulating stride familiar to anyone who had ever seen a herd of mustangs flowing over the land, their backs rising and falling as easy and regularly as watery waves. Trot for the next half hour in that swinging double-beat stride mustangs themselves favoured for making maximum distance with minimum effort. It was hard, not knowing what was happening ahead, to hold down, to keep from ramming into full gallop. But there was still a long way to go.

'Let's see,' said the farmer who was working on a stretch of fence along the roadside. 'There was two together. A black and a bay. I'd make that a shade under two hours ago. Then along comes a grey. I'd call that just a mite over one hour.'

Only half of the meagre contents of the bag for Jimmie Dun at this nooning. Only one of the two sandwiches in the saddlebag for himself.

But there was no water. Nowhere along the last miles had they come on a stream or a farmhouse with its well. Nothing but barren sandy friendless country and one rickety farm wagon drawn by two bony horses with a pinch-faced man and a pursed-mouth woman on the driving seat who failed out of meanness or lethargy to return a passing word.

Only half an hour of resting. 'Short rations all around,' said Young Jake as he retied the bag behind the cantle. Jimmie Dun whiffled softly in response and turned his head to push gently against him and stood steady as a rock while he swung up into saddle again.

They could see it far ahead, a cluster of weathered board buildings, a house and small barn and shed. And there, in front of the house, a pump and a water trough.

He held Jimmie Dun to a trot then to a walk as they approached. He dismounted twenty feet from the pump and Jimmie Dun stood, ground-reined, waiting. He looked around. There was no sign of life anywhere. He strode to the pump and worked with the handle and a stream of water ran into the trough. He strode back to Jimmie Dun and led him to the trough and let him drink sparingly. 'Enough's enough,' he said and led Jimmie about twenty feet away again and left him again, ground-reined, waiting. He returned to the trough and leaned down and scooped water in his hands and drank.

'Howdy, cowboy. Reckon you're one of those racers.'

A man had stepped out of the house, smiling in friendly fashion, very friendly. He held in one hand a bottle two thirds full of an amber liquid. 'Water's all right,' he said. 'Whiskey's better. Perk you up.' He moved a few steps forward and held out the hand with the bottle.

Young Jake suddenly realized he had not had a real drink for five days and more. That was what he needed, something stronger than water to rake the dust of five days' riding out of his throat. 'Thanks,' he said and moved towards the man and took the bottle.

He raised it high and let a satisfying slug of the amber liquid gurgle into his mouth. He sloshed this around inside before he let it slide raw and tingling down his throat. 'Thanks again,' he said and raised the bottle again.

Out of the corner of one eye he saw movement over by Jimmie Dun. Two men had slipped quietly, very quietly, around from the other side of the house. One had hold of Jimmie Dun's reins and the other was stretching out a hand under Jimmie Dun's nose, palm flat, and something showed on the flattened palm.

Young Jake jerked around, dropping the bottle.

'Hey,' he shouted, 'Get away from—' The rest of that breath was jolted out of him. The first man had jumped to grab him from behind.

He struggled to free himself but the man had arms clamped around him. He tried to whistle, high and shrill. Only a desperate small sound came from him—but Jimmie Dun heard. And Jimmie Dun reared back, away from the flattened palm and whatever was on it, jerking on the reins, and the man who held them clung to them and Jimmie Dun reared again, plunging forward, forehoofs striking, and one struck the man in the chest and knocked him away and down and loosened his hold on the reins, and Jimmie Dun was swinging in a fast arc, head high, dodging the third man, aiming for Young Jake.

'I'm acomin'!' gasped Young Jake. He smashed backward with booted heel on the left instep of the man holding him and heaved upward and forward and broke loose and as Jimmie Dun, true to his old training, swung to move past him, broadside to him, his hands fastened on the horn and he vaulted into the saddle. Only his grip on the horn held him there as Jimmie Dun surged ahead, picking up speed, away from the men and the house. His feet found the stirrups. Secure in the seat, he leaned forward to take the trailing reins.

Out in the road, moving away, he looked back. No one was following. If the men had horses with them, these were still in the barn or hidden behind the house. Two of the men were bending over the third, who still lay flat on the ground. 'You sure did it up right,' he said, reaching to rub along Jimmie Dun's neck. 'An' I sure got me a kick comin'.'

The wind of motion was ruffling his hair. 'Lost my hat,' he muttered. Somehow that seemed the final ultimate insult. 'From now on,' he said, 'we ain't trustin' nobody on nothin'.'

He became aware that Jimmie Dun was pounding in full gallop. 'Easy,' he said, tightening on reins. 'Easy. Save it for when it counts.'

And then he was aware of a nagging ache inside him, under his ribs, growing, increasing, and a nausea creeping through him. He swayed in the saddle and his throat constricted in dry retching. He could feel a weakness taking him and his vision blurred.

Time passed and he did not know it. Hunched forward, head hanging down, hands clenched on the forward edge of the saddle blanket, he rode in a kind of coma, aware of nothing, not even of the insistent joggle of Jimmie Dun's swinging trot or of the habitual ingrained response of his own muscles holding him there in the saddle. Then gradually awareness fought through the fog gripping him and he knew where he was. He was on Jimmie Dun and he was riding a race, Jimmie Dun's race, and he was the damnedest stupidest fool in the whole of the world and he was letting Jimmie Dun down. He tried to straighten in the saddle, be less of spineless blob of dead weight on Jimmie Dun's back, and he managed to do so a bit.

He felt Jimmie Dun moving strong and steady under him and suddenly, out of nowhere, he wanted to do something he had not done for too many years. He wanted to cry, to blubber like a snot-nosed kid. And then, somehow, it seemed to him that Jimmie Dun was saying something to him, saying it in the ceaseless steadiness of stride, in the flex and flow of muscles under the dusty dun-coloured hide, in the tireless rhythmic thuddings of hoofs. 'Quit frettin',' Jimmie Dun was saying. 'I'm adoin' this. You're all right for a man. But you never could do what I'm doin' now. I can. So I'm fool enough in my turn to do it for you.'

And time passed and Young Jake began to feel better. He was a tough one too. He was straight in the saddle again, a true horseman helping his horse by the instinctive coordination and balance of his riding.

The sign was nailed to a tree by the roadside. The legend was faded and worn. Young Jake could barely make it out in the dimness of dusk. 'Omaha 90 Miles.'

In the clean dark of night, several hundred yards from a lonely stretch of the road, well screened by clumps of bushes

121

and trees, Jimmie Dun munched on the last grains of the remnants of the meagre contents of the bag and Young Jake chewed on his one remaining sandwich. 'Just about enough to make us hungrier'n ever,' he said.

He swallowed the last crumbs. He took the end of the rope trailing from Jimmie Dun's neck and tied this to his left arm. 'Half an hour,' he said. 'Make it any longer an' I'll fall asleep sure.' He leaned back against the saddle on the ground behind him and thoughts about a dun-coloured maverick mustang and about three strong big horses somewhere along the same road in the dark of the same night chased themselves through his mind.

Twenty feet away Jimmie Dun stood, motionless, head low. He was gaunted some along the ribs and sunk in some at the flanks. He was a dirtied clumsy-looking caricature of a horse that seemed dead on its feet. He looked finished, done for, ready to collapse into a heap of bones and hide. He was not. He was resting. He was relaxed all over, drooped, sagged, into absolute limpness. He knew. He was wasting no energy in twitchings or stompings or movings about. He was making the most of a brief resting. He was a smallish southwestern mustang who was just about ready to begin to fight.

Young Jake struggled out of a doze and forced himself to his feet. 'All right, Jimmie boy,' he said. 'Omaha the next stop.'

There was only the dark of night and the tracery of road ghostly in faint starlight and the wind of their own motion as they moved at a fast lope into the lonely miles. Houses were more frequent now, but these were nothing more than blank eyeless shapes along the way. Urgency talked along the reins, stretching Jimmie Dun's stride.

Tiredness was an ache in Young Jake and hunger a hollowness in his belly. Giddiness took him now and again and he felt strangely light-headed. He would never remember the rest of this ride in clear sequence, only in snatches as if full awareness caught him only at certain intervals.

It seemed to him that this supposedly short summer night would never end and suddenly he realized that objects by the roadside were sharper, more distinct, and somewhere a rooster was crowing and he could make out a sign on a fencepost: 'Omaha 40 Miles.'

This little settlement showed activity in the morning sun-light. A dog ran out barking at Jimmie Dun's heels. Two wagons and a pinto saddlehorse stood by a tie-rail and half a dozen people were in front of the general store, four men and two women.

'Here's another of them Black Hills buckaroos!'

He held Jimmie Dun to a trot passing by, but he was ready to strike with spurs at any instant. He kept straight on, ignoring the people. After what had happened yesterday, he was in no mood even to wave at anyone, even to a pretty woman like one of those back there.

He heard hoofbeats behind him and twisted to look around. The pinto was coming up fast. It came alongside and slowed to Jimmie Dun's pace. The man was lean and hard and a piece with his saddle and he had a sun-and-wind tanned face with crinkles at the eye-corners from squinting into sun and dis-tance. Young Jake relaxed some. One of his own breed.

'What in holy hell you doin' without a hat?'

Young Jake relaxed even more. He knew that tone too, an echo out of the distances of the cattle country. 'Lost it,' he said, 'Ain't had time to steal me another.'

'Sun's got muscles hereabouts,' said the man. 'You'll fry what few brains you got. Here, take mine. I'll get another at the store.' He reined the pinto in closer, pulled off his high-crowned broad-brimmed hat that was battered by weather and work into a proper dirty greasy shape and general bedraggled consistency and reached to pop it on Young Jake's head.

'Likely you don't know it,' he said. 'But one of 'em's in that barn back there. Mean-lookin' gent. Big grey of his gave out. Could be he'll be movin' on after a while but he won't get much more'n a walk out of that hoss. If he can sit a saddle hisself. He's done beat.'

Young Jake was adjusting the hat to firm position. A bit tight, but it had the right feel.

'You ain't got exactly the look of a fresh-picked daisy your-self,' said the man. 'But them two on ahead look worse. Can't have more'n two-three miles on you. Go get 'em.' He swung the pinto and headed back towards the settlement.

Young Jake sat up straight in the saddle as a man should. Somehow he was not as tired as he had been. He waved at a farmer who was doing something with a hoe in a field off to the left. He reached to slap Jimmie Dun on the neck. 'One down, Jimmie boy,' he said. 'Only two more. You heard 'im. Go get 'em.' And Jimmie Dun warmed through to the very marrow of his bones now, fully into this race if it should last through all eternity, leaned forward again into a fast long-reaching lope.

There was plenty of activity along the way now. Houses and more houses between cultivated fields and people by the roadside shouting and waving and sometimes a man or two or even a boy on horses loping alongside for a while yipping advice and encouragement. Jimmie Dun ignored them all. He was intent on this day's work, strong and steady, eating the wind, gobbling the miles.

'Win or lose,' shouted a man on a stocky sorrel that was working hard to stay alongside. 'I'll give you two hundred dollars for that horse!'

'Go soak your head,' shouted Young Jake. 'There ain't enough money in the whole of the world to buy him!'

They clattered over a wooden bridge and slowed some on an up-slope. Jimmie Dun shifted his lead from right forefoot to the left, sure sign he was feeling the strain. His eyes were beginning to show red-rimmed. His chest heaved in long slow rhythm and sweaty lather dampened his flanks and stretched-out neck. But still that reassuring refrain came from his pounding rock-hard range hoofs. 'Quit frettin'. I'm adoin' this. You want it done, so I'm doin' it.'

'Omaha 12 Miles,' said the sign a small boy held up high over his small head.

A dark shape blotted the road in front of them, moving slowly. They came closer and it was a big bay, lathered, gaunted, head hanging, reduced to a shuffling jogtrot. The black-bearded man in the saddle heard them coming and looked back and exploded into frantic action, slapping with his rein ends, raking with his spurs, and the big bay rallied some, trying, trying, and broke into a jerky gallop.

Young Jake was debating with himself whether to use his own spurs or hold his pace and wear the bay down—and Jimmie Dun took charge. He shifted to right forefoot lead again and surged full gallop, belly low, legs striving for distance in lengthening stride. Young Jake felt the power pulsing under him, the message of urgency suddenly reversed and coming back to him now along the reins from Jimmie Dun's hammering hammer-head. 'Yahoo!' he yelled, leaning to throw his weight forward in the saddle. 'Get 'im, Jimmie boy! Get 'im!'

Closer they came. And closer. Alongside. Young Jake heard the black-bearded man cursing him and Jimmie Dun and the bay and then they were out in front, the gap between steadily widening.

Young Jake looked back. He saw the bay stumble and almost fall. He saw the black-bearded man yank savagely on the reins and the bay slow to a dragging walk.

Young Jake heard cheers and shouts from the roadside. None of them meant anything to him except the shrill yipping from a lanky overalled farmer. 'Yowee, cowboy! Five miles to go!'

There was no break in the steady long-reaching lope, but Young Jake could sense the labouring in it. He could feel the extra jolting as the hoofs hit and the straining muscles no longer cushioned the shocks in instant springy response. Jimmie Dun's breath came in long sobbing gasps. Sweat drenched his dun-coloured hide and a dingy froth dropped from the side-bars of the bit in his mouth. But there was no break, no falter in that steady stride.

'Three miles!' shouted someone on the edge of vision.

Strange, there was no one loping alongside, no mounted escort, and had not been for a mile and more. Houses clustered close along the way and people in front of them were excited, shouting, waving, jumping up and down, the sense of their shouts drowned in their own clamour. But there was no one on horseback.

Around a sharp bend in the road—and there they were, twenty and more mounted men not fifty yards ahead, trotting forward in a group. And there, in the midst of them, the big black Thoroughbred known as Cannonball. Black no longer, streaked and discoloured by dust and dirt and sweaty lather. Head hung low. Moving jerkily in a shuffling foot-dragging trot. But moving. Forward.

The others scattered sideways, clearing the way, and Jimmie Dun swept past, holding hard to his fast lope. 'Yahoo!' yelled Young Jake, forgetting the rawness of his throat and the tiredness bedded in him. 'Omaha, here we come!' And the escort was with him now, pulling away with him and Jimmie Dun from a bitter cursing thin-faced man and a big black horse dropping even further behind.

'Two miles!'

Young Jake was fighting himself now, fighting to hold himself straight in the saddle as a man should. He had this race won. He was intent on just one thing, to finish it in proper style.

Suddenly he was aware that the escort was scattering again, was shouting at him, was pointing back along the road. He swung in saddle to see.

The big black named Cannonball was coming up! The thin-faced man was lashing with a quirt, jabbing with spurs. Frenzied, foam-spattering, head high and tossing, wild-eyed, running on breeding and nerve alone, dragging the last burst of power and speed out of the great Thoroughbred heart in him. Cannonball was coming up fast!

Jimmie Dun heard. Through the tangle of hoofbeats about him he heard. He turned his head to place the big black coming up and there for a flashing instant Young Jake saw it, the look of eagles in the red-rimmed bloodshot eye. And out of the long past of his kind in the wide stripped barren land of the far southwest, out of the stubborn endurance bred into him through the generations, came the surge of strength in lean hard gaunted flanks and rock-hard hammering hoofs.

The big black, longer-legged, covering more ground with each frantic leap, crept up, was nose to flank. Alongside. Nose to nose they pounded on and the striving escort was left behind and Young Jake saw the bloody froth flying from the big black's mouth and heard its breath whistling and rattling in its throat. A rush of anger he could never have put into words stabbed through him that men should do such things to fellow creatures finer and nobler than themselves and then all that was forgotten and he was crouched forward jockey-style in stirrups shouting encouragement at Jimmie Dun's hammering head.

It was Jimmie Dun creeping out in front now, inch by inch, foot by foot, yard by yard. The big black broke stride and stumbled and caught itself and came on but the distance between was widening. Young Jake looked back and saw the big black stumble again and go down and the man be thrown free, rolling in the road dust.

'Easy, Jimmie boy,' he said, tightening on reins. 'It's all over but the shoutin'. Easy does it. We got to come in proud.'

And Jimmie Dun came in proud, tired and worn and dingy-looking, but strong and steady in stride, head up, ears perked, listening to the cheers from the crowd lining the way as he breasted the string stretched across the street at the finish line.

It was Buffalo Bill Cody, whose Wild West Show was in town, who stepped up to shake Young Jake's hand and give him a small slip of paper, a certified cheque for one thousand dollars.

It was the pretty daughter of the man who ran the leading leather goods store who kissed him smack on the dusty unshaven cheek and made an equally pretty little speech presenting him with a fine new double-cinch A-fork high-cantle free-swinging-stirrup saddle whose silver-topped horn gleamed in the Nebraska sunlight.

The Horse Show

CLARE LEIGHTON

THE PLACE seemed changed. But there stood the familiar hills. Thanks to them one was certain that one had not strayed into an unknown district. Yet as the hills were lost from time to time in the deep mist of the rain, even that certainty grew dim. What was it that had happened?

For the quiet road on the outskirt of the little town was clogged and choked with cars. Strange police controlled the traffic, abrupt and ill-tempered in the wet heat of the September day; they were impatient with all who passed, respecting nobody. 'And who do you think *you* are?' Stanley Peabody swore back at them. 'I've lived here, in this place, pretty nigh on eighty-five year, and nobody ain't never stopped me from walking along my own road. "Pass along please!" And why, I asks you?'

The unending line of cars, horse-boxes and show animals pushed Stanley Peabody close against the hedge, and blocked his passage. But even here, in the shelter of the hawthorns, tranquillity was not possible: to his right, with pictures propped against the weeds at the foot of the hedge, sat a pavement artist, caught up and brought along in the tide of the urban invasion. Stanley Peabody looked all around him, but he could not escape. He glanced in curious disgust at the chalk drawings of loaves of bread and bunches of flowers, swans on lakes, and sailing ships.

It was cruel of it to be so sopping wet to-day. On this everyone was agreed. The rain had started during the night, and in places the grass of the show-ground was already hidden under pools of water, reflecting the heavy dull grey of the sky. The gatemen swore with impatience as cars stuck in the churned mud of the entrance. Vendors of fruit and ices anticipated a useless day.

But the worst sufferers were the men who tended the animals. In the early hours of the morning they had wakened to the drip of rain, as they lay in bed in obscure farms among the folds of the hills. Tom Grainger thought of Duke, whom he had so groomed and polished that you could almost see your face in the shire's great flanks. He thought of the miles to go before you reached the show-ground. He knew how thick the mud would stand in the lanes around Brampton Bottom, how blinding the rain would be after you passed the top of Stourton Hill. As he braided Duke's mane with blue ribbons and knotted his tail with straw, he cursed the weather that had played him such a trick.

'And the hair round your hocks white and pure-like, as though you'd stepped out of a bowl of cream. And it'll be a sight to see you when we get you there to-day, what with that mud all sticking to your legs and your body streaming with rain. Now if you was a hunter, old man, instead of a great mighty shire, what earns his living on the farm, you'd be taken to the show in a horse-box, you would, and arrive there all dainty and dandy-like, as if you'd come straight out of a barber's shop, as you might say. Here, now, quiet, Duke, quiet while I do this last pigtail. '

And Tom Grainger and his shire Duke had set off along the hilly lanes in the ceaseless downpour, man and horse both covered with sacks in the endeavour to keep dry. The man walked by his horse's side, looking up from time to time to the smoothness of the great neck. He guided him carefully, that they might avoid all possible puddles. Mile after mile of drenched road brought them at last within sight of the show. But just when they turned the corner of the lane that led to the show-ground, they were overtaken by a horse-box. It was going at a great speed, and as it passed them it splashed through an enormous puddle, sending the muddy water over Tom Grainger and Duke. They were soaked to the skin as they entered the gates of the field. The animals were grouped in the second meadow, protected from the wet by the fringe of great chestnuts. Tom Grainger and his shire were not the only ones to have suffered. Beneath the shelter of the trees men cleaned their cows, bending over hindquarters, stooping to wash mud from leg and udder, stepping back as they drew cloths along

the length of swishing tail. And as the cows were cleaned, the large bodies shifted the weight from leg to leg and the eyes stared into the darkness of the chestnut under-growth. There was a feeling of peace among the animals.

Tom Grainger tied Duke to the fence, in line with the other shire horses. He washed the mud from his legs, and combed the white hair on his hocks. His movements, in bending down to clean the horse, were slow, attuned to the world of animal and plough-land. And as they tended the horses—he and Jim Webster and the new farm-hand from Morland's over Hughenden way—they seemed part of the earth itself, and the lines of back and neck of the mighty shires repeated the lines of the distant hills. A rhythm ran from horse to hill, and caught up in its sweep Tom Grainger and his bucket of water; it eternalized man and horse and mud. Here, this morning, among the animals, nothing was discordant.

It was an abrupt shock to walk from the peace of the chestnut meadow to the front part of the Horse Show. If the Village Flower Show were the great social leveller of the year, the Horse Show dug a blatant social cleavage. The difference that separated the heavy lines of the shire horses from the delicate, spare grace of the hunter spread from horse to man, and isolated the flowing tranquillity of Tom Grainger from the taut handsomeness of the aristocrat. While each kept to his separate meadow, there was no meeting-point.

Handsome the aristocrats most certainly were, as they paraded the show-ground with proprietary step and jerky talk. The well-made faces spoke of a life of wealth and ease, the assurance of their bearing told of the habit of command. But with all their fineness of clothing and bony structure, they yet had drifted from the earth, and it was with spiky discord that they stood out upon the show-ground against the quiet curve of the hills. Tom Grainger, with his stumpy figure and shabby overcoat, had the greater understanding of the eternal values.

But if the Flower Show belonged, essentially, to the villager, the Horse Show to-day was dominated by the aristocrat. Eddies of chance would sweep the world of the animals across that of the 'county', as cows or bulls or horses were brought into the judging-ring. But it would be for a brief few moments, and back to the chestnut meadows would go shire or bull. In this idle crowd they were of fleeting importance compared with hunter and horsemanship.

As the morning drew on towards midday, the gentry preponderated yet more. Cars banked the race-course, in position for the afternoon's sport. With the stopping of the rain the air grew still heavier, as though sky and earth were bound together by steam. Into this close atmosphere rose and clung the hot smell of cars and motor tyres, and odour of countless mackintoshes, subduing the scent of the trodden grass.

Tom Grainger had left Duke for a short while in the care of Jim Webster. He had to see a man about some wurzels. He walked dazed among the gentry, seeking the root marquee.

'Whew!' he thought. 'And this is the smell of all them what has motor-cars. It's enough to drive you sick, what with they rubber tyres and the petrol and all. What I say is, give me the smell of a hot wet horse or a cow as is being milked with your head against her flank. That's what you might call natural. But all these noises and shouts and smells don't suit me, they don't. Nor the women don't, neither. '

He was indifferent to the finely-cut beauty of the young horsewomen, as they strode in the field in their riding-habits. He was unable to appreciate the grace of their cared-for bodies or the scent of their well-groomed hair. He saw only the hard tense look in their faces and the crimson gash of their lipsticked mouths. And they, if they had even bothered to notice him, would have thought what a scrubby-looking little creature he was, with a smell of wet clothes about him. He returned to Duke and the chestnut trees and sighed with relief as he lowered himself on to a heap of dry straw.

'There's none of they hunters as comes up to you, old man,' he thought. 'They may shine and quiver and their veins do stand out like little rivers, but there weren't none of them, no, not even one of they heavyweights nor three-year-olds, what could gather at the headland as you do. They be only for show, they be. And they women too.'

But all Duke cared for was the sweet hay that lay before him, and he munched in peace.

Perhaps it was the quiet of the animals' feeding that made Mr Hampton's bull sound so terrifying. The huge red monster puffed and roared and blew, making a gigantic noise. It was humiliating for him to be tethered like this at a show, and he seemed to know it. From time to time the rising wind blew a spiky horse-chestnut upon his back from the trees above, vexing him still further. He tugged at his chain, he lowered his head to charge; but there was nothing before him but wooden palings and undergrowth. Miss Agatha and Miss Christina Mayhew were passing at this moment, enjoying the thrill of looking at dangerous animals that were safety tethered. Never before had they seen such a mighty bull so close at hand. They examined his woolly head, his heavy shoulders, silently admiring his virility. The bull felt the ignominy, and resented it. He snorted through his nostrils and gave one enormous bellow. Miss Agatha and Miss Christina Mayhew fled.

'Dear, dear,' said Miss Agatha. 'I really think one more moment and he'd have broken loose and been upon us. They're quite right in saying that you can never trust those animals. I believe he must have known you were wearing a red petticoat. They say that bulls go mad when they see something red. It must have been showing beneath your skirt. Here, Chrissie, turn round and let me have a look. And then we'll go back and see the mangolds.'

It was the time of the midday meal. The judging was over. Destinies were decided. Picnic-baskets were opened in the

shelter of the cars, and the gentry ate. Among the shire horses Tom Grainger and Jim Webster and the new farm-hand from Morland's also ate, sitting on straw at the feet of the animals, or leaning against the palings. Further along, where the cattle were tethered, Andrew Rogers sat milking his judged cow. By his side stood his young wife with their child in her arms, searching among her packages for a tin mug.

'There now, that's better, Daisy, ain't it?' said Andrew Rogers. 'And it weren't my fault as I had to bring you all that way unmilked, with your udders that full that they did drip on the roads. Here, Mary, give us the mug.'

And the Rogers family sat down, also, on a heap of straw, and ate.

But Steve Duncan wanted something stronger than milk. He wanted to celebrate. He had won first prize for the best pen of three ewes, first prize for the best pen of three theaves, and second prize for his wether lambs. He hurried back from the town, bearing two bottles of beer with him.

'Come on, boys,' he shouted. 'Here's no offence meant to any of you, but here's to my health.' The cheering from the sheep-pens floated over the meadow to Tom Grainger as he sat beside his shire. He needed no beer. He hardly knew what it was he was eating. For Duke had won first prize.

So happy was Tom Grainger that afternoon, that the events of the show around him passed unremarked. He stood by the side of his shire, alert for the praise of passers-by. But they were few, and those who did walk through the chestnut meadow had mostly been there during the morning, and knew already about Duke. Not much need to tell Farmer Lucas about it, when he'd been certain all along that Duke would get that first prize. For Farmer Lucas knew a good horse when he saw one. And as for all his friends—well, they couldn't come and see him and Duke; they hadn't got the two shillings entrance fee. He'd have to tell them all about it that night, at the Three Crowns.

No, the admiring crowds that Tom Grainger waited for in vain were crushed together in the first field, between white wooden railings of race-course and banked cars. If the morning had been the time for business, the afternoon was dedicated to sport. Clapping and cheering punctuated the end of each item, whether it were riding or jumping or obstacle race. Proud frightened children rode their ponies into the ring; high-stepping, graceful yearling colts excited ripples of admiration. Lest there should be one moment's pause in the excitement, the afternoon's programme included the arrival of the local fire-engine, looking like a flaming sacrificial animal at a procession. And still the large crowd cheered, and still Tom puffed his pipe in the quiet of the chestnut field, against the side of his shire.

Then the hunt arrived, and the flutter of excitement grew reverent before pink coats and hunting-horn and the moving pattern of up-tailed hounds. Among the gentry stood a strange tramp-like creature; how he had arrived there, was a puzzle to the well-dressed crowd. His face glowed and his eyes gleamed and he waved his thorn stick high in the air, nearly knocking off the hats of the ladies as he did so. 'They'll be over the hill in the morning!' he shouted. The gentry turned and glared at him, unable any longer to ignore him. It wasn't done to behave like this. A mere common tramp, what right had he to concern himself with the hunt? It was their affair—they who attended each meet, who themselves rode to hounds. But to the tramp-like creature the hunt meant running over fields and through copses at the sound of the distant horn, and in his nostrils he smelt the sting of an autumn morning, with the mist hanging over the ploughed fields, and dewdrops enchaining the thorns of the bramble. He became the fox itself, chased and hunted and lost, slinking to earth at nightfall. In sympathy, his feet felt sore. But someone was touching his arm. He turned and saw a swell, who glared at him. 'You mustn't go on like this, sir, don't you know. We can't hear what's happening. Don't you know it isn't done?'

The tramp's stick fell limply to his side, and he moved off.

The rain had started again, and the parade of prize-winners took place in a steamy downpour. The animals looked strangely like the procession into the ark, as they passed in varying size. Mr Wilkin's prize sow lumbered after Mr Hampton's monster bull, to be followed by Ted Lowrie's pair of gilts. It was Tom Grainger's moment, and he led in Duke with proud dignity, his stumpy body erect and transfigured. He did not notice the rain now, for it did not matter. Duke might get his hocks splashed till the white hair looked dappled with mud:

nothing could remove the rosette of triumph. But the rain by now was falling so fast that it thinned the crowds, who ran for shelter to the surrounding marquees. Tom Grainger never knew that he led Duke round the ring before a preoccupied audience. He walked beside the horse in a state of exaltation, his feet mechanically following in the thread of the three wether lambs before him, his eyes gazing in pride at the glossy neck above him.

There was no point in staying any longer. Gradually, as the afternoon wore on, the animals in the chestnut field melted away. The sheep and the pigs disappeared into the vans under the fringe of the trees. But they left the field unobserved, for the rain had lifted and the people had gathered once more round the ring, where the jumping was in progress.

But as the animals left, it was a chance for those in the road outside the show. Throughout the day, in rain and heat, a crowd had stood at the entrance to the fields, feeding with excitement upon every stray happening. And now, as pig and cow and horse filed out, they noted each prize-winner.

'Coo! There goes Steve Duncan with his sheep. Wouldn't I 'arf have liked to have seen the judge's face as he looked at they ewes of his'n. And to think as I helped feed 'em and as I did the shearing of 'em, and all for the blessed two shillings as I can't afford, I has to stand here instead of watching them be judged.'

Along the hilly lanes, at dusk, clumps of animals might be seen going home to obscure farms among the folds of the hills. And this time the farm-hands do not scruple to ride the horses, as they dared not on their way to the show in the morning. For their destiny now is fixed. It is slow work, reaching home, for the lanes are narrow and twisting, and the horses have continually to be moved to the ditch, against the hedge, to give place to overtaking cars that carry the owners of the hunters, or to horse-boxes containing the hunters themselves. But the cars move so quickly that they have all passed while Tom has yet another mile and a half to go. The rain wets the bright blue of the ribbons that deck Duke's mane, and drips down Tom Grainger's neck. Man and horse are tired and wet, but as Tom jumps to the ground to open the farm gate, pride banishes fatigue.

First Money

WILL JAMES

I T WAS natural that we was feeling pretty good when we walked in the Rodeo headquarters that evening and heard the reports. We got our 'daily money' and then we holds our breaths while we listen who all so far had qualified for the finals. There was only three and *I was one of 'em*.

Tom near went through hisself when he heard my name was on that list and a grin spread on his face that sure disguised it. 'Good boy, Bill,' he hollers at the same time giving me a slap on the back that give me to understand he meant all what he said.

The eight or nine riders left what hadn't competed for the finals and due to ride the next day was drawing their horses and I edged in to draw my 'final' horse, I closed my eyes and near prayed as I reaches in the hat, gets one envelope and steps out where Tom and me can read it together.

We pulls the paper out of the little envelope like it was going to be either real bad news or else information that we'd inherited a million, and hesitating we unfolds it. — 'Slippery Elm' is all that little piece of paper said, but that was enough and meant a plenty. It meant that tomorrow I was to ride a horse by that name and that nine chances out of ten it was up to that horse whether I'd win first, second, or third money or nothing.

We'd seen that horse bucked out the second day. He was a big black and reminded me some of Angel Face, back there on the range. His mane was roached and from what we'd seen of him he wasn't near as good a bucking horse as our old Angel Face, he wasn't as honest and we remembered that he throwed himself a purpose and near killed a good cowboy on that second day. What's more we learn that he can't be depended on to buck everytime he's rode, sometimes he just stampedes, and it was told that one time he run through two railings and halfway up the grandstand where he broke through the steps and near broke his neck.

Putting all that together and thinking it over, me and Tom was looking mighty solemn. Of course, chances was that he might buck and buck good but the biggest part of them chances was that he'd just stampede and crowhop and then fall, and we knowed if it happened the important judges would take advantage of that and instead of giving me another horse they'd grin and just put a line across my name.

Tom ain't saying nothing, but I can see he's doing a heap of thinking instead, and watching him I can't help but grin a little and remark that everything may turn out all right. 'Can't tell about that horse, Tom,' I says, 'he might buck like hell.'

'Yes, he might and he might *not*,' says Tom, looking gloomy, 'and I sure hate to see you take a chance on a scrub like that horse after you getting as far as the finals. If you'd drawed a good one like that Ragtime horse for instance, I don't mean the one I rode and got disqualified on, I mean the one they cheated me out of, well, if you'd got a horse like that you'd have a chance for your money, but who do you suppose has drawed that horse?' he asks.

'I don't know,' I says, wondering.

'That pet cowboy of Colter's got him—and do you think he could of drawed that horse on the square? Not by a damn sight! That cowboy is a good rider and being he is Colter's drawcard same as some of his horses he advertises and claims can't be rode, Colter is naturally going to see that that cowboy wins first. It's a safe bet so far cause when he drawed Ragtime he drawed the best bucking horse in the outfit.'

'Now I'll tell you Bill,' says Tom, all het up on the subject, 'it's not the prize money nor the honours we're after so much, if they can out-ride us and do it on the square we'd be glad to shake hands with 'em and congratulate, but they're trying to put something over on us and on all the riders of this part of the country. Other outfits like Colter's done the same thing last two years and got away with the money when there was boys from here that could of outrode 'em two to one, and it looks like the same thing is going to be done this year, but if you had a good horse, Bill, we'd sure make them circus hands look up to a cowboy.'

It's after supper when Tom, still looking mighty sour, tells me he's going to the stable to get his horse and go visiting out of town a ways. I see his mind is still on the subject as he's saddling, and giving the latigo a jerk remarks that he can lose a square deal and laugh about it, 'but I'll be daggone', he says, 'if it don't hurt to get cheated out of what's yours, have it done right under your nose and not have no say acoming.'

The next day was the last day, the big day, the grounds was sizzling hot and dust that was stirred up stayed in the air looking for a cooler atmosphere. It was past noon and Tom hadn't showed up yet. I was beginning to wonder of the whereabouts of that cowboy and started looking for him. I was still at it when the parade drifted in and the Grand Entree was over, every kid that could borrow a horse was in it, some wore red silk shirts and they sure thought they was cowboys far as the clothes was concerned.

The riders what still had to ride for the finals went hard at it and I was busy watching and judging for myself how many of them would make them finals. I hears when it's over that only two had qualified and them two was of Colter's outfit, that made six of us who are still to ride for the grand prize, four of Colter's men and two of us outsiders and by that I figgers that Colter is sure making it a cinch of *keeping the money in the family*.

'All the bulldoggers on the track,' hollers the Rodeo boss, and knowing that Tom is in on that event I take another look for him, but I can't see hair nor hide of that son-of-a-gun nowheres, so I was getting real worried.

My name is called and I rides up to the shute. My steer is let out and for the time being I forgets everything but what I'd rose up there for. I done good time, the best time of that day so far, and I sure did wish that old Tom was there and seen it, cause I know it'd tickled him.

A half dozen or so other bulldoggers are called on to take their chance and then Tom's name comes, but he's still among the missing and I see no way but offer to substitute for him. I had a mighty hard time to get the judges to agree to that, but with Pete on my side and me atalking my head off, they finally decide to let me take his place.

I glances towards the shutes and notices a steer *just my size* already there and waiting to come out, and I also notices that they're trying to drive him back and put another steer in the place of him, a great big short-horned Durham. I rides up there right now and begins to object, remarking that I'd take on any steer as they come but at the same time I wasn't letting any skunk stack the cards on me by going to the special trouble of picking me the hardest steer they can find. I object so strong that they finally let me have the first steer.

I was mad and when that steer come out I figgered there was something to work my hard feelings out on, I made a reach for them horns that I wouldn't of made if I'd been normal, the critter kept me up for a good airing, but when my boot heels finally connected with the sod the programme wasn't long in ending. I stopped him good so there wouldn't be no danger of being disqualified and imagining that I was bulldogging a Rodeo boss or a judge instead of a steer, it wasn't long before I had him down.

'Old critter,' I says to the steer as I lets him up, 'you play square which is more than I can say for some folks.'

I shakes the dust off myself, locates my hat, and being I was through on bulldogging I struts out round and towards the saddling shutes trying to get a peek at that long lean pardner of mine—a vision of his expression as he was leaving the night before came to me and I'm beginning to wonder if he didn't try to even scores with the Colter outfit. 'But daggone it,' I thinks, 'he should of let me tag along.'

'You'll soon be riding now, Bill,' says one of the local boys breaking in on my thoughts, 'and if you don't bring home the bacon with first money you better keep on riding and never let me see your homely phizog again.'

'Bet your life,' I says, 'and that goes for two judges too.'

Comes the time when they're introducing Colter's pet cowboy to the crowd in the grandstand and telling all about his riding abilities on the worst horses, etc., etc. A few bows in answer to the cheers and that same *hombre* rides to the shutes graceful and prepares to get ready.

The Ragtime horse (the one Tom drawed and didn't get) came out like a real bucker, he wiped up the earth pretty and Colter's top hand was a setting up there as easy as though he was using shock absorbers. None of the hard hitting jumps seemed to faze him and his long lean legs was a reefing that pony from the root of his tail to the tips of his ears and a keeping time with motions that wasn't at all easy to even see.

I felt kind of dubious as I watched the proceedings. If I only had a horse like that, I thought, for as it was I didn't see no chance and things was made worse when I hear one of the riders next to me remark: 'You know, Bill, we got to hand it to that feller, he may be with Colter's outfit and all that, *but he sure can ride.*'

A couple other boys came out on their ponies and they done fine but it was plain to see who was up for first money. I didn't put much heart to the job when I gets near the shutes to straddle that roach-maned scrub I'd drawed, but I figgers to do the best I can, there was no use quitting now and maybe after all that horse might buck pretty good, good enough to get me into second or third money but dammit, I didn't want second or third money. I wanted first or nothing and it was my intention to *ride* for that.

The judges, all excepting Pete, didn't seem interested when it was announced that I was next to come out and I reckoned they'd already figured me out of it as they knowed I'd drawed Slippery Elm.

'Judges,' hollers a voice that sounds mighty familiar, 'watch this cowboy ride, he's after first money.'

The shute gate was about to be opened, but I had to turn and see who's just spoke—and there, a few feet back stood Tom, a glance of him kept me wondering or asking where he'd been, his features was kinda set, and I finds myself listening mighty close as he looks at me and says—sort of low: 'Careful of the first jump, Bill, and ride like you would if old Angel Face was under you.'

I had no time to talk back and that got me to setting pretty close, but I had to grin at the thought of the scrub I was setting on being anything like the good bucker old Angel Face could be, but I was going to play safe anyway and get ready to *ride*. If this horse bucked good, all the better—then, the shute gate flies open.

That horse came out like the combination of a ton of dyna-mite and a lighted match, I lost the grin I'd been packing, I kinda felt the cantle crack as that pony took me up to I don't know where and I was flying instead of riding.

Instinct, or maybe past experience warned me that somehow mighty soon we was going to come down again and natural like I prepares for it. A human can think fast sometimes, and you can tell that I did by the fact that all I've described so far of that pony's movements was done in about the length of time it took you to read a couple of these words. That roach mane horse was sure surprising.

When the horse hit the ground I felt as though Saint Peter and all the guards of the Pearly Gates who I'd been to see just a second before, had put their foot down on me and was trying to push me through the earth to the hot place. The saddle horn was tickling me under the chin and one of my feet touched the ground, the other one was alongside the horse's jaw.

I hear a snorting beller that sounds away off and I gets a hazy glimpse of the roman-nosed lantern-jawed head that was making it—I'd recognized the whole if it was in hell and instead of Slippery Elm, *old Angel Face was under me.*

Right then and there the tune changed, the spirits I'd lost came back along with memories of first money. A full grown war-whoop was heard, Angel Face answers with a beller and all the world was bright once more.

The judges had no chance to direct me to scratch forward and back, I was doing that aplenty and they was busy turning their ponies and just keeping track of me. I'd look over my shoulder at 'em and laugh in their face at the same time place one of my feet between the pony's ears or reach back and put the III (hundred and eleven) spur mark on the back of the cantle of the saddle.

All through the performance old faithful Angel Face kept up a standard of that first jump I tried to describe. He was wicked but true and it was a miracle that his feel always touched the ground instead of his body. There was none of that high rearing show stuff with that old boy, only just plain honest-to-God bucking that only a horse of his kind could put out—one in a thousand of his kind.

I got to loving that horse right then. He was carrying me, kinda rough of course, but straight to my ambitions, and even though my feet was in the motion of scratching and covering a lot of territory on his hide my spurs didn't touch him nor leave a mark on him nowheres, he was my friend in need.

There's cheers from the grandstand, cheers from the cowboys. As far as I can see in my wild ride everybody is up and ahollering, everybody but the Colter crowd. The shot is fired that marks the end of my ride and Tom is right there to pick Angel Face's head up out of the dust, that old pony hated to quit and tries to buck even after he's snubbed.

'He's *some* horse,' Tom says real serious, 'and Bill, you're *some* rider.'

Late that night finds me and Tom leading Slippery Elm and headed for the grounds, we was going to steal back Slippery Elm's double, Angel Face.

'Too bad,' I remark, 'that his mane had to be roached to get him to look like this scrub we're leading. The boss'll have seventeen fits when he sees that.'

Tom didn't seem worried. 'What I'd like to know,' he says, 'is how come I was handed the championship bulldogging. I wasn't even there the last day.'

'I substituted for you, and even went and broke my own record doing it but,' I goes on before Tom can speak, 'if you hadn't brought in Angel Face I'd never got first money. If the Colter outfit hadn't switched horses on us we wouldn't of switched horses on them, so there you are, Tom. Turn about is fair play and that goes all round.'

145

Tale of the Gipsy Horse

DONN BYRNE

> O saddle me my milk white steed,
> Go and fetch me my pony, O!
> That I may ride and seek my bride,
> *Who is gone with the raggle-taggle gipsies, O!*

I THOUGHT first of the old lady's face, in the candlelight of the dinner table at Destiny Bay, as some fine precious coin, a spade guinea perhaps, well and truly minted. How old she was I could not venture to guess, but I knew well that when she was young men's heads must have turned as she passed. Age had boldened the features much, the proud nose and definite chin. Her hair was grey, virtually grey, like a grey wave curling in to crash on the sands of Destiny. And I knew that in another woman that hair would be white as scutched flax. When she spoke, the thought of the spade guinea came to me again, so rich and golden was her voice.

'Lady Clontarf,' said my uncle Valentine, 'this is Kerry, Hector's boy.'

'May I call you Kerry? I am so old a woman and you are so much a boy. Also I knew your father. He was of that great line of soldiers who read their Bibles in their tents, and go into battle with a prayer in their hearts. I always seem to have known,' she said, 'that he would fondle no grey beard.'

'Madame,' I said, 'what should I be but Kerry to my father's friends!'

It seemed to me that I must know her because of her proud high face, and her eyes of a great lady, but the title Clontarf made little impress on my brain. Our Irish titles have become so hawked and shop-worn that the most hallowed names in Ireland may be borne by a porter brewer or former soap boiler. O'Connor Don and MacCarthy More mean so much more to us than the Duke of This or the Marquis of There, now the politics have so muddled chivalry. We may resent the presentation of this title or that to a foreigner, but what can you do? The loyalty of the Northern Irishman to the Crown is a loyalty of head and not of heart. Out of our Northern country came the United Men, if you remember. But for whom should our hearts beat faster? The Stuarts were never fond of us, and the Prince of Orange came over to us, talked a deal about liberty, was with us at a few battles, and went off to grow asparagus in England. It is so long since O'Neill and O'Donnell sailed for Spain!

Who Lady Clontarf was I did not know. My uncle Valentine is so off-hand in his presentations. Were you to come on him closeted with a heavenly visitant he would just say: 'Kerry, the Angel Gabriel.' Though as to what his Angelicness was doing with my uncle Valentine, you would be left to surmise. My uncle Valentine will tell you just as much as he feel you ought to know and no more—a quality that stood my uncle in good stead in the days when he raced and bred horses for racing. I did know one thing: Lady Clontarf was not Irish. There is a feeling of kindness between all us Irish that we recognize without speaking. One felt courtesy, gravity, dignity in her, but not that quality that makes your troubles another Irish person's troubles, if only for the instant. Nor was she English. One felt her spiritual roots went too deep for that. Nor had she that brilliant armour of the Latin. Her speech was the ordinary speech of a gentlewoman, unaccented. Yet that remark about knowing my father would never fondle a grey beard!

Who she was and all about her I knew I would find out later from my dear aunt Jenepher. But about the old drawing-room of Destiny there was a strange air of formality. My uncle Valentine is most courteous, but tonight he was courtly. He was like some Hungarian or Russian noble welcoming an empress. There was an air of deference about my dear aunt Jenepher that informed me that Lady Clontarf was very great indeed. Whom my aunt Jenepher likes is lovable, and whom she respects is clean and great. But the most extraordinary part of the setting was our butler James Carabine. He looked as if royalty were present, and I began to say to myself: 'By damn, but royalty it is! Lady Clontarf is only a racing name. I know that there's a queen or princess in Germany who's held by the Jacobites to be Queen of England. Can it be herself that's in it? It sounds impossible, but sure there's nothing impossible where my uncle Valentine's concerned.'

* * *

At dinner the talk turned on racing, and my uncle Valentine inveighed bitterly against the new innovations on the track; the starting gate, and the new seat introduced by certain American jockeys, the crouch now recognized as orthodox in flat-racing. As to the value of the starting gate my uncle was open to conviction. He recognized how unfairly the apprentice was treated by the crack jockey with the old method of the flag, but he dilated on his favourite theme: that machinery was the curse of man. All these innovations—

'But it isn't an innovation, sir. The Romans used it.'

'You're a liar!' said my uncle Valentine.

My uncle Valentine, or any other Irishman for the matter of that only means that he doesn't believe you. There is a wide difference.

'I think I'm right, sir. The Romans used it for their chariot races. They dropped the barrier instead of raising it.' A tag of my classics came back to me, as tags will. '*Rapagula submitten-tur*, Pausanias writes.'

'Pausanias, begob!' My uncle Valentine was visibly impressed.

But as to the new seat he was adamant. I told him competent

judges had placed it about seven pounds' advantage to the horse.

'There is only one place on a horse's back for a saddle,' said my uncle Valentine. 'The shorter your leathers, Kerry, the less you know about your mount. You are only aware whether or not he is winning. With the ordinary seat, you know whether he is lazy, and can make proper use of your spur. You can stick to his head and help him.'

'Races are won with that seat, sir.'

'Be damned to that!' said my uncle Valentine. 'If the horse is good enough, he'll win with the rider facing his tail.'

'But we are boring you, Madame,' I said, 'with our country talk of horses.'

'There are three things that are never boring to see: a swift swimmer swimming, a young girl dancing, and a young horse running. And three things that are never tiring to speak of: God, and love, and the racing of horses.'

'A *kushto jukel* is also *rinkeno, mi pen*,' suddenly spoke our butler, James Carabine.

'*Dabla*, James Carabine, you *roker* like a *didakai*. A *jukel* to catch *kanangre*!' And Lady Clontarf laughed. 'What in all the *tem* is as *dinkeno* as a *kushti-dikin grai*?'

'A *tatsheno jukel, mi pen*, like Rory Bosville's,' James Carabine evidently stood his ground, 'that *noshered* the Waterloo Cup through *wafro bok*!'

'*Avali*! You are right, James Carabine.' And then she must have seen my astonished face, for she laughed, that small golden laughter that was like the ringing of an acolyte's bell. 'Are you surprised to hear me speak the *tawlo tshib*, the black language, Kerry? I am a gipsy woman.'

'Lady Clontarf, Mister Kerry,' said James Carabine, 'is saying there is nothing in the world like a fine horse. I told her a fine greyhound is a good thing too. Like Rory Bosville's, that should have won the Waterloo Cup in Princess Dagmar's year.'

'Lady Clontarf wants to talk to you about a horse, Kerry,' said my uncle Valentine. 'So if you would like us to go into the gunroom, Jenepher, instead of the withdrawing-room while you play—'

'May I not hear about the horse too?' asked my aunt Jenepher.

'My very, very dear,' said the gipsy lady to my blind Jenepher, 'I would wish you to, for where you are sitting, there a blessing will be.'

* * *

My uncle Valentine had given up race-horses for as long as I can remember. Except with Limerick Pride, he had never had any luck, and so he had quitted racing as an owner, and gone in for harness ponies, of which, it is admitted, he bred and showed the finest of their class. My own two chasers, while winning many good Irish races, were not quite up to Aintree form, but in the last year I happened to buy, for a couple of hundred guineas, a handicap horse that had failed signally as a three-year-old in classic races, and of which a fashionable stable wanted to get rid. It was Ducks and Drakes, by Drake's Drum out of Little Duck, a beautifully shaped, dark grey horse, rather short in the neck, but the English stable was convinced he was a hack. However, as often happens, with a change of trainers and jockeys, Ducks and Drakes became a different horse and won five good races, giving me so much in hand that I was able to purchase for a matter of nine hundred guineas a colt I was optimistic about, a son of Saint Simon's. Both horses were in training with Robinson at the Curragh. And now it occurred to me that the gipsy lady wanted to buy one or the other of them. I decided beforehand that it would be across my dead body.

'Would you be surprised,' asked my uncle Valentine, 'to hear that Lady Clontarf has a horse she expects to win the Derby with?'

'I should be delighted, sir, if she did,' I answered warily. There were a hundred people who had hopes of their nominations in the greatest of races.

'Kerry,' the gipsy lady said quietly, 'I think I will win.' She had a way of clearing the air with her voice, with her eyes. What was a vague hope now became an issue.

'What is the horse, Madam?'

'It is as yet unnamed, and has never run as a two-year-old. It is a son of Irlandais, who has sired many winners on the Continent, and who broke down sixteen years ago in prep-

150

aration for the Derby and was sold to one of the Festetics. Its dam is Iseult III, who won the *Priz de Diane* four years ago.'

'I know little about Continental horses,' I explained.

'The strain is great-hearted, and with the dam, strong as an oak tree. I am a gipsy woman, and I know a horse, and I am an old, studious woman,' she said, and she looked at her beautiful, unringed golden hands, as if she were embarrassed, speaking of something we, not Romanies, could hardly understand, 'and I think I know propitious hours and days.'

'Where is he now, Madame?'

'He is at Dax, in the Basse-Pyrénées, with Romany folk.'

'Here's the whole thing in a nutshell, Kerry: Lady Clontarf wants her colt trained in Ireland. Do you think the old stables of your grandfather are still good?'

'The best in Ireland, sir, but sure there's no horse been trained there for forty years, barring jumpers.'

'Are the gallops good?'

'Sure, you know yourself, sir, how good they are. But you couldn't train without a trainer, and stable boys—'

'We'll come to that,' said my uncle Valentine. 'Tell me, what odds will you get against an unknown, untried horse in the winter books?'

I thought for an instant. It had been an exceptionally good year for two-year-olds, the big English breeders' stakes having been bitterly contested. Lord Shere had a good horse; Mr Paris a dangerous colt. I should say there were fifteen good colts, if they wintered well, two with outstanding chances.

'I should say you could really write your own ticket. The ring will be only too glad to get money. There's so much up on Sir James and Toison d'Or.'

'To win a quarter-million pounds?' asked my uncle Valentine.

'It would have to be done very carefully, sir, here and there, in ponies and fifties and hundreds, but I think between four and five thousand pounds would do it.'

'Now if this horse of Lady Clontarf's wins the Two Thousand and the Derby, and the Saint Leger—'

Something in my face must have shown a lively distaste for the company of lunatics, for James Carabine spoke quietly from the door by which he was standing.

'Will your young Honour be easy, and listen to your uncle and my lady.'

My uncle Valentine is most grandiose, and though he has lived in epic times, a giant among giants, his schemes are too big for practical business days. And I was beginning to think that the gipsy lady, for all her beauty and dignity, was but an old woman crazed by gambling and tarot cards, but James Carabine is so wise, so beautifully sane, facing all events, spiritual and material, foursquare to the wind.

'—what would he command in stud fees?' continued quietly my uncle Valentine.

'If he did this tremendous triple thing, sir, five hundred guineas would not be exorbitant.'

'I am not asking ycu out of idle curiosity, Kerry, or for information,' said my uncle Valentine. 'I merely wish to know if the ordinary brain arrives at these conclusions of mine; if they are, to use a word of Mr Thackeray's, apparent.'

'I quite understand, sir,' I said politely.

'And now,' said my uncle Valentine, 'whom would you suggest to come to Destiny Bay as trainer?'

'None of the big trainers will leave their stables to come here, sir. And the small ones I don't know sufficiently. If Sir Arthur Pollexfen were still training, and not so old—'

'Sir Arthur Pollexfen is not old,' said my uncle Valentine. 'He cannot be more than seventy-two or seventy-three.'

'But at that age you cannot expect a man to turn out at five in the morning and oversee gallops.'

'How little you know Mayo men,' said my uncle Valentine. 'And Sir Arthur with all his triumphs never won a Derby. He will come.'

'Even at that, sir, how are you going to get a crack jockey? Most owners have first or second call on them. And the great free lances, you cannot engage one of those and ensure secrecy.'

'That,' said my uncle Valentine, 'is already arranged. Lady Clontarf has a Gitano, or Spanish gipsy in whom her confidence is boundless. And now,' said my uncle Valentine, 'we come to the really diplomatic part of the proceeding. Trial horses are needed, so that I am commissioned to approach you with delicacy and ask you if you will bring up your two

152

excellent horses Ducks and Drakes and the Saint Simon colt and help train Lady Clontarf's horse. I don't see why you should object.'

To bring up the two darlings of my heart, and put them under the care of a trainer who had won the Gold Cup at Ascot fifty years before, and hadn't run a horse for twelve years, and have them ridden by this Gitano or Spanish gipsy, as my uncle called him; to have them used as trial horses to this colt which might not be good enough for a starter's hack. Ah, no! Not damned likely. I hardened my heart against the pleading gaze of James Carabine.

'Will you or won't you?' roared my uncle diplomatically.

My aunt Jenepher laid down the lace she was making, and reaching across, her fingers caught my sleeve and ran down to my hand, and her hand caught mine.

'Kerry will,' she said.

So that was decided.

*　　*　　*

'Kerry,' said uncle Valentine, 'will you see Lady Clontarf home?'

I was rather surprised. I had thought she was staying with us. And I was a bit bothered, for it is not hospitality to allow the visitor to Destiny to put up at the local pub. But James Carabine whispered: ''Tis on the downs she's staying, Master Kerry, in her own great van with four horses.' It was difficult to believe that the tall graceful lady in the golden and red Spanish shawl, with the quiet speech of our own people, was a roaming gipsy, with the whole world as her home.

'Good night, Jenepher. Good night, Valentine. *Boshto dok*, good luck, James Carabine!'

'*Boshto dok, mi pen*. Good luck, sister.'

We went into the October night of the full moon—the hunter's moon—and away from the great fire of turf and bog-wood in our drawing-room the night was vital with an electric cold. One could sense the film of ice in the bogs, and the drumming of snipe's wings, disturbed by some roving dog, come to our ears. So bright was the moon that each white-washed apple tree stood out clear in the orchard, and as we took the road toward Grey River, we could see a barkentine off shore, with sails of polished silver—some boat from Bilbao probably, making for the Clyde, in the daytime a scrubby ore carrier but tonight a ship out of some old sea story, as of Magellan, or our own Saint Brendan:

'*Feach air muir lionadh gealach buidhe mar ór,*' she quoted in Gaelic; 'See on the filling sea the full moon yellow as gold . . . It is full moon and full tide, Kerry; if you make a wish, it will come true.'

'I wish you success in the Derby, Madam.'

Ahead of us down the road moved a little group to the sound of fiddle and mouth organ. It was the Romany bodyguard ready to protect their chieftainess on her way home.

'You mean that, I know, but you dislike the idea. Why?'

'Madame' I said, 'if you can read my thoughts as easily as that, it's no more impertinent to speak than think. I have heard a lot about a great colt tonight, and of his chance for the greatest race in the world, and that warms my heart. But I have heard more about money, and that chills me.'

'I am so old, Kerry, that the glory of winning the Derby means little to me. Do you know how old I am? I am six years short of an hundred old.'

'Then the less—' I began, and stopped short, and could have chucked myself over the cliff for my unpardonable discourtesy.

'Then the less reason for my wanting money,' the old lady said. 'Is that not so?'

'Exactly, Madam.'

'Kerry,' she said, 'does my name mean anything to you?'

'It has bothered me all evening. Lady Clontarf, I am so sorry my father's son should appear to you so rude and ignorant a lout.'

'Mifanwy, Countess Clontarf and Kincora.'

I gaped like an idiot. 'The line of great Brian Boru. But I thought—'

'Did you really ever think of it, Kerry?'

'Not really, Madame,' I said. 'It's so long ago, so wonderful. It's like that old city they speak of in the country tales, under Ownaglass, the grey river, with its spires and great squares. It seems to me to have vanished like that, in rolling clouds of thunder.'

'The last O'Neill has vanished, and the last Plantagenet. But great Brian's strain remains. When I married my lord,' she said quietly, 'it was in a troubled time. Our ears had not forgotten the musketry of Waterloo, and England was still shaken by fear of the Emperor, and poor Ireland was hurt and wounded. As you know, Kerry, no peer of the older faith sat in College Green. It is no new thing to ennoble, and steal an ancient name. Pitt and Napoleon passed their leisure hours at it. So that of O'Briens, Kerry, sirred and lorded, there are a score, but my lord was Earl of Clontarf and Kincora since before the English came.

'If my lord was of the great blood of Kincora, myself was not lacking in blood. We Romanies are old, Kerry, so old that no man knows our beginning, but that we came from the uplands of India centuries before history. We are a strong, vital race, and we remain with our language, our own customs, our own laws until this day. And to certain families of us, the Romanies all over the world do reverence, as to our own, the old Lovells. There are three Lovells, Kerry, the *dinelo* or foolish Lovells, the *gozvero* or cunning Lovells, and the *puro* Lovells, the old Lovells. I am of the old Lovells. My father was the great Mairik Lovell. So you see I am of great stock too.'

'Dear Madame, one has only to see you to know that.'

'My lord had a small place left him near the Village of Swords, and it was near there I met him. He wished to buy a horse from my father Mairik, a stallion my father had brought all the way from Nejd in Arabia. My lord could not buy the horse. But when I married my lord, it was part of my dowry, that and two handfuls of uncut Russian emeralds, and a chest of gold coins, Russian and Indian and Turkish coins, all gold. So I did not come empty-handed to my lord.'

'Madame, do you wish to tell me this?'

'I wish to tell it to you, Kerry, because I want you for a friend to my little people, the sons of my son's son. You must know everything about friends to understand them.

'My lord was rich only in himself and in his ancestry. But with the great Arab stallion and the emeralds and the gold coins we were well. We did a foolish thing, Kerry; we went to London. My lord wished it, and his wishes were my wishes, although something told me we should not have gone. In

London I made my lord sell the great Arab. He did not wish to, because it came with me, nor did I wish to, because my father had loved it so, but I made him sell it. All the Selim horses of today are descended from him, Sheykh Selim.

'My lord loved horses, Kerry. He knew horses, but he had no luck. Newmarket Heath is a bad spot for those out of luck. And my lord grew worried. When one is worried, Kerry, the heart contracts a little—is it not so? Or don't you want to know yet? Also another thing bothered my lord. He was with English people, and English people have their codes and ordinances. They are good people, Kerry, very honest. They go to churches, and like sad songs, but whether they believe in God, or whether they have hearts or have no hearts, I do not know. Each thing they do by rote and custom, and they are curious in this: they will make excuses for a man who has done a great crime, but no excuses for a man who neglects trivial things. An eccentricity of dress is not forgiven. An eccentric is an outsider. So that English are not good for Irish folk.

'My own people,' she said proudly, 'are simple people, kindly and loyal as your family know. A marriage to them is a deep thing, not the selfish love of one person for another, but involving many factors. A man will say: "Mifanwy Lovell's father saved my honour once. What can I do for Mifanwy Lovell and Mifanwy Lovell's man?" And the Lovells said when we were married: "Brothers, the *gawjo rai*, the foreign gentleman, may not understand the gipsy way, that our sorrows are his sorrows, and our joys his, but we understand that his fights are our fights, and his interests the interests of the Lovell Clan."

'My people were always about my lord, and my lord hated it. In our London house in the morning, there were always gipsies waiting to tell my lord of a great fight coming off quietly on Epsom Downs, which it might interest him to see, or of a good horse to be bought cheaply, or some news of a dog soon to run in a coursing match for a great stake, and of the dog's excellences or his defects. They wanted no money. They only wished to do him a kindness. But my lord was embarrassed, until he began to loathe the sight of a gipsy neckerchief. Also, in the race-courses, in the betting ring where my lord would be, a gipsy would pay hard-earned entrance money to tell my lord quietly of something they had noticed that morning in the gallops, or horses to be avoided in betting, or of neglected horses which would win. All kindnesses to my lord. But my lord was with fashionable English folk, who do not understand one's having a strange friend. Their uplifted eyebrows made my lord ashamed of the poor Romanies. These things are things you might laugh at, with laughter like sunshine, but there would be clouds in your heart.

'The end came at Ascot, Kerry, where the young queen was, and the Belgian king, and the great nobles of the court. Into the paddock came one of the greatest of gipsies, Tyso Herne, who had gone before my marriage with a great draft of Norman trotting horses to Mexico, and came back with a squadron of ponies, suitable for polo. Tyso was a vast man, a *pawni Romany*, a fair gipsy. His hair was red, and his moustache was long and curling, like a Hungarian pandour's. He had a flaunting *diklo* of fine yellow silk about his neck, and the buttons on his coat were gold Indian mohurs, and on his bell-shaped trousers were braids of silver bells, and the spurs on his Wellingtons were fine silver, and his hands were covered with rings, Kerry, with stones in them such as even the young queen did not have. It was not vulgar ostentation. It was just that Tyso felt rich and merry, and no stone on his hand was as fine as his heart.

'When he saw me he let a roar out of him that was like the roar of the ring when the horses are coming in to the stretch.

' "Before God," he shouted, "it's Mifanwy Lovell." And, though I am not a small woman, Kerry, he tossed me in the air, and caught me in the air. And he laughed and kissed me, and I laughed and kissed him, so happy was I to see great Tyso once more, safe from over the sea.

' "Go get your *rom*, *mi tshai*, your husband, my lass, and we'll go to the *kitshima* and have a Jeroboam of Champagne wine."

'But I saw my lord walk off with thunder in his face, and all the English folk staring and some women laughing. So I said: "I will go with you alone, Tyso." For Tyso Herne had been my father's best friend and my mother's cousin, and had held me as a baby, and no matter how he looked, or who laughed, he was well come for me.

'Of what my lord said, and of what I said in rebuttal, we will not speak. One says foolish things in anger, but, foolish or not, they leave scars. For out of the mouth comes things forgotten, things one thinks dead. But before the end of the meeting, I went to Tyso Herne's van. He was braiding a whip with fingers light as a woman's, and when he saw me he spoke quietly.

' "Is all well with thee, Mifanwy?"

' "Nothing is well with me, father's friend."

'And so I went back to my people, and I never saw my lord any more.'

We had gone along until in the distance I could see the gipsy fire, and turning the headland we saw the light on Farewell Point. A white flash; a second's rest: a red flash; three second occultation; then white and red again. There is something heartening and brave in Farewell Light. Ireland keeps watch over her share of the Atlantic sea.

'When I left my lord, I was with child, and when I was delivered of him, and the child weaned and strong, I sent him to my lord, for every man wants his man child, and every family its heir. But when he was four and twenty he came back to me, for the roving gipsy blood and the fighting Irish blood were too much for him. He was never Earl of Clontarf. He died while my lord still lived. He married a Herne, a grandchild of Tyso, a brave golden girl. And he got killed charging in the Balkan Wars.

'Niall's wife—my son's name was Niall—understood, and when young Niall was old enough, we sent him to my lord. My lord was old at this time, older than his years, and very poor. But of my share of money he would have nothing. My lord died when Niall's Niall was at school, so the little lad became Earl of Clontarf and Kincora. I saw to it he had sufficient money, but he married no rich woman. He married a poor Irish girl, and by her had two children, Niall and Alick. He was interested in horses, and rode well, my English friends tell me. But mounted on a brute in the Punchestown races, he made a mistake at the stone wall. He did not know the horse very well. So he let it have its head at the stone wall. It threw its head up, took the jump by the roots, and so Niall's Niall was killed. His wife, the little Irish girl, turned her face away from life and died.

'The boys are fifteen and thirteen now, and soon they will go into the world. I want them to have a fair chance, and it is for this reason I wish them to have money. I have been rich and then poor, and then very rich and again poor, and rich again and now poor. But if this venture succeeds, the boys will be all right.'

'Ye-s,' I said.

'You don't seem very enthusiastic, Kerry.'

'We have a saying,' I told her, 'that money won from a book-maker is only lent.'

'If you were down on a race-meeting and on the last race of the last day you won a little what would you say?'

'I'd say I only got a little of my own back.'

'Then we only get a little of our own back over the losses of a thousand years.'

We had come to the encampment. Around the great fire were tall swarthy men with coloured neckchiefs, who seemed more reserved, cleaner than the English gipsy. They rose quietly as the gipsy lady came. The great spotted Dalmatian dogs rose too. In the half light the picketed horses could be seen, quiet as trees.

'This is the Younger of Destiny Bay,' said the old lady, 'who is kind enough to be our friend.'

'*Sa shan, rai!*' they spoke with quiet courtesy. 'How are you, sir?'

Lady Clontarf's maid hurried forward with a wrap, scolding and speaking English with beautiful courtesy. 'You are dreadful, sister. You go walking the roads at night like a courting girl in spring. Gentlemen, you are wrong to keep the *rawnee* out, and she an old woman and not well.'

'Supplistia,' Lady Clontarf chided, 'you have no more manners than a growling dog.'

'I am the *rawnee's* watch-dog,' the girl answered.

'Madame, your maid is right, I will go now.'

'Kerry,' she stopped me, 'will you be friends with my little people?'

'I will be their true friend,' I promised, and I kissed her hand.

'God bless you!' she said. And I left the camp for my people's house. The hunter's moon was dropping toward the edge of the world, and the light on Farewell Point flashed seaward its white and red, and as I walked along, I noticed that a wind from Ireland had sprung up, and the Bilbao boat was bowling along nor'east on the starboard tack. It seemed to me an augury.

* * *

In those days, before my aunt Jenepher's marriage to Patrick Herne, the work of Destiny Bay was divided in this manner: my dear aunt Jenepher was, as was right, supreme in the house. My uncle Valentine planned and superintended the breeding of the harness ponies, and sheep, and black Dexter cattle which made Destiny Bay so feared at the Dublin Horse Show and at the Bath and West. My own work was the farms. To me fell the task of preparing the stables and training grounds for Lady Clontarf's and my own horses. It was a relief and an adventure to give up thinking of turnips, wheat, barley, and seeds, and to examine the downs for training ground. In my great-grandfather's time, in pre-Union days, many a winner at the Curragh had been bred and trained at Destiny Bay. The soil of the downs is chalky, and the matted roots of the woven herbage have a certain give in them in the driest weather. I found out my great-grandfather's mile and a half, and two miles and a half with a turn and shorter gallops of various gradients. My grandfather had used them as a young man, but mainly for hunters, horses which he sold for the great Spanish and Austrian regiments. But to my delight the stables were as good as ever. Covered with reed thatch, they required few repairs. The floors were of chalk, and the boxes beautifully ventilated. There were also great tanks for rain-water, which is of all water the best for horses in training. There were also a few stalls for restless horses. I was worried a little about lighting, but my uncle Valentine told me that Sir Arthur Pollexfen allowed no artificial lights when he trained. Horses went to bed with the fowls and got up at cock-crow.

My own horses I got from Robinson without hurting his feelings. 'It's this way, Robinson,' I told him. 'We're trying to do a crazy thing at Destiny, and I'm not bringing them to another trainer. I'm bringing another trainer there. I can tell you no more.'

'Not another word, Mr Kerry. Bring them back when you

want to. I'm sorry to say good-bye to the wee colt. But I wish you luck.'

We bought three more horses, and a horse for Ann-Dolly. So that with the six we had a rattling good little stable. When I saw Sir Arthur Pollexfen, my heart sank a little, for he seemed so much out of a former century. Small, ruddy-cheeked, with the white hair of a bishop, and a bishop's courtesy, I never thought he could run a stable. I thought, perhaps, he had grown too old and had been thinking for a long time now of the Place whither he was going, and that we had brought him back from his thoughts and he had left his vitality behind. His own servant came with him to Destiny Bay, and though we wished to have him in the house with us, yet he preferred to stay in a cottage by the stables. I don't know what there was about his clothes, but they were all of an antique though a beautiful cut. He never wore riding breeches but trousers of a bluish cloth and strapped beneath his varnished boots. A flowered waistcoat with a satin stock, a short covert coat, a grey bowler hat and gloves. Always there was a freshly cut flower in his buttonhole, which his servant got every evening from the green-houses at Destiny Bay, and kept overnight in a glass of water into which the least drop of whisky had been poured. I mention this as extraordinary, as most racing men will not wear flowers. They believe flowers bring bad luck, though how the superstition arose I cannot tell. His evening trousers also buckled under his shoes, or rather half Wellingtons, such as army men wear, and though there was never a crease in them there was never a wrinkle. He would never drink port after dinner when the ladies had left, but a little whisky punch which James Carabine would compose for him. Compared to the hard shrewd-eyed trainers I knew, this bland, soft-spoken old gentleman filled me with misgiving.

I got a different idea of the old man the first morning I went out to the gallops. The sun had hardly risen when the old gentleman appeared, as beautifully turned out as though he were entering the Show Ring at Ballsbridge. His servant held his horse, a big grey, while he swung into the saddle as light as a boy. His hack was feeling good that morning, and he and I went off toward the training ground at a swinging canter, the old gentleman half standing in his stirrups, with a light firm grip of his knees, riding as Cossacks do, his red terrier galloping behind him. When we settled down to walk he told me the pedigree of his horse, descended through Matchem and Whalebone from Oliver Cromwell's great charger The White Turk, or Place's White Turk, as it was called from the Lord Protector's stud manager. To hear him follow the intricacies of breeding was a revelation. Then I understood what a great horseman he was. On the training ground he was like a marshal commanding an army, such respect did everyone accord him. The lads perched on the horses' withers, his head man, the grooms, all watched the apple-ruddy face, while he said little or nothing. He must have had eyes in the back of his head, though. For when a colt we had brought from Mr Gubbins, a son of Galtee More's, started lashing out and the lad up seemed like taking a toss, the old man's voice came low and sharp: 'Don't fall off, boy.' And the boy did not fall off. The red terrier watched the trials with a keen eye, and I believe honestly that he knew as much about horses as any one of us and certainly more than any of us about his owner. When my lovely Ducks and Drakes went out at the lad's call to beat the field by two lengths over five furlongs, the dog looked up at Sir Arthur and Sir Arthur looked back at the dog, and what they thought toward each other, God knoweth.

I expected when we rode away that the old gentleman would have some words to say about my horses, but coming home his remarks were of the country. 'Your Derry is a beautiful country, young Mister Kerry,' he said, 'though it would be treason to say that in my own country of Mayo.' Of my horses not a syllable.

He could be the most silent man I have ever known though giving the illusion of keeping up a conversation. You could talk to him, and he would smile, and nod at the proper times, as though he were devouring every word you said. In the end you thought you had a very interesting conversation. But as to whether he had even heard you, you were never sure. On the other hand when he wished to speak, he spoke to the point and beautifully. Our bishop, on one of his pastoral visitations, if that be the term, stayed at Destiny Bay, and because my uncle Cosimo is a bishop too, and because he felt he ought to do something for our souls he remonstrated with us for starting our stable. My uncle Valentine was livid, but said nothing, for no guest must be contradicted in Destiny Bay.

'For surely, Sir Valentine, no man of breeding can mingle with the rogues, cut-purses and their womenfolk who infest race-courses, drunkards, bawds and common gamblers, without lowering himself to some extent to their level,' his Lordship purred. 'Yourself, one of the wardens of Irish chivalry, must give an example to the common people.'

'Your Lordship,' broke in old Sir Arthur Pollexfen, 'is egregiously misinformed. In all periods of the world's history, eminent personages have concerned themselves with the racing of horses. We read of Philip of Macedon, that while campaigning in Asia Minor, a courier brought him news of two events, of the birth of his son Alexander and of the winning, by his favourite horse, of the chief race at Athens, and we may reasonably infer that his joy over the winning of the race was equal to if not greater than that over the birth of Alexander. In the life of Charles the Second, the traits which do most credit to that careless monarch are his notable and gentlemanly death and his affection for his great race-horse Old Rowley. Your Lordship is, I am sure,' said Sir Arthur, more blandly than any ecclesiastic could, 'too sound a Greek scholar not to remember the epigrams of Maecius and Philodemus, which show what interest these antique poets took in the racing of horses. And coming to present times, your Lordship must have heard that his Majesty (whom God preserve!) has won two Derbies, once with the leased horse Minoru, and again with his own great Persimmon. The premier peer of Scotland, the Duke of Hamilton, Duke of Chastellerault in France, Duke of Brandon in England, hereditary prince of Braden, is prouder of his fine mare Eau de Vie than of all his titles. As to the Irish families, the Persses of Galway, the Dawsons of Dublin, and my own, the Pollexfens of Mayo, have always been so interested in the breeding and racing of horses. And none of these—my punch, if you please, James Carabine!—are, as your Lordship puts it, drunkards, bawds, and common gamblers. I fear your Lordship has been reading—'and he cocked his eye, bright as a wren's, at the bishop, 'religious publications of the sensational and morbid type.'

It was all I could do to keep from leaping on the table and giving three loud cheers for the County of Mayo.

*   *   *

Now, on those occasions, none too rare, when my uncle Valentine and I differed on questions of agricultural economy, or of national polity, or of mere faith and morals, he poured torrents of invective over my head, which mattered little. But when he was really aroused to bitterness he called me 'modern'. And by modern my uncle Valentine meant the quality inherent in brown button boots, in white waistcoats worn with dinner jackets, in nasty little motor-cars—in fine, those things before which the angels of God recoil in horror. While I am not modern in that sense, I am modern in this, that I like to see folk getting on with things. Of Lady Clontarf and of Irlandais colt, I heard no more. On the morning after seeing her home I called over to the caravan but it was no longer there. There was hardly a trace of it. I found a broken fern and a slip of oak-tree, the gipsy pattern. But what it betokened or whither it pointed I could not tell. I had gone to no end of trouble in getting the stables and training ground ready, and Sir Arthur Pollexfen had been brought out of his retirement in the County of Mayo. But still no word of the horse. I could see my uncle Valentine and Sir Arthur taking their disappointment bravely, if it never arrived, and murmuring some courteous platitude, out of the reign of good Queen Victoria, that it was a lady's privilege to change her mind. That might console them in their philosophy, but it would only make me hot with rage. For to me there is no sex in people of standards. They do not let one another down.

Then one evening the horse arrived.

It arrived at sundown in a large van drawn by four horses, a van belonging evidently to some circus. It was yellow and covered with paintings of nymphs being wooed by swains, in clothes hardly fitted to agricultural pursuits: of lions of terrifying aspect being put through their paces by a trainer of an aspect still more terrifying: of an Indian gentleman with a vast turban and a small loin-cloth playing a penny whistle to a snake that would have put the heart crosswise in Saint Patrick himself; of a most adipose lady in tights swinging from a ring while the husband and seven sons hung on to her like bees in a swarm. Floridly painted over the van was 'Arsène Bombaudiac, Prop., Bayonne.' The whole added no dignity to Destiny Bay, and if some sorceress had disclosed to Mr Bombaudiac of Bayonne that he was about to lose a van by fire at low tide on the beach of Destiny in Ireland within forty-eight hours— The driver was a burly gipsy, while two of the most utter scoundrels I have ever laid eyes on sat beside him on the wide seat.

'Do you speak English?' I asked the driver.

'Yes, sir,' he answered, 'I am Petulengro.'

'Which of these beauties beside you is the jockey?'

'Neither, sir. These two are just gipsy fighting men. The jockey is inside with the horse.'

My uncle Valentine came down stroking his great red beard. He seemed fascinated by the pictures on the van. 'What your poor aunt Jenepher, Kerry,' he said, 'misses by being blind!'

'What is she spared, sir! Boy,' I called one of the servants, 'go get Sir Arthur Pollexfen. Where do you come from?' I asked the driver.

'From Dax, sir, in the South of France.'

'You're a liar,' I said. 'Your horses are half-bred Clydesdale. There's no team like that in the South of France.'

'We came to Dieppe with an *attelage basque*, six yoked oxen. But I was told they would not be allowed in England, so I telegraphed our chief, Piramus Petulengro, to have a team at Newhaven. So I am not a liar, sir.'

'I am sorry.'

'Sir, that is all right.'

Sir Arthur Pollexfen came down from where he had been speaking to my aunt Jenepher. I could see he was tremendously excited, because he walked more slowly than was usual, spoke with more deliberation. He winced a little as he saw the van. But he was of the old heroic school. He said nothing.

'I think, Sir Valentine,' he said, 'we might have the horse out.'

'Aye, we might as well know the worst,' said my uncle Valentine.

A man jumped from the box, and swung the crossbar up. The door opened and into the road stepped a small man in dark clothes. Never on this green earth of God's have I seen such dignity. He was dressed in dark clothes with a wide dark hat, and his face was brown as soil. White starched cuffs covered half of his hands. He took off his hat and bowed first to my uncle Valentine, then to Sir Arthur, and to myself last. His hair was plastered down on his forehead, and the impression you got was of an ugly rugged face, with piercing black eyes. He seemed to say: 'Laugh, if you dare!' But laughter was the furthest thing from us, such tremendous masculinity did the small man have. He looked at us searchingly, and I had the feeling that if he didn't like us, for two pins he would have the bar across the van door again and be off with the horse. Then he turned and spoke gutturally to someone inside.

A boy as rugged as himself, in a Basque cap and with a Basque sash, led first a small donkey, round as a barrel, out of the outrageous van. One of the gipsies took it, and the next moment the boy led out the Irlandais colt.

He came out confidently, quietly, approaching gentlemen as a gentleman, a beautiful brown horse, small, standing perfectly. I had just one glance at the sound strong legs and the firm ribs, before his head caught my eye. The graceful neck, the beautiful small muzzle, the gallant eyes. In every inch of him you could see breeding. While Sir Arthur was examining his hocks, and my uncle Valentine was standing weightily considering strength of lungs and heart, my own heart went out to the lovely eyes that seemed to ask: 'Are these folk friends?'

Now I think you could parade the Queen of Sheba in a show ring before me without extracting more than an off-hand compliment out of me, but there is something about a gallant thoroughbred that makes me sing. I can understand the trainer who, pointing to Manifesto, said that if ever he found a woman with a shape like that, he'd marry her. So out of my heart through my lips came the cry: *'Och, asthore!'* which is, in our Gaelic, 'Oh, my dear!'

The Spanish jockey, whose brown face was rugged and impassive as a Pyrenee, looked at me, and broke into a wide, understanding smile.

'*Si, si, Señor,*' he uttered, '*si, si!*'

* * *

Never did a winter pass so merrily, so advantageously at Destiny Bay. Usually there is fun enough with the hunting, but with a racing stable in winter there is always anxiety. Is there a suspicion of a cough in the stables? Is the ground too hard for gallops? Will snow come and hold the gallops up for a week? Fortunately we are right on the edge of the great Atlantic drift, and you can catch at times the mild amazing atmosphere of the Caribbean. While Scotland sleeps beneath its coverlet of snow, and England shivers in its ghastly fog, we on the north-east seaboard of Ireland go through a winter that is short as a mid-summer night in Lofoden. The trees have hardly put off their gold and brown until we perceive their cheeping green. And one soft day we say: 'Soon on that bank will be the fairy gold of the primrose.' And behold, while you are looking the primrose is there!

Each morning at sun-up, the first string of horses were out. Quietly as a general officer reviewing a parade old Sir Arthur sat on his grey horse, his red dog beside him, while Geraghty, his head man, galloped about with his instructions. Hares bolted from their forms in the grass. The sun rolled away the mists from the blue mountains of Donegal. At the starting gate, which Sir Arthur had set up, the red-faced Irish boys steered their mounts from a walk towards the tapes. A pull at the lever and they were off. The old man seemed to notice everything. 'Go easy, boy, don't force that horse!' His low voice would carry across the downs. 'Don't lag there, Murphy, ride him!' And when the gallop was done, he would trot across to the horses, his red dog trotting beside him, asking how Sarsfield went. Did Ducks and Drakes seem interested? Did Rustum go up to his bit? Then they were off at a slow walk towards their sand bath, where they rolled like dogs. Then the sponging and the rubbing, and the fresh hay in the mangers kept as clean as a hospital. At eleven the second string came out. At half-past three the lads were called to their horses, and a quarter of an hour's light walking was given to them. At four, Sir Arthur made his 'stables', questioning the lads in each detail as to how the horses had fed, running his hand over their legs to feel for any heat in the joints that might betoken trouble.

Small as our stable was, I doubt if there was one in Great Britain and Ireland to compare with it in each fitting and necessity for training a race-horse. Sir Arthur pinned his faith to old black tartar oats, of about forty-two pounds to the bushel, bran mashes with a little linseed, and sweet old meadow hay.

The Irlandais colt went beautifully. The Spanish jockey's small brother, Joselito, usually rode it, while the jockey's self, whose name we were told was Frasco, Frasco Moreno—usually called, he told us, Don Frasco—looked on. He constituted himself a sort of sub-trainer for the colt, allowing none else to attend to its feeding. The small donkey was its invariable stable companion, and had to be led out to exercise with it. The donkey belonged to Joselito. Don Frasco rode many trials on the other horses. He might appear small standing, but on horseback he seemed a large man, so straight did he sit in the saddle. The little boys rode with a fairly short stirrup, but the *gitano* scorned anything but the traditional seat. He never seemed to move on a horse. Yet he could do what he liked with it.

The Irlandais colt was at last named Romany Baw, or 'gipsy friend' in English, as James Carabine explained to us, and Lady Clontarf's colours registered, quartered red and gold. When the winter lists came out, we saw the horse quoted at a hundred to one, and later at the call over of the Victoria Club, saw the price offered but not taken. My uncle Valentine made a journey to Dublin, to arrange for Lady Clontarf's commission being placed, putting it in the hands of a Derry man who had become big in the affairs of Tattersall's. What he himself and Sir Arthur Pollexfen and the jockey had on I do not know, but he arranged to place an hundred pounds of mine, and fifty of Ann-Dolly's. As the months went by, the odds crept down gradually to thirty-three to one, stood there for a while and went out to fifty. Meanwhile Sir James became a sensational favourite at fives, and Toison d'Or varied between tens and one hundred to eight. Some news of a great trial of Lord Shire's horse had leaked out which accounted for the ridiculously short price. But no word did or could get out about Lady

Clontarf's colt. The two gipsy fighters from Dax patrolled
Destiny Bay, and God help any poor tipster or wretched newspaper tout who tried to plumb the mysteries of training. I
honestly believe a bar of iron and a bog hole would have been
his end.

The most fascinating figure in this crazy world was the gipsy
jockey. To see him talk to Sir Arthur Pollexfen was a phenom-
enon. Sir Arthur would speak in English and the gipsy answer
in Spanish, neither knowing a word of the other's language,
yet each perfectly understanding the other. I must say that this
only referred to how a horse ran, or how Romany Baw was
feeding and feeling. As to more complicated problems, Ann-
Dolly was called in, to translate his Spanish.

'Ask him,' said Sir Arthur, 'has he ever ridden in France?'

'*Oiga, Frasco,*' and Ann-Dolly would burst into a torrent of
gutturals.

'*Si, si, Doña Anna.*'

'Ask him has he got his clearance from the Jockey Club of
France?'

'*Seguro, Don Arturo!*' And out of his capacious pocket he
extracted the French Jockey Club's 'character'. They made a
picture I will never forget, the old horseman ageing so gently,

the vivid boyish beauty of Ann-Dolly, and the overpowering dignity and manliness of the jockey. Always, except when he was riding or working at his anvil—for he was a smith too—he wore the dark clothes, which evidently some village tailor of the Pyrenees made for him—the very short coat, the trousers tubed like cigarettes, his stiff shirt with the vast cuffs. He never wore a collar, nor a neckerchief. Always his back was flat as the side of a house.

When he worked at the anvil, with his young ruffian of a brother at the bellows, he sang. He had shakes and grace notes enough to make a thrush quit. Ann-Dolly translated one of his songs for us.

> *No tengo padre ni madre . . .*
> *Que desgraciado soy yo*
> *Soy como el arbol solo*
> *Que echas frutas y no echa flo . . .*

'He sings he has no father or mother. How out of luck he is! He is like a lonely tree, which bears the fruit and not the flower.'

'God bless my soul, Kerry,' my uncle was shocked. 'The little man is homesick.'

'No, no!' Ann-Dolly protested. 'He is very happy. That is why he sings a sad song.'

One of the reasons of the little man's happiness was the discovery of our national game of handball. He strolled over to the Irish Village and discovered the court back of the Inniskillen Dragoon, that most notable of rural pubs. He was tremendously excited, and getting some gipsy to translate for him, challenged the local champion for the stake of a barrel of porter. He made the local champion look like a cart-horse in the Grand National. When it was told to me I couldn't believe it. Ann-Dolly explained to me that the great game of the Basque country was *pelota*.

'But don't they place *pelota* with a basket?'

'Real *pelota* is *à mains nues*, "with the hands naked".'

'You mean Irish handball,' I told her.

I regret that the population of Destiny made rather a good thing out of Don Frasco's prowess on the court, going from village to village, and betting on a certain wine. The end was a match between Mick Tierney, the Portrush Jarvey and the jockey. The match was billed for the champion of Ulster, and Don Frasco was put down on the card, to explain his lack of English, as Danny Frask, the Glenties Miracle, the Glenties being a district of Donegal where Erse is the native speech. The match was poor, the Portrush Jarvey, after the first game, standing and watching the bill hiss past him with his eyes on his cheek bones. All Donegal seemed to have turned out for the fray. When the contest was over, a big Glenties man pushed his way towards the jockey.

'Dublin and London and New York are prime cities,' he chanted, 'but Glenties is truly magnificent. *Kir do lauv anshin, a railt na hooee*, "Put your hand there, Star of the North".'

'*No entiendo, señor*,' said Don Frasco. And with that the fight began.

James Carabine was quick enough to get the jockey out of the court before he was lynched. But Destiny Bay men, gipsies, fishers, citizens of Derry, bookmakers and their clerks and the fighting tribes of Donegal went to it with a vengeance. Indeed, according to the experts, nothing like it, for spirit or results, had been since or before the Prentice Boys had chased King James (to whom God give his deserts!) from Derry Walls. The removal of the stunned and wounded from the court drew the attention of the police, for the fight was continued in grim silence. But on the entrance of half a dozen peelers commanded by a huge sergeant, Joselito, the jockey's young brother, covered himself with glory. Leaping on the reserved seats, he brought his right hand over hard and true to the sergeant's jaw, and the sergeant was out for half an hour. Joselito was arrested, but the case was laughed out of court. The idea of a minuscule jockey who could ride at ninety pounds knocking out six foot three of Royal Irish Constabulary was too much. Nothing was found on him but his bare hands, a packet of cigarettes and thirty sovereigns he had won over the match. But I knew better. I decided to prove him with hard questions.

'Ask him in Romany, James Carabine, what he had wrapped around that horseshoe he threw away.'

'He says: "Tow, Mister Kerry".'

'Give me my riding crop,' I said; 'I'll take him behind the

stables.' And the training camp lost its best light-weight jockey for ten days, the saddle suddenly becoming repulsive to him. I believe he slept on his face.

But the one who was really wild about the affair was Ann-Dolly. She came across from Spanish Men's Rest flaming with anger.

'Because a Spanish wins, there is fighting, there is anger. If an Irish wins, there is joy, there is drinking. Oh, shame of sportsmanship!'

'Oh, shut your gab, Ann-Dolly,' I told her. 'They didn't know he was a Spanish, as you call it.'

'What did they think he was if not a Spanish? Tell me. I demand it of you.'

'They thought he was Welsh.'

'Oh, in that case . . .' said Ann-Dolly, completely mollified. *Ipsa hibernis hiberniora!*

* * *

I wouldn't have you think that all was beer and skittles, as the English say, in training Romany Baw for the Derby. As spring came closer, the face of the old trainer showed signs of strain. The Lincoln Handicap was run and the Grand National passed, and suddenly flat-racing was on us. And now not the Kohinoor was watched more carefully than the Derby horse. We had a spanking trial on a course as nearly approaching the Two Thousand Guineas route as Destiny Downs would allow, and when Romany Baw flew past us, beating Ducks and Drakes who had picked him up at the mile for the uphill dash, and Sir Arthur clicked his watch, I saw his tense face relax.

'He ran well,' said the old man.

'He'll walk in,' said my uncle Valentine.

My uncle Valentine and Jenico and Ann-Dolly were going across to Newmarket Heath for the big race, but the spring of the year is the time that the farmer must stay by his land, and nurse it like a child. All farewells, even for a week, are sad, and I was loath to see the horses go into the races. Romany Baw had a regular summer bloom on him and his companion, the donkey, was corpulent as an alderman. Ducks and Drakes looked rough and backward, but that didn't matter.

'You've got the best-looking horse in the United Kingdom,' I told Sir Arthur.

'Thank you, Kerry.' The old man was pleased. 'And as to Ducks and Drakes, looks aren't everything.'

'Sure, I know that,' I told him.

'I wouldn't be rash,' he told me, 'but I'd have a little on both. That is, if they go to the post fit and well.'

I put in the days as well as I could, getting ready for the Spring Show at Dublin. But my heart and my thoughts were with my people and the horses at Newmarket. I could see my uncle Valentine's deep bow with his hat in his hand as they passed the Roman ditch at Newmarket, giving that squat wall the reverence that racing men have accorded it since races were run there, though why, none know. A letter from Ann-Dolly apprised me that the horses had made a good crossing and that Romany Baw was well—'and you mustn't think, my dear, that your colt is not as much and more to us than the Derby horse, no, Kerry, not for one moment. Lady Clontarf is here, in her caravan, and oh, Kerry, she looks ill. Only her burning spirit keeps her frail body alive. Jenico and I are going down to Eastbourne to see the little Earl and his brother . . . You will get this letter, cousin, on the morning of the race . . .'

At noon that day I could stand it no longer so I had James Carabine put the trotter in the dogcart. 'There are some things I want in Derry,' I told myself, 'and I may as well get them today as tomorrow.' And we went spinning towards Derry Walls. Ducks and Drakes' race was the two-thirty. And after lunch I looked at reapers I might be wanting in July until the time of the race. I went along to the club, and had hardly entered it when I saw the boy putting up the telegrams on the notice board.

1, Ducks and Drakes, a hundred to eight; 2, Geneva, four to six; 3, Ally Sloper, three to one. 'That's that!' I said. Another telegram gave the betting for the Two Thousand: Threes, Sir James; seven to two, Toison d'Or; eights, Ca'Canny, Greek Singer, Germanicus; tens, six or seven horses; twenty to one any other. No word in the betting of the gipsy horse, and I wondered had anything happened. Surely a horse looking as well as he did must have attracted backers' attention. And as I was worrying the result came in, Romany Baw, first; Sir James, second; Toison d'Or, third.

'Kerry,' somebody called.

'I haven't a minute,' I shouted. Neither I had, for James Carabine was outside, waiting to hear the result. When I told him he said: 'There's a lot due to you, Mister Kerry, in laying out those gallops. 'Be damned to that!' I said, but I was pleased all the same.

I was on tenterhooks until I got the papers describing the race. Ducks and Drakes' win was dismissed summarily, as that of an Irish outsider, and the jockey, Flory Cantillon (Frasco could not manage the weight), was credited with a clever win of two lengths. But the account of Romany Baw's race filled me with indignation. According to it, the winner got away well, but the favourites were hampered at the start and either could have beaten the Irish trained horse, only that they just didn't. The race was won by half a length, a head separating second and third, and most of the account was given to how the favourites chased the lucky outsider, and in a few more strides would have caught him. There were a few dirty backhanders given at Romany's jockey, who, they said, would be more at home in a circus than on a modern race track. He sat like a rider of a century back, they described it, more like an exponent of the old manége than a modern jockey, and even while the others were thundering at his horse's hind-quarters he never moved his seat or used his whip. The experts' judgement of the race was that the Irish colt was forward in a backward field, and that Romany would be lost on Epsom Downs, especially with its 'postillion rider'.

But the newspaper criticisms of the jockey and his mount did not seem to bother my uncle Valentine or the trainer or the jockey's self. They came back elated; even the round white donkey had a humorous happy look in his full Latin eye.

'Did he go well?' I asked.

'He trotted it,' said my uncle Valentine.

'But the accounts read, sir,' I protested, 'that the favourites would have caught him in another couple of strides.'

'Of course they would,' said my uncle Valentine, 'at the pace he was going,' he added.

'I see,' said I.

'You see nothing,' said my uncle Valentine. 'But if you had seen the race you might talk. The horse is a picture. It goes so sweetly that you wouldn't think it was going at all. And as for the gipsy jockey—'

'The papers say he's antiquated.'

'He's seven pounds better than Flory Cantillon,' said my uncle Valentine.

I whistled. Cantillon is our best Irish jockey, and his retaining fees are enormous, and justified. 'They said he was nearly caught napping—'

'Napping be damned!' exploded my uncle Valentine. 'This Spanish gipsy is the finest judge of pace I ever saw. He knew he had the race won, and he never bothered.'

'If the horse is as good as that, and you have as high an opinion of the rider, well, sir, I won a hatful over the Newmarket meeting, and as the price hasn't gone below twenties for the Derby, I'm going after the Ring. There's many a bookmaker will wish he'd stuck to his father's old-clothes business.'

'I wouldn't, Kerry,' said my uncle Valentine. 'I'm not sure I wouldn't hedge a bit of what I have on, if I were you.'

I was still with amazement.

'I saw Mifanwy Clontarf,' said my uncle Valentine, 'and only God and herself and myself and now you, know how ill that woman is.'

'But ill or not ill, she won't scratch the horse.'

'She won't,' said my uncle Valentine, and his emphasis on 'she' chilled me to the hear. 'You're forgetting, Kerry,' he said very quietly, 'the Derby Rule.'

* * *

Of the Derby itself on Epsom Downs, everybody knows. It is supposed to be the greatest test of a three-year-old in the world, though old William Day used to hold it was easy. The course may have been easy for Lord George Bentinck's famous and unbeaten mare Crucifix, when she won the Oaks in 1840, but most winners over the full course justify their victory in other races. The course starts up a heartbreaking hill, and swinging around the top, comes down again towards

Tattenham Corner. If a horse waits to steady itself coming down it is beaten. The famous Fred Archer (whose tortured soul God rest!) used to take Tattenham Corner with one leg over the rails. The straight is uphill. A mile and a half of the trickiest, most heartbreaking ground in the world. Such is Epsom. Its turf has been consecrated by the hoofs of great horses since James I established there a race for the Silver Bell: by Cromwell's great Coffin Mare; by the Arabs, Godolphin and Darby; by the great bay, Malton; by the prodigious Eclipse; by Diomed, son of Florizel, who went to America . . .

Over the Derby what sums are wagered no man knows. On it is won the Calcutta Sweepstake, a prize of which makes a man rich for life, and the Stock Exchange sweep, and other sweeps innumerable. Someone has ventured the belief that on it annually are five million of pounds sterling, and whether he is millions short, or millions over none knows. Because betting is illegal.

There are curious customs in regard to it, as this: that when the result is sent over the ticker to clubs, in case of a dead heat, the word 'dead heat' must come first, because within recent years a trusted lawyer, wagering trust funds on a certain horse, was waiting by the tape to read the result, and seeing another horse's name come up, went away and forthwith blew his brains out. Had he been less volatile he would have seen his own fancy's name follow that, with 'dead heat' after it and been to this day rich and respected. So now, for the protection of such, 'dead heat' comes first. A dead heat in the Derby is are rare a thing as there is in the world, but you can't be too cautious. But the quaintest rule of the Derby is this: that if the nominator of a horse for the Derby Stakes dies, his horse is automatically scratched. There is a legend to the effect that an heir-at-law purposed to kill the owner of an entry, and to run a prime favourite crookedly, and that on hearing this the Stewards of the Jockey Club made the rule. Perhaps it has a more prosaic reason. The Jockey Club may have considered that when a man died, in the trouble of fixing his estates, forfeits would not be paid, and that it was best for all concerned to have the entry scratched. How it came about does not matter, it exists. Whether it is good in law is not certain. Racing folk will quarrel with His Majesty's Lord Justices of Appeal, with the Privy Council, but they will not quarrel with the Jockey Club. Whether it is good in fact is indisputable, for certain owners can tell stories of narrow escapes from racing gangs, in those old days before the Turf was cleaner than the Church, when attempts were made to nobble favourites, when jockeys had not the wings of angels under their silken jackets, when harsh words were spoken about trainers—very, very long ago. There it is, good or bad, the Derby Rule!

*   *   *

As to our bets on the race, they didn't matter. It was just bad luck. But to see the old lady's quarter million of pounds and more go down the pike was a tragedy. We had seen so much of shabby great names that I trembled for young Clontarf and his brother. Armenian and Greek families of doubtful antecedents were always on the lookout for a title for their daughters, and crooked businesses always needed directors of title to catch gulls, so much in the United Kingdom do the poor trust their peers. The boys would not exactly be poor, because the horse, whether or not it ran in the Derby, would be worth a good round sum. If it were as good as my uncle Valentine said, it would win the Leger and the Gold Cup at Ascot. But even with these triumphs it wouldn't be a Derby winner. And the Derby means so much. There are so many people in England who remember dates by the Derby winner's names, as 'I was married in Bend Or's year', or 'the Achilles was lost in the China seas, let me see when—that was in Sainfoin's year.' Also I wasn't sure that the Spanish gipsy would stay to ride him at Doncaster, or return for Ascot. I found him one day standing on the cliffs of Destiny and looking long at the sea, and I knew what that meant. And perhaps Romany Baw would not run for another jockey as he ran for him.

I could not think that Death could be so cruel as to come between us and triumph. In Destiny we have a friendliness for the Change which most folk dread. One of our songs says:

> 'When Mother Death in her warm arms shall embrace me,
> Low lull me to sleep with sweet Erin-go-bragh—'

We look upon it as a kind friend who comes when one is

tired and twisted with pain, and says: 'Listen, *avourneen*, soon the dawn will come, and the tide is on the ebb. We must be going.' And we trust him to take us, by a short road or a long road to a place of birds and bees, of which even lovely Destiny is but a clumsy seeming. He could not be such a poor sportsman as to come before the aged gallant lady had won her last gamble. And poor Sir Arthur, who had come out of his old age in Mayo to win a Derby! It would break his heart. And the great horse, it would be hard on him. Nothing will convince me that a thoroughbred does not know a great race when he runs one. The streaming competitors, the crackle of silk, the roar as they come into the straight, and the sense of the jockey calling on the great heart that the writer of Job knew so well. 'The glory of his nostril is terrible,' says the greatest of poets. 'He pauseth in the valley and rejoiceth in his strength: he goeth on to meet the armed man.' Your intellectual will claim that the thoroughbred is an artificial brainless animal evolved by men for their amusement. Your intellectual, here again, is a liar.

Spring came in blue and gold. Blue of sea and fields and trees; gold of sun and sand and buttercup. Blue of wild hyacinth and bluebell; gold of primrose and laburnum tree. The old gipsy lady was with her caravan near Bordeaux, and from the occasional letter my uncle Valentine got, and from the few words he dropped to me, she was just holding her own. May drowsed by with the cheeping of the little life in the hedgerows. The laburnum floated in a cloud of gold and each day Romany Baw grew stronger. When his blankets were stripped from him he looked a mass of fighting muscle under a covering of satin, and his eye showed that his heart was fighting too. Old Sir Arthur looked at him a few days before we were to go to England, and he turned to me.

'Kerry,' he said, very quietly.

'Yes, Sir Arthur.'

'All my life I have been breeding and training horses, and it just goes to show,' he told me, 'that goodness of God that he let me handle this great horse before I died.'

The morning before we left my uncle Valentine received a letter which I could see moved him. He swore a little as he does when moved and stroked his vast red beard and looked fiercely at nothing at all.

'Is it bad news, sir?' I asked.

He didn't answer me directly. 'Lady Clontarf is coming to the Derby,' he told me.

Then it was my turn to swear a little. It seemed to me to be but little short of maniacal to risk a Channel crossing and the treacherous English climate in her stage of health. If she should die on the way or on the downs, then all her planning and our work was for nothing. Why could she not have remained in the soft French air, husbanding her share of life until the event was past!

'She comes of ancient, violent blood,' thundered my uncle Valentine, 'and where should she be but present when her people or her horses go forth to battle?'

'You are right, sir,' I said.

The epithet of 'flaming' which the English apply to their June was in this year of grace well deserved. The rhododendrons were bursting into great fountains of scarlet, and near the swans and cygnets paddled, unbelievably small. The larks fluttered in the air above the downs, singing so gallantly that when you heard the trill of the nightingale in the thicket giving his noontime song, you felt inclined to say: 'Be damned to that Italian bird; my money's on the wee fellow!' All through Surrey the green walls of spring rose high and thick, and then suddenly coming, as we came, through Leatherhead and topping the hill, in the distance the black colony of the downs showed like a thundercloud. At a quarter mile away, the clamour came to you, like the vibration when great bells have been struck.

The stands and enclosures were packed so thickly that one wondered how movement was possible, how people could enjoy themselves, close as herrings. My uncle Valentine had brought his beautiful harness ponies across from Ireland, 'to encourage English interest in the Irish horse' he explained it, but with his beautifully cut clothes, his grey high hat, it seemed to me that more people looked at him as we spun along the road than looked at the horses. Behind us sat James Carabine, with his face brown as autumn and the gold rings in his thickened ears. We got out near the paddock and Carabine took the ribbons. My uncle Valentine said quietly to him: 'Find out how things are, James Carabine.' And I knew he was referring to the gipsy lady. Her caravan was somewhere on the Downs guarded by her gipsies, but my uncle had been there the first day of the meeting, and on Monday night, at the National Sporting, some of the gipsies had waited for him coming out and given him news. I asked him how she was, but all his answer was: 'It's in the Hands of God.'

Along the track towards the grandstand we made our way. On the railings across the track the bookmakers were proclaiming their market: 'I'll give fives the field. I'll give nine to one bar two. I'll give twenty to one bar five. Outsiders! Outsiders! Fives Sir James. Seven to one Toison d'Or. Nines Honey Bee. Nines Welsh Melody. Ten to one the gipsy horse.

'It runs all right,' said my uncle Valentine, 'up to now.'

'Twenty to one Maureen Roe! Twenties Asclepiades! Twenty-five Rifle Ranger. Here thirty-three to one Rifle Ranger, Monk of Sussex, or Presumptuous—'

'Gentlemen, I am here to plead with you not to back the favourite. In this small envelope you will find the number of the winner. For the contemptible sum of two shillings or half a dollar, you may amass a fortune. Who gave the winner of last year's Derby?' a tipster was calling. 'Who gave the winner of the Oaks? Who gave the winner of the Steward's Cup?'

'All right, guv'nor, I'll bite. 'Oo the 'ell did?'

Opposite the grandstand the band of the Salvation Army was blaring the music of 'Work, for the Night is Coming.' Gipsy girls were going around *dukkering* or telling fortunes, 'Ah, gentleman, you've got a lucky face. Cross the poor gipsy's hand with silver—'

'You better cut along and see your horse saddled,' said my uncle Valentine. Ducks and Drakes was in the Ranmore Plate and with the penalty he received after Newmarket, Frasco could ride him. As I went towards the paddock I saw the numbers go up, and I saw we were drawn third, which I think is best of all on the tricky Epsom five-furlong dash. I got there in time to see the gipsy swing into the saddle in the green silk jacket and orange cap, and Sir Arthur giving him his orders. 'Keep back of the Fusilier,' he pointed to the horse, 'and then come out. Hit him once if you have to, and no more.'

'Si, si, Don Arturo!' And he grinned at me.

'Kerry, read this,' said the old trainer, and gave me a newspaper, 'and tell me before the race,' his voice was trembling a little, 'if there's truth in it.'

I pushed the paper into my pocket and went back to the box where my uncle Valentine and Jenico and Ann-Dolly were. 'What price my horse?' I asked in Tattersall's. 'Sixes, Mister MacFarlane.' 'I'll take six hundred to a hundred twice.' As I moved away there was a rush to back it. It tumbled in five minutes to five to two.

'And I thought I'd get tens,' I said to my uncle Valentine, 'with the Fusilier and Bonny Hortense in the race. I wonder who's been backing it.'

'I have,' said Ann-Dolly. 'I got twelves.'

'You might have the decency to wait until the owner gets on,' I said bitterly. And as I watched the tapes went up. It was a beautiful start. Everything except those on the outside seemed to have a chance as they raced for the rails. I could distinguish the green jacket but vaguely until they came to Tattenham Corner, when I could see Fusilier pull out, and Bonny Hortense follow. But back of Fusilier, racing quietly beside the filly, was the jacket green.

'I wish he'd go up,' I said.

'The favourite wins,' they were shouting. And a woman in the box next to us began to clap her hands calling: 'Fusilier's won. Fusilier wins it.'

'You're a damn fool, woman,' said Ann-Dolly. 'Ducks and Drakes has it.' And as she spoke, I could see Frasco hunch forward slightly and dust his mount's neck with his whip. He crept pass the hard-pressed Fusilier to win by half a length.

In my joy I nearly forgot the newspaper, and I glanced at it rapidly. My heart sank. 'Gipsy Owner Dying as Horse runs in Derby,' I read, and reading down I felt furious. Where had the man got his information from I don't know, but he drew a picturesque account of the old gipsy lady on her deathbed on the downs as Romany Baw was waiting in his stall. The account was written the evening before, and 'it is improbable she will last the night,' it ended. I gave it to my uncle Valentine, who had been strangely silent over my win.

'What shall I say to Sir Arthur Pollexfen?'

'Say she's ill, but it's all rot she's dying.'

I noticed as I went to the paddock a murmur among the

racegoers. The attention of all had been drawn to the gipsy horse by its jockey having won the Ranmore Plate. Everywhere I heard questions being asked as to whether she were dead. Sir James had hardened to fours. And on the heath I heard a woman proffer a sovereign to a bookmaker on Romany Baw, and he said: 'That horse don't run, lady.' I forgot my own little triumph in the tragedy of the scratching of the great horse.

In the paddock Sir Arthur was standing watching the lads leading the horses around. Twenty-seven entries, glossy as silk, muscled like athletes of old Greece, ready to run for the Derby stakes. The jockeys, with their hard wizened faces, stood talking to trainers and owners, saying nothing about the race, all already having been said, but just putting in the time until the order came to go to the gate. I moved across to the old Irish trainer and the gipsy jockey. Sir Arthur was saying nothing, but his hand trembled as he took a pinch of snuff from his old-fashioned silver horn. The gipsy jockey stood erect, with his overcoat over his silk. It was a heart-rendering five minutes standing there beside them, waiting for the message that they were not to go.

My uncle Valentine was standing with a couple of the Stewards. A small race official was explaining something to them. They nodded him away. There was another minute's conversation and my uncle came towards us. The old trainer was fumbling pitifully with his silver snuff horn, trying to find the pocket in which to put it.

'It's queer,' said my uncle Valentine, 'but nobody seems to know where Lady Clontarf is. She's not in her caravan.'

'So—' questioned the old trainer.

'So you run,' said my uncle Valentine. 'The horse comes under starter's orders. You may have an objection, Arthur, but you run.'

The old man put on youth and grandeur before my eyes. He stood erect. With an eye like an eagle's he looked around the paddock.

'Leg up, boy!' he snapped at Frasco.

'Here, give me your coat.' I helped throw the golden-and-red shirted figure into the saddle. Then the head lad led the horse out.

We moved down the track and into the stand, and the

parade began. Lord Shire's great horse, and the French hope Toison d'Or; the brown colt owned by the richest merchant in the world, and the little horse owned by the Leicester butcher, who served in his own shop; the horse owned by the peer of last year's making; and the bay filly owned by the first baroness in England. they went down past the stand, and turning breezed off at a gallop back, to cross the downs towards the starting gate, and as they went with each went someone's heart. All eyes seemed turned on the gipsy horse, with his rider erect as a Life Guardsman. As Frasco raised his whip to his cap in the direction of our box, I heard in one of the neighbouring boxes a man say: 'But that horse's owner is dead!'

'Is that so, Uncle Valentine?' asked Ann-Dolly. There were tears in her eyes. 'Is that true?'

'Nothing is true until you see it yourself,' parried my uncle Valentine. And as she seemed to be about to cry openly— 'Don't you see the horse running?' he said. 'Don't you know the rule?' But his eyes were riveted through his glasses on the starting gate. I could see deep furrows of anxiety on his bronze brow. In the distance, over the crowd's heads, over the book-maker's banners, over the tents, we could see the dancing horses at the tapes, the gay colours of the riders moving here and there in an intricate pattern, the massed hundreds of black figures at the start. Near us, across the rails, some religious zealots let fly little balloons carrying banners reminding us that doom was waiting. Their band broke into a lugubrious hymn, while nasal voices took it up. In the silence of the crowded downs, breathless for the start, the religious demonstration seemed startlingly trivial. The line of horses, formed for the gate, broke, and wheeled. My uncle snapped his fingers in vexation.

'Why can't the fool get them away?'

Then out of a seemingly inextricable maze, the line formed suddenly and advanced on the tape. And the heavy silence exploded into a low roar like growling thunder. Each man shouted: 'They're off!' The Derby had started.

It seemed like a river of satin, with iridescent foam, pouring, against all nature, uphill. And for one instant you could dis-tinguish nothing. You looked to see if your horse had got away well, had not been kicked or cut into at the start, and as you were disentangling them, the banks of gorse shut them from your view, and when you saw them again they were racing for the turn of the hill. The erect figure of the jockey caught my eye before his colours did.

'He's lying fifth,' I told my uncle Valentine.

'He's running well,' my uncle remarked quietly.

They swung round the top of the hill, appearing above the rails and gorse, like something tremendously artificial, like some theatrical illusion, as of a boat going across the stage. There were three horses grouped together, then a black horse —Esterhazy's fine colt—then Romany Baw, then after that a stretching line of horses. Something came out of the pack at the top of the hill, and passed the gipsy horse and the fourth.

'Toison d'Or is going up,' Jenico told me.

But the gallant French colt's bolt was flown. He fell back, and now one of the leaders dropped back. And Romany was fourth as they started downhill for Tattenham Corner. 'How slow they go!' I thought.

'What a pace!' said Jenico, his watch in his hand.

At Tattenham Corner the butcher's lovely little horse was beaten, and a sort of moan came from the rails where the poor people stood. Above the religious band's outrageous nasal tones, the ring began roaring: 'Sir James! Sir James has it. Twenty to one bar Sir James!'

As they came flying up the stretch I could see the favourite going along, like some bird flying low, his jockey hunched like an ape on his withers. Beside him raced an outsider, a French-bred horse owned by Kazoutlian, an Armenian banker. Close to his heels came the gipsy horse on the inside, Frasco sitting as though the horse were standing still. Before him raced the favourite and the rank outsider.

'It's all over,' I said. 'He can't get through. And he can't pull around. Luck of the game!'

And then the rider on the Armenian's horse tried his last effort. He brought his whip high in the air. My uncle Valentine thundered a great oath.

'Look, Kerry!' His fingers gripped my shoulder.

I knew, when I saw the French horse throw his head up, that he was going to swerve at the whip, but I never expected

Frasco's mad rush. He seemed to jump the opening, and land the horse past Sir James.

'The favourite's beat!' went up the cry of dismay.

Romany Baw, with Frasco forward on his neck, passed the winning post first by a clear length.

Then a sort of stunned silence fell on the Derby crowd. Nobody knew what would happen. If, as the rumour went around, the owner was dead, then the second automatically won. All eyes were on the horse as the trainer let him into the paddock, followed by second and third. All eyes turned from the horse towards the notice board as the numbers went up: 17, 1, 26. All folk were waiting for the red objection signal. The owner of the second led his horse in, the burly Yorkshire peer. An old gnarled man, with a face like a walnut, Kazoutlian's self, led in the third.

'I say, Kerry,' Jenico called quietly, 'something's up near the paddock.'

I turned and noticed a milling mob down the course on our right. The mounted policeman set off at a trot towards the commotion. Then cheering went into the air like a peal of bells.

Down the course came all the gipsies, all the gipsies in the world, it seemed to me. Big-striding, black men with gold earrings and coloured neckerchiefs, and staves in their hands. And gipsy women, a-jingle with coins, dancing. Their tambourines jangled as they danced forward in a strange East Indian rhythm. There was a loud order barked by the police officer, and the men stood by to let them pass. And the solid English police began cheering too. It seemed to me that even the little trees of the downs were cheering, and in an instant I cheered too.

For back of an escort of mounted gipsies, big foreign men with moustaches, saddleless on their shaggy mounts, came a gipsy cart with its cover down, drawn by four prancing horses. A wild-looking gipsy man was holding the reins. On the cart, for all to see, seated in a great armchair, propped up by cushions, was Lady Clontarf. Her head was laid back on a pillow, and her eyes were closed, as if the strain of appearing had been too much for her. Her little maid was crouched at her feet.

For an instance we saw her, and noticed the aged beauty of her face, noticed the peace like twilight on it. There was an order from a big Roumanian gipsy and the Romany people made a lane. The driver stood up on his perch and manoeuvring his long snakelike whip in the air, made it crack like a musket. The horses broke into a gallop, and the gipsy cart went over the turfed course towards Tattenham Corner, passed it, and went up the hill and disappeared over the Surrey downs. All the world was cheering.

*   *   *

'Come in here,' said my uncle Valentine, and he took me into the cool beauty of our little church of Saint Columba's-in-Paganry. 'Now what do you think of that?' And he pointed out a brass tablet on the wall.

'In Memory of Mifanwy, Countess of Clontarf and Kincora,' I read. Then came the dates of her birth and death, 'and who is buried after the Romany manner, no man know where.' And then came the strange text, 'In death she was not divided.'

'But surely,' I objected, 'the quotation is: "In death they were not divided".'

'It may be,' said my uncle Valentine, 'or it may not be. But as the living of Saint Columba's-in-Paganry is in my gift, surely to God!' he broke out, 'a man can have a text the way he wants it in his own Church.'

This was arguable, but something serious caught my eye.

'See, sir,' I said, 'the date of her death is wrong. She died on the evening of Derby Day, June the second. And here it is given as June the first.'

'She did not die on the evening of Derby Day. She died on the first.'

'Then,' I said, 'when she rode down the course on her gipsy cart,' and a little chill came over me, 'she was—'

'As a herring, Kerry, as a gutted herring,' my uncle Valentine said.

'Then the rule was really infringed, and the horse should not have won.'

'Wasn't the best horse there?'

'Undoubtedly, sir, but as to the betting.'

'The bookmakers lost less than they would have lost on the favourite.'

'But the backers of the favourite.'

'The small backer in the silver ring is paid on the first past the post, so they'd have lost, anyway. At any rate, they all should have lost. They backed their opinion as to which was the best horse, and it wasn't.'

'But damn it all, sir! and God forgive me for swearing in this holy place—there's the Derby Rule.'

' "The letter killeth," Kerry,' quoted my uncle gravely, even piously. ' "The letter killeth".'

How Mr Pickwick Undertook to Drive and Mr Winkle to Ride

CHARLES DICKENS

'Now, about Manor Farm,' said Mr Pickwick. 'How shall we go?'

'We had better consult the waiter, perhaps,' said Mr Tupman, and the waiter was summoned accordingly.

'Dingley Dell, gentlemen—fifteen miles, gentlemen—cross road—post-chaise, sir?'

'Post-chaise won't hold more than two,' said Mr Pickwick.

'True, sir—beg your pardon sir.—Very nice four-wheeled chaise, sir—seat for two behind—one in front for the gentleman that drives—oh! beg your pardon, sir—that'll only hold three.'

'What's to be done?' said Mr Snodgrass.

'Perhaps one of the gentlemen would like to ride, sir?' suggested the waiter, looking towards Mr Winkle; 'very good saddle horses, sir—any of Mr Wardle's men coming to Rochester bring 'em back, sir.'

'The very thing,' said Mr Pickwick. 'Winkle, will you go on horseback?'

Mr Winkle did entertain considerable misgivings in the very lowest recesses of his own heart, relative to his equestrian skill; but, as he would not have them even suspect on any account, he at once replied with great hardihood, 'Certainly, I should enjoy it, of all things.'

Mr Winkle had rushed upon his fate; there was no resource. 'Let them be at the door by eleven,' said Mr Pickwick.

'Very well, sir,' replied the waiter.

The waiter retired; the breakfast concluded; and the travellers ascended to their respective bedrooms, to prepare a change of clothing, to take with them on their approaching expedition.

Mr Pickwick had made his preliminary arrangements, and was looking over the coffee-room blinds at the passengers in the street, when the waiter entered, and announced that the chaise was ready—an announcement which the vehicle itself confirmed, by forthwith appearing before the coffee-room blinds aforesaid.

It was a curious little green box on four wheels, with a low place like a wine-bin for two behind, and an elevated perch for one in front, drawn by an immense brown horse, displaying great symmetry of bone. An hostler stood near, holding by the bridle another immense horse—apparently a near relative of the animal in the chaise-ready saddled for Mr Winkle.

'Bless my soul!' said Mr Pickwick, as they stood upon the pavement while the coats were being put in. 'Bless my soul! who's to drive? I never thought of that.'

'Oh! you, of course,' said Mr Tupman.

'Of course,' said Mr Snodgrass.

'I!' exclaimed Mr Pickwick.

'Not the slightest fear, sir,' interposed the hostler. 'Warrant him quiet, sir; a hinfant in arms might drive him.'

'He don't shy, does he?' inquired Mr Pickwick. 'Shy, sir?— He wouldn't shy if he was to meet a vaggin-load of monkeys with their tails burnt off.'

The last recommendation was indisputable. Mr Tupman and Mr Snodgrass got into the bin; Mr Pickwick ascended to his perch, and deposited his feet on a floor-clothed shelf, erected beneath it for that purpose.

'Now, shiny Villiam,' said the hostler to the deputy hostler, 'give the gen'l'm'n the ribbins.' 'Shiny Villiam'—so called, probably, from his sleek hair and oily countenance—placed the reins in Mr Pickwick's left hand; and the upper hostler thrust a whip in his right.

'Wo—o!' cried Mr Pickwick, as the tall quadruped evinced a decided inclination to back into the coffee-room window.

'Wo—o!' echoed Mr Tupman and Mr Snodgrass, from the bin.

'Only his playfulness, gen'l'm'n,' said the head hostler encouragingly; 'jist kitch hold of him, Villiam.' The deputy restrained the animal's impetuosity, and the principal ran to assist Mr Winkle in mounting.

'T'other side, sir, if you please.'

'Blowed if the gen'l'm'n worn't a gettin' up on the wrong side,' whispered a grinning post-boy to the inexpressibly gratified waiter.

Mr Winkle, thus instructed, climbed into his saddle, with about as much difficulty as he would have experienced in getting up the side of a first-rate man-of-war.

'All right?' inquired Mr Pickwick, with an inward presentiment that it was all wrong.

'All right,' replied Mr Winkle faintly.

'Let 'em go,' cried the hostler—'Hold him in, sir,' and away went the chaise, and the saddle-horse, with Mr Pickwick on the box of one, and Mr Winkle on the back of the other, to the delight and gratification of the whole inn yard.

'What makes him go sideways?' said Mr Snodgrass in the bin, to Mr Winkle in the saddle.

'I can't imagine,' replied Mr Winkle. His horse was drifting up the street in the most mysterious manner—side first, with his head towards one side of the way, and his tail towards the other.

Mr Pickwick had no leisure to observe either this or any other particular, the whole of his facilities being concentrated on the management of the animal attached to the chaise, who displayed various peculiarities, highly interesting to a bystander, but by no means equally amusing to any one seated behind him. Besides constantly jerking his head up, in a very unpleasant and uncomfortable manner, and tugging at the reins to an extent which rendered it a matter of great difficulty for Mr Pickwick to hold them, he had a singular propensity for darting suddenly every now and then to the side of the road, then stopping short, and then rushing forward for some minutes, at a speed which it was wholly impossible to control.

'What *can* he mean by this?' said Mr Snodgrass, when the horse had executed this manoeuvre for the twentieth time.

'I don't know,' replied Mr Tupman; 'it *looks* very like shying, don't it?' Mr Snodgrass was about to reply, when he was interrupted by a shout from Mr Pickwick.

'Woo!' said that gentleman; 'I have dropped my whip.'

'Winkle,' said Mr Snodgrass, as the equestrian came trotting up on the tall horse, with his hat over his ears, and shaking all over, as if he would shake to pieces, with the violence of the exercise, 'pick up the whip, there's a good fellow.' Mr Winkle pulled at the bridle of the tall horse till he was black in the face; and having at length succeeded in stopping him, dismounted, handed the whip to Mr Pickwick, and grasping the reins, prepared to remount.

Now whether the tall horse, in the natural playfulness of his disposition, was desirous of having a little innocent recreation with Mr Winkle, or whether it occurred to him that he could perform the journey as much to his own satisfaction without a rider as with one, are points upon which, of course, we can arrive at no definite and distinct conclusion. By whatever motives the animal was actuated, certain it is that Mr Winkle had no sooner touched the reins, than he slipped them over his head, and darted backwards to their full length.

'Poor fellow,' said Mr Winkle, soothingly—'poor fellow— good old horse.' The 'poor fellow' was proof against flattery: the more Mr Winkle tried to get near him, the more he sidled away; and, notwithstanding all kinds of coaxing and whee- dling, there were Mr Winkle and the horse going round and round each other for ten minutes, at the end of which time each was at precisely the same distance from the other as when they first commenced—an unsatisfactory sort of thing under any circumstances, but particularly so in a lonely road, where no assistance can be procured.

'What am I to do?' shouted Mr Winkle, after the dodging had been prolonged for a considerable time. 'What am I to do? I can't get on him.'

'You had better lead him till we come to a turnpike,' replied Mr Pickwick from the chaise.

'But he won't come!' roared Mr Winkle. 'Do come, and hold him.'

Mr Pickwick was the very personation of kindness and humanity: he threw the reins on the horse's back, and having descended from his seat, carefully drew the chaise into the hedge, less anything should come along the road, and stepped back to the assistance of his distressed companion, leaving Mr Tupman and Mr Snodgrass in the vehicle.

The horse no sooner beheld Mr Pickwick advancing towards him with the chaise whip in his hand, than he exchanged the rotary motion in which he had previously indulged, for a retrograde movement of so very determined a character, that it at once drew Mr Winkle, who was still at the end of the bridle, at a rather quicker rate than fast walking, in the direction from which they had just come. Mr Pickwick ran to his assistance, but the faster Mr Pickwick ran forward, the faster the horse ran backward. There was a great scraping of feet, and kicking up of the dust; and at last Mr Winkle, his arms being nearly pulled out of their sockets, fairly let go his hold. The horse paused, stared, shook his head, turned round, and quietly trotted home to Rochester, leaving Mr Winkle and Mr Pickwick gazing on each other with countenances of blank dismay. A rattling noise at a little distance attracted their attention. They looked up.

'Bless my soul!' exclaimed the agonised Mr Pickwick, 'there's the other horse running away!'

It was but too true. The animal was startled by the noise, and the reins were on his back. The result may be guessed. He tore off with the four-wheeled chaise behind him, and Mr Tupman and Mr Snodgrass in the four-wheeled chaise. The heat was a short one. Mr Tupman threw himself into the hedge. Mr Snodgrass followed his example, the horse dashed the four-wheeled chaise against a wooden bridge, separated the wheels from the body, and the bin from the perch: and finally stood stock still to gaze upon the ruin he had made.

The first care of the two unspilt friends was to extricate their unfortunate companions from their bed of quickset—a process which gave them the unspeakable satisfaction off discovering that they had sustained no injury, beyond sundry rents in their garments, and various lacerations from the brambles. The next thing to be done was, to unharness the horse. This complicated process having been effected, the party walked slowly forward, leading the horse among them, and abandoning the chaise to its fate.

An hour's walking brought the travellers to a little roadside public-house, with two elm trees, a horse trough, and a sign-post in front; one or two deformed hayricks behind, a kitchen garden at the side, and rotten sheds and mouldering outhouses jumbled in strange confusion all about it. A red-headed man was working in the garden; and to him Mr Pickwick called lustily—'Hallo there!'

The red-headed man raised his body, shaded his eyes with his hand, and stared, long and coolly, at Mr Pickwick, and his companions.

'Hallo there!' repeated Mr Pickwick.

'Hallo!' was the red-headed man's reply.

'How far is it to Dingley Dell?'

'Better er seven mile.'

'Is it a good road?'

'No t'aint.' Having uttered this brief reply, and apparently satisfied himself with another scrutiny, the red-headed man resumed his work.

'We want to put this horse up here,' said Mr Pickwick; 'I suppose we can, can't we?'

'Want to put that ere horse up, do ee?' repeated the red-headed man, leaning on his spade.

'Of course,' replied Mr Pickwick, who had by this time advanced, horse in hand, to the garden rails.

'Missus'—roared the man with the red head, emerging from the garden, and looking very hard at the horse—'Missus!'

A tall bony woman—straight all the way down—in a coarse blue pelisse, with the waist an inch or two below her armpits, responded to the call.

'Can we put this horse up here, my good woman?' said Mr Tupman, advancing, and speaking in his most seductive tones. The woman looked very hard at the whole party; and the red-headed man whispered something in her ear.

'No,' replied the woman, after a little consideration, 'I'm afeered on it.'

'Afraid!' exclaimed Mr Pickwick, 'what's the woman afraid of?'

'It got us into trouble last time,' said the woman, turning into the house: 'I woant have nothin' to say to 'un.'

'Most extraordinary thing I ever met with in my life,' said the astonished Mr Pickwick.

'I—I—really believe,' whispered Mr Winkle, as his friends gathered round him, 'that they think we have come by this horse in some dishonest manner.'

'What!' exclaimed Mr Pickwick, in a storm of indignation. Mr Winkle modestly repeated his suggestion.

'Hallo, you fellow!' said the angry Mr Pickwick, 'do you think we stole this horse?'

'I'm sure ye did,' replied the red-headed man, with a grin which agitated his countenance from one auricular organ to the other. Saying which, he turned into the house, and banged the door after him.

'It's like a dream,' ejaculated Mr Pickwick, 'a hideous dream. The idea of a man's walking about, all day, with a dreadful horse that he can't get rid of!' The depressed Pickwickians turned moodily away, with the tall quadruped, for which they all felt the most unmitigated disgust, following slowly at their heels.

It was late in the afternoon when the four friends and their four-footed companion turned into the lane leading to Manor Farm; and even when they were so near their place of destination, the pleasure they would otherwise have experienced was materially damped as they reflected on the singularity of their appearance, and the absurdity of their situation. Torn clothes, lacerated faces, dusty shoes, exhausted looks, and, above all, the horse. Oh, how Mr Pickwick cursed that horse: he had eyed the noble animal from time to time with looks expressive of hatred and revenge; more than once he had calculated the probable amount of expense he would incur by cutting his throat; and now the temptation to destroy him, or to cast him loose upon the world, rushed upon his mind with tenfold force. He was roused from a meditation on these dire imaginings, by the sudden appearance of two figures at a turn of the lane. It was Mr Wardle, and his faithful attendant, the fat boy.

'Why, where *have* you been?' said the hospitable old gentleman, 'I've been waiting for you all day. Well, you *do* look tired. What! Scratches! Not hurt, I hope—eh? Well, I *am* glad to hear that—very. So you've been spilt, eh? Never mind. Common accident in these parts. Joe—he's asleep again!—Joe, take that horse from the gentleman, and lead it into the stable.'

The fat boy sauntered heavily behind them with the animal; and the old gentleman, condoling with his guests in homely phrase on so much of the day's adventures as they thought proper to communicate, led the way to the kitchen.

'We'll have you put to rights here,' said the old gentleman, 'and then I'll introduce you to the people in the parlour. Emma, bring out the cherry brandy; now, Jane, a needle and thread here; towels and water, Mary. Come, girls, bustle about.'

Three or four buxom girls speedily dispersed in search of the different articles in requisition, while a couple of large-headed, circular-visaged males rose from their seats in the chimney-corner (for although it was a May evening, their attachment to the wood fire appeared as cordial as if it were Christmas), and dived into some obscure recesses, from which they speedily produced a bottle of blacking, and some half-dozen brushes.

'Bustle!' said the old gentleman again, but the admonition was quite unnecessary, for one of the girls poured out the cherry brandy, and another brought in towels, and one of the men suddenly seizing Mr Pickwick by the leg, at imminent hazard of throwing him off his balance, brushed away at his boots, till his corns were red-hot; while the other shampoo'd Mr Winkle with a heavy clothes-brush, indulging, during the operation, in that hissing sound which hostlers are wont to produce when engaged in rubbing down a horse.

Mr Snodgrass, having concluded his ablutions, took a survey of the room, while standing with his back to the fire, sipping his cherry brandy with heartfelt satisfaction. He describes it as a large apartment, with a red brick floor and a capacious chimney; the ceiling garnished with hams, sides of bacon, and ropes of onions. The walls were decorated with several hunting-whips, two or three bridles, a saddle and an old rusty blunderbuss, with an inscription below it, intimating that it was 'Loaded'—as it had been, on the same authority, for half a century at least. An old eight-day clock, of solemn and sedate demeanour, ticked gravely in one corner; and a silver watch, of equal antiquity, dangled from one of the many hooks which ornamented the dresser.

'Ready?' said the old gentleman inquiringly, when his guests had been washed, mended, brushed, and brandied.

'Quite,' replied Mr Pickwick.

'Come along, then,' said the party having traversed several dark passages, and being joined by Mr Tupman, who had lingered behind to snatch a kiss from Emma, for which he had been duly rewarded with sundry pushings and scratchings, arrived at the parlour door.

'Welcome,' said their hospitable host, throwing it open and stepping forward to announce them, 'Welcome, gentlemen, to Manor Farm.'

Philippa's Fox-Hunt

E. SOMERVILLE AND MARTIN ROSS

> It isn't the 'unting as 'urts the horse's 'oofs,
> It's the 'ammer, 'ammer, 'ammer on the 'ard
>   'igh road!
>
> OLD ENGLISH ADAGE

NO ONE can accuse Philippa and me of having married in haste. As a matter of fact, it was but little under five years from that autumn evening on the river when I had said what is called in Ireland 'the hard word,' to the day in August when I was led to the altar by my best man, and was subsequently led away from it by Mrs Sinclair Yeates. About two years out of the five had been spent by me at Shreelane in ceaseless warfare with drains, eaveshoots, chimneys, pumps; all those fundamentals, in short, that the ingenuous and improving tenant expects to find established as a basis from which to rise to higher things. As far as rising to higher things went, frequent ascents to the roof to search for leaks summed up my achievements; in fact, I suffered so general a shrinkage of my ideals that the triumph of making the hall-door bell ring blinded me to the fact that the rat-holes in the hall floor were nailed up with pieces of tin biscuit boxes, and that the casual visitor could, instead of leaving a card, have easily written his name in the damp on the walls.

Philippa, however, proved adorably callous to these and similar shortcomings. She regarded Shreelane and its floundering, foundering ménage of incapables in the light of a gigantic picnic in a foreign land; she held long conversations daily with Mrs Cadogan, in order, as she informed me, to acquire the language; without any ulterior domestic intention she engaged kitchenmaids because of the beauty of their eyes, and housemaids because they had such delightfully picturesque old mothers, and she declined to correct the phraseology of the parlourmaid, whose painful habit it was to whisper 'Do ye choose cherry or clarry?' when proffering the wine. Fast-days, perhaps, afforded my wife her first insight into the sterner realities of Irish housekeeping. Philippa had what are known as High Church proclivities, and took the matter seriously.

'I don't know how we are going to manage for the servants' dinner tomorrow, Sinclair,' she said, coming into my office one Thursday morning; 'Julia says she "promised God this long time that she wouldn't eat an egg on a fast-day" and the kitchenmaid says she won't eat herrings "without they're fried with onions," and Mrs Cadogan says she will "not go to them extremes for servants." '

'I should let Mrs Cadogan settle the menu herself,' I suggested.

'I asked her to do that,' replied Philippa, 'and she only said she "thanked God *she* had no appetite!" '

The lady of the house here fell away into unseasonable laughter.

I made the demoralizing suggestion that, as we were going away for a couple of nights, we might safely leave them to fight it out, and the problem was abandoned.

Philippa had been much called on by the neighbourhood in all its shades and grades, and daily she and her trousseau frocks presented themselves at hall-doors of varying dimensions in due acknowledgment of civilities. In Ireland, it may be noted, the process known in England as 'summering and wintering' a newcomer does not obtain; sociability and curiosity alike forbid delay. The visit to which we owed our escape from the intricacies of the fast-day was to the Knoxes of Castle Knox, relations in some remote and tribal way of my landlord, Mr Flurry of that ilk. It involved a short journey by train, and my wife's longest basket-trunk; it also, which was more serious, involved my being lent a horse to go out cubbing the following morning.

At Castle Knox we sank into an almost forgotten environment of draught-proof windows and doors, of deep carpets, of silent servants instead of clattering belligerents. Philippa told me afterwards that it had been by an effort that she had restrained herself from snatching up the train of her wedding-gown as she paced across the wide hall on little Sir Valentine's arm. After three weeks at Shreelane she found it difficult to remember that the floor was neither damp nor dusty.

I had the good fortune to be of the limited number of those who got on with Lady Knox, chiefly, I imagine, because I was as a worm before her, and thankfully permitted her to do all the talking.

'Your wife is extremely pretty,' she pronounced autocratically, surveying Philippa through the candle-shades; 'does she ride?'

Lady Knox was a short square lady, with a weather-beaten face, and an eye decisive from long habit of taking her own line across country and elsewhere. She would have made a very imposing little coachman, and would have caused her stable helpers to rue the day they had the presumption to be born; it struck me that Sir Valentine sometimes did so.

'I am glad you like her looks,' I replied, 'as I fear you will find her thoroughly despicable otherwise; for one thing, she not only can't ride, but she belies that I can!'

'Oh come, you're not as bad as all that!' my hostess was good enough to say; 'I'm going to put you up on Sorcerer tomorrow, and we'll see you at the top of the hunt—if there is one. That young Knox hasn't a notion how to draw these woods.'

'Well, the best run we had last year out of this place was with Flurry's hounds,' struck in Miss Sally, the sole daughter of Sir Valentine's house, and home, from her place half-way down the table. It was not difficult to see that she and her mother held different views on the subject of Mr Flurry Knox.

'I call it a criminal thing in any one's great-great-grandfather to rear up a preposterous troop of sons and plant them all out in his own country,' Lady Knox said to me with apparent irrelevance. 'I detest collaterals. Blood may be thicker than water, but it is also a great deal nastier. In this country I find that fifteenth cousins consider themselves near relations if they live within twenty miles of one!'

Having before now taken in the position with regard to Flurry Knox, I took care to accept these remarks as generalities, and turned the conversation to other themes.

'I see Mrs Yeates is doing wonders with Mr Hamilton,' said

Lady Knox presently, following the direction of my eyes, which had strayed away to where Philippa was beaming upon her left-hand neighbour, a mildewed-looking old clergyman, who was delivering a long dissertation, the purport of which we were happily unable to catch.

'She has always had a gift for the Church,' I said.

'Not curates?' said Lady Knox, in her deep voice.

I made haste to reply that it was the elders of the Church who were venerated by my wife.

'Well, she has her fancy in old Eustace Hamilton; he's elderly enough!' said Lady Knox. 'I wonder if she'd venerate him as much if she knew that he had fought with his sister-in-law, and they haven't spoken for thirty years! though for the matter of that,' she added, 'I think it shows his good sense!'

'Mrs Knox is rather a friend of mine,' I ventured.

'Is she? H'm! Well, she's not one of mine!' replied my hostess, with her usual definiteness. 'I'll say one thing for her, I believe she's always been a sportswoman. She's very rich you know, and they say she only married old Badger Knox to save his hounds from being sold to pay his debts, and then she took the horn from him and hunted them herself. Has she been rude to your wife yet? No? Oh, well, she will. It's a mere question of time. She hates all English people. You know the story they tell of her? She was coming home from London, and when she was getting her ticket the man asked if she had said a ticket for York. "No, thank God, Cork!" says Mrs Knox.'

'Well, I rather agree with her!' said I; 'but why did she fight with Mr Hamilton?'

'Oh, nobody knows. I don't believe they know themselves! Whatever it was, the old lady drives five miles to Fortwilliam every Sunday, rather than go to his church, just outside her own back gates,' Lady Knox said with a laugh like a terrier's bark. 'I wish I'd fought with him myself,' she said; 'he gives us forty minutes every Sunday.'

As I struggled with my boots the following morning, I felt that Sir Valentine's acid confidences on cub-hunting, bestowed on me at midnight, did credit to his judgement. 'A very moderate amusement, my dear Major,' he had said, in his dry little voice; 'you should stick to shooting. No one expects you to shoot before daybreak.'

It was six o'clock as I crept downstairs, and found Lady Knox and Miss Sally at breakfast, with two lamps on the table, and a foggy daylight oozing in from under the half-raised blinds. Philippa was already in the hall, pumping up her bicycle, in a state of excitement at the prospect of her first experience of hunting that would have been more comprehensible to me had she been going to ride a strange horse, as I was. As I bolted my food I saw the horses being led past the windows, and a faint twang of a horn told that Flurry Knox and his hounds were not far off.

Miss Sally jumped up.

'If I'm not on the Cockatoo before the hounds come up, I shall never get there!' she said, hobbling out of the room in the toils of her safety habit. Her small, alert face looked very childish under her riding-hat; the lamp-light struck sparks out of her thick coil of golden-red hair: I wondered how I had ever thought her like her prim little father.

She was already on her white cob when I got to the hall-door, and Flurry Knox was riding over the glistening wet grass with his hounds, while his whip, Dr Jerome Hickey, was having a stirring time with the young entry and the rabbit-holes. They moved on without stopping, up a back avenue, under tall and dripping trees, to a thick laurel covert, at some distance from the house. Into this the hounds were thrown, and the usual period of fidgety inaction set in for the riders, of whom, all told, there were about half a dozen. Lady Knox, square and solid, on her big, confidential iron-grey, was near me, and her eyes were on me and my mount; with her rubicund face and white collar she was more than ever like a coachman.

'Sorcerer looks as if he suited you well,' she said, after a few minutes of silence, during which the hounds rustled and crackled steadily through the laurels; 'he's a little high on the leg and so are you, you know, so you show each other off.'

Sorcerer was standing like a rock, with his good-looking head in the air and his eyes fastened on the covert. His manners, so far, had been those of a perfect gentleman, and were in marked contrast to those of Miss Sally's cob, who was sidling, hopping, and snatching unappeasably at his bit. Philippa had disappeared from view down the avenue ahead. The fog was melting, and the sun threw long blades of light through the trees; everything was quiet, and in the distance the curtained windows of the house marked the warm repose of Sir Valentine, and those of the party who shared his opinion of cubbing.

'Hark! hark to cry there!'

It was Flurry's voice, away at the other side of the covert. The rustling and brushing through the laurels became more vehement, then passed out of hearing.

Miss Sally and the Cockatoo moved away in a series of heraldic capers towards the end of the laurel plantation, and at the same moment I saw Philippa on her bicycle shoot into view on the drive ahead of us.

'I've seen a fox!' she screamed, white with what I believe to have been personal terror, though she says it was excitement; 'it passed quite close to me!'

'Which way did he go?' bellowed a voice which I recognized as Dr Hickey's, somewhere in the deep of the laurels.

'Down the drive!' returned Philippa, with a pea-hen quality in her tones with which I was quite unacquainted.

An electrifying screech of 'Gone away!' was projected from the laurels by Dr Hickey.

'Gone away!' chanted Flurry's horn at the top of the covert.

'This is what he calls cubbing!' said Lady Knox, 'a mere farce!' but none the less she loosed her sedate monster into a canter.

Sorcerer got his hind-legs under him, and hardened his crest against the bit, as we all hustled along the drive after the flying figure of my wife. I knew very little about horses, but I realized that even with the hounds tumbling hysterically out of the covert, and the Cockatoo kicking the gravel into his face, Sorcerer comported himself with the manners of the best society. Up a side road I saw Flurry Knox opening half of a gate and cramming through it; in a moment we also had crammed through, and the turf of a pasture field was under our feet Dr Hickey leaned forward and took hold of his horse; I did likewise, with a trifling difference that my horse took hold of me, and I steered for Flurry Knox with single-hearted purpose, the hounds, already a field ahead, being merely an exciting and noisy accompaniment of this endeavour. A heavy stone wall was the first occurrence of note. Flurry chose a place where the

top was loose, and his clumsy-looking brown mare changed feet on the rattling stones like a fairy. Sorcerer came at it, tense and collected as a bow at full stretch, and sailed steeply into the air; I saw the wall far beneath me, with an unsuspected ditch on the far side, and I felt my hat following me at the full stretch of its guard as we swept over it, then, with a long slant, we descended to earth some sixteen feet from where we had left it, and I was possessor of the gratifying fact that I had achieved a good-sized 'fly' and had not perceptibly moved in my saddle. Subsequent disillusioning experience has taught me that but few horses jump like Sorcerer, so gallantly, so sympathetically, and with such supreme mastery of the subject; but none the less the enthusiasm that he imparted to me has never been extinguished, and that October morning ride revealed to me the unsuspected intoxication of fox-hunting.

Behind me I heard the scrabbling of the Cockatoo's little hoofs among the loose stones, and Lady Knox, galloping on my left jerked a maternal chin over her shoulder to mark her daughter's progress. For my part, had there been an entire circus behind me, I was far too much occupied with ramming on my hat and trying to hold Sorcerer, to have looked round, and all my spare faculties were devoted to steering for Flurry, who had taken a right-handed turn, and was at that moment surmounting a bank of uncertain and briary aspect. I surmounted it also, with the swiftness and simplicity for which the Quaker's methods of bank jumping had not prepared me, and two or three fields, traversed at the same steeplechase pace, brought us to a road and to an abrupt check. There, suddenly, were the hounds, scrambling in baffled silence down into the road from the opposite bank, to look for the line they had overrun, and there, amazingly, was Philippa, engaged in excited converse with several men with spades over their shoulders.

'Did ye see the fox, boys?' shouted Flurry, addressing the group.

'We did! we did!' cried my wife and her friends in chorus; 'he ran up the road!'

'We'd be badly off without Mrs Yeates!' said Flurry, as he whirled his mare round and clattered up the road with a hustle of hounds after him.

It occurred to me as forcibly as any mere earthly thing can occur to those who are wrapped in the sublimities of a run, that, for a young woman who had never before seen a fox out of a cage at the Zoo, Philippa was taking to hunting very kindly. Her cheeks were a most brilliant pink, her blue eyes shone.

'Oh, Sinclair!' she exclaimed, 'they say he's going for Aussolas, and there's a road I can ride all the way!'

'Ye can, Miss! Sure we'll show you!' chorused her *cortège*.

Her foot was on the pedal ready to mount. Decidedly my wife was in no need of assistance from me.

Up the road a hound gave a yelp of discovery, and flung himself over a stile into the fields; the rest of the pack went squealing and jostling after him, and I followed Flurry over one of those infinitely varied erections, pleasantly termed 'gaps' in Ireland. On this occasion the gap was made of three razor-edged slabs of slate leaning against an iron bar, and Sorcerer conveyed to me his thorough knowledge of the matter by a lift of his hind-quarters that made me feel as if I were being skilfully kicked downstairs. To what extent I looked it, I cannot say, nor providentially can Philippa, as she had already started. I only know that undeserved good luck restored me to my stirrup before Sorcerer got away with me in the next field.

What followed was, I am told, a very fast fifteen minutes; for me time was not; the empty fields rushed past uncounted, fences came and went in a flash, while the wind sang in my ears, and the dazzle of the early sun was in my eyes. I saw the hounds occasionally, sometimes pouring over a green bank, as the charging breaker lifts and flings itself, sometimes driving across a field, as the white tongues of foam slide racing over the sand; and always ahead of me was Flurry Knox, going as a man who knows his country, who knows his horse, and whose heart is wholly and absolutely in the right place.

Do what I would, Sorcerer's implacable stride carried me closer and closer to the brown mare, till, as I thundered down the slope of a long field, I was not twenty yards behind Flurry. Sorcerer had stiffened his neck to iron, and to slow him now was beyond me; but I fought his head away to the right, and found myself coming hard and steady at a stonefaced bank with broken ground in front of it. Flurry bore away to the left,

shouting something that I did not understand. That Sorcerer shortened his stride at the right moment was entirely due to his own judgement; standing well away from the jump, he rose like a stag out of the tussocky ground, and as he swung my twelve stone six into the air the obstacle revealed itself to him and me as consisting not of one bank but of two, and between the two lay a deep grassy lane, half choked with furze. I have often been asked to state the width of the bohereen, and can only reply that in my opinion it was at least eighteen feet; Flurry Knox and Dr Hickey, who did not jump it, say that it is not more than five. What Sorcerer did with it I cannot say; the sensation was of a towering flight with a kick back in it; a biggish drop, and a landing on cee-springs, still on the downward grade. That was how one of the best horses in Ireland took one of Ireland's most ignorant riders over a very nasty place.

A sombre line of fir-wood lay ahead, rimmed with a grey wall, and in another couple of minutes we had pulled up on the Aussolas road and were watching the hounds struggling over the wall into Aussolas demesne.

'No hurry now,' said Flurry, turning in his saddle to watch the Cockatoo jump into the road, 'he's to ground in the big earth inside. Well, Major, it's well for you that's a big-jumped horse. I thought you were a dead man a while ago when you faced him at the bohereen!'

I was disclaiming intention in the matter when Lady Knox and the others joined us.

'I thought you told me your wife was no sportswoman,' she said to me, critically scanning Sorcerer's legs for cuts the while, 'but when I saw her a minute ago she had abandoned her bicycle and was running across country like—'

'Look at her now!' interrupted Miss Sally. 'Oh!—oh!' In the interval between these exclamations my incredulous eyes beheld my wife in mid-air, hand in hand with a couple of stalwart country boys, with whom she was leaping in unison from the top of the bank on to the road.

Everyone, even the saturnine Dr Hickey, began to laugh; I rode back to Philippa, who was exchanging compliments and congratulations with her escort.

'Oh, Sinclair!' she cried, 'wasn't it splendid? I saw you jumping, and everything! Where are they going now?'

'My dear girl,' I said with marital disapproval, 'you're killing yourself. Where's your bicycle?'

'Oh, it's punctured in a sort of lane, back there. It's all right; and then they'—she breathlessly waved her hand at her attendants—'they showed me the way.'

'Begor! you proved very good, Miss!' said a grinning cavalier.

'Faith she did!' said another, polishing his shining brow with his white flannel coat-sleeve, 'she lepped like a haarse!'

'And may I ask how you propose to go home?' said I.

'I don't know and I don't care! I'm not going home!' she cast an entirely disobedient eye at me. 'And your eye-glass is hanging down your back and your tie is bulging out over your waistcoat!'

The little group of riders had begun to move away.

'We're going on into Aussolas,' called out Flurry; 'come on, and make my grandmother give you some breakfast, Mrs Yeates; she always has it at eight o'clock.'

The front gates were close at hand, and we turned in under the tall beech-trees, with the unswept leaves rustling round the horses' feet, and the lovely blue of the October morning sky filling the spaces between smooth grey branches and golden leaves. The woods rang with the voices of the hounds, enjoying an untrammelled rabbit hunt, while the Master and the Whip, both on foot, strolled along unconcernedly with their bridles under their arms, making themselves agreeable to my wife, an occasional touch of Flurry's horn, or a crack of Dr Hickey's whip, just indicating to the pack the authorities still took a friendly interest in their doings.

Down a grassy glade in the wood a party of old Mrs Knox's young horses suddenly swept into view, headed by an old mare, who, with her tail over her back, stampeded ponderously past our cavalcade, shaking and swinging her handsome old head, while her youthful friends bucked and kicked and snapped at each other round her with the ferocious humour of their kind.

'Here, Jerome, take the horn,' said Flurry to Dr Hickey; 'I'm going to see Mrs Yeates up to the house, the way these tomfools won't gallop on top of her.'

From this point it seems to me that Philippa's adventures are more worthy of record than mine, and as she has favoured me with a full account of them, I venture to think my version may be relied on.

Mrs Knox was already at breakfast when Philippa was led, quaking, into her formidable presence. My wife's acquaintance with Mrs Knox, was, so far, limited to a state visit on either side, and she found but little comfort in Flurry's assurances that his grandmother wouldn't mind if he brought all the hounds in to breakfast, coupled with the statement that she would put her eyes on sticks for the Major.

Whatever the truth of this may have been, Mrs Knox received her guests with an equanimity quite unshaken by the fact that her boots were in the fender instead of on her feet, and that a couple of shawls of varying dimensions and degrees of age did not conceal the inner presence of a magenta flannel dressing-jacket. She installed Philippa at the table and plied her with food, oblivious as to whether the needful implements with which to eat it were forthcoming or no. She told Flurry where a vixen had reared her family, and she watched him ride away with some biting comments on his mare's hocks screamed after him from the window.

The dining-room at Aussolas Castle is one of the many rooms in Ireland in which Cromwell is said to have stabled his horse (and probably no one would have objected less than Mrs Knox had she been consulted in the matter). Philippa questions if the room had ever been tidied up since, and she endorses Flurry's observations that 'there wasn't a day in the year you wouldn't get feeding for a hen and chicken on the floor.' Opposite to Philippa, on a Louise Quinze chair, sat Mrs Knox's woolly dog, its suspicious little eyes peering at her out of their setting of pink lids and dirty white wool. A couple of young horses outside the window tore at the matted creepers on the walls, or thrust faces that were half-shy, half-impudent, into the room. Portly pigeons waddled to and fro on the broad window-sill, sometimes flying in to perch on the picture-frames, while they kept up incessantly a hoarse and pompous cooing.

Animals and children are, as a rule, alike destructive to conversation; but Mrs Knox, when she chose, *bien entendu*, could have made herself agreeable in a Noah's ark, and Philippa has a gift of sympathetic attention that personal experience has taught me to regard with distrust as well as respect, while it has often made me realize the worldly wisdom of Kingsley's injunction:

'Be good, sweet maid, and let who will be clever.'

Family prayers, declaimed by Mrs Knox with alarming austerity, followed close on breakfast, Philippa and a vinegar-faced henchwoman forming the family. The prayers were long, and through the open window as they progressed came distantly a whoop or two; the declamatory tones staggered a little, and then continued at a distinctly higher rate of speed.

'Ma'am! Ma'am!' whispered a small voice at the window.

Mrs Knox made a repressive gesture and held on her way. A sudden outcry of hounds followed, and the owner of the whisper, a small boy with a face freckled like a turkey's egg, darted from the window and dragged a donkey and bath-chair into view. Philippa admits to having lost the thread of the discourse, but thinks that the 'Amen' that immediately ensued can hardly have come in its usual place. Mrs Knox shut the book abruptly, scrambled up from her knees, and said, 'They've found!'

In a surprising short time she had added to her attire her boots, a fur cape, and a garden hat, and was in the bath-chair, the small boy stimulating the donkey with the success peculiar to his class, while Philippa hung on behind.

The woods of Aussolas are hilly and extensive, and on that particular morning it seemed that they held as many foxes as hounds. In vain was the horn blown and the whips cracked, small rejoicing parties of hounds, each with a fox of its own, scoured to and fro; every labourer in the vicinity had left his work, and was sedulously heading every fox with yells that would have befitted a tiger hunt, and sticks and stones when occasion served.

'Will I pull out as far as the big rosy-dandhrum, ma'am?' inquired the small boy; 'I seen three of the dogs go in it, and they yowling.'

'You will,' said Mrs Knox, thumping the donkey on the back with her umbrella; 'here! Jeremiah Regan! Come down out of that with that pitchfork! Do you want to kill the fox, you fool?'

'I do not, your honour, ma'am,' responded Jeremiah Regan, a tall, young countryman, emerging from a bramble brake.

'Did you see him?' said Mrs Knox eagerly.

'I seen himself and his ten pups drinking below at the lake ere yesterday, your honour, ma'am, and he as big as a chestnut horse!' said Jeremiah.

'Faugh! Yesterday!' snorted Mrs Knox; 'go on to the rhododendrons, Johnny!'

The party, reinforced by Jeremiah and the pitchfork, progressed at a high rate of speed along the shrubbery path, encountering *en route* Lady Knox, stooping on her horse's neck under the sweeping branches of the laurels.

'Your horse is too high for my coverts, Lady Knox,' said the Lady of the Manor, with a malicious eye at Lady Knox's flushed face and dinged hat; 'I'm afraid you will be left behind like Absalom when the hounds go away!'

'As they never do anything here but hunt rabbits,' retorted her ladyship, 'I don't think that's likely.'

Mrs Knox gave her donkey another whack, and passed on.

'Rabbits, my dear!' she said scornfully to Philippa. 'That's all she knows about it. I declare it disgusts me to see a woman of that age making such a Judy of herself! Rabbits indeed!'

Down in the thicket of rhododendron everything was very quiet for a time. Philippa strained her eyes in vain to see any of the riders; the horn blowing and the whip cracking passed on almost out of hearing. Once or twice a hound worked through the rhododendrons, glanced at the party, and hurried on, immersed in business. All at once Johnny, the donkey-boy, whispered excitedly:

'Look at he! Look at he!' and pointed to a boulder of grey rock that stood out among the dark evergreens. A big yellow cub was crouching on it; he instantly slid into the shelter of the bushes, and the irrepressible Jeremiah, uttering a rendering shriek, plunged into the thicket after him. Two or three hounds came rushing at the sound, and after this Philippa says she finds some difficulty in recalling the proper order of events; chiefly, she confesses, because of the wholly ridiculous tears of excitement that blurred her eyes.

'We ran,' she said, 'we simply tore, and the donkey galloped, and as for that old Mrs Knox, she was giving cracked screams to the hounds all the time, and they were screaming too; and then somehow we were all out on the road!'

What seems to have occurred was that three couple of hounds, Jeremiah Regan, and Mrs Knox's equipage, amongst them somehow hustled the cub out of the Aussolas demesne and up on to a hill on the farther side of the road. Jeremiah was sent back by his mistress to fetch Flurry, and the rest of the party pursued a thrilling course along the road, parallel with that of the hounds, who were hunting slowly through the gorse on the hillside.

'Upon my honour and word, Mrs Yeates, my dear, we have the hunt to ourselves!' said Mrs Knox to the panting Philippa, as they pounded along the road. 'Johnny, d'ye see the fox?'

'I do, ma'am!' shrieked Johnny, who possessed the usual field-glass vision bestowed upon his kind. 'Look at him overright us on the hill above! Hi! The spotty dog have him! No, he's gone from him! *Gwan out o' that*' This to the donkey, with blows that sounded like the beating of carpets, and produced rather more dust.

They had left Aussolas some half a mile behind, when, from a strip of wood on their right, the fox suddenly slipped over the bank on to the road just ahead of them, ran up it for a few yards and whisked in at a small entrance gate, with three couple of hounds yelling on a red-hot scent, not thirty yards behind. The bath-chair party whirled in at their heels, Philippa and the donkey considerably blown, Johnny scarlet through his freckles, but as fresh as paint, the old lady blind and deaf to all things save the chase. The hounds went raging through the shrubs beside the drive, and away down a grassy slope towards a shallow glen, in the bottom of which ran a little stream, and after them over the grass bumped the bath-chair. At the stream they turned sharply and run up the glen towards the avenue, which crossed it by means of a rough stone viaduct.

'Pon me conscience, he's into the old culvert!' exclaimed Mrs Knox; 'there was one of my hounds choked there once, long ago! Beat on the donkey, Johnny!'

At this juncture Philippa's narrative again becomes incoherent, not to say breathless. She is, however, positive that it was somewhere about here that the upset of the bath-chair occurred, but she cannot be clear as to whether she picked up the donkey or Mrs Knox, or whether she herself was picked up by Johnny while Mrs Knox picked up the donkey. From my knowledge of Mrs Knox I should say she picked herself up and no one else. At all events, the next salient point is the palpitating moment when Mrs Knox, Johnny and Philippa successively applying an eye to the opening of the culvert by which the stream trickled under the viaduct, while five dripping hounds bayed and leaped around them, discovered by more senses than that of sight that the fox was in it, and furthermore that one of the hounds was in it too.

'There's a sthrong grating before him at the far end,' said Johnny, his head in at the mouth of the hole, his voice sounding as if he were talking into a jug, 'the two of them's fighting in it; they' be choked surely!'

'Then don't stand gabbling there, you little fool, but get in and pull the hound out!' exclaimed Mrs Knox, who was balancing herself on a stone in the stream.

'I'd be in dread, ma'am,' whined Johnny.

'Balderdash!' said the implacable Mrs Knox. 'In with you!'

I understand that Philippa assisted Johnny into the culvert, and presume that it was in so doing that she acquired the two Robinson Crusoe bare footprints which decorated her jacket when I next met her.

'Have you got hold of him yet, Johnny?' cried Mrs Knox up the culvert.

'I have, ma'am, by the tail,' responded Johnny's voice, sepulchral in the depths.

'Can you stir him, Johnny?'

'I cannot, ma'am, and the wather is rising in it.'

'Well, please God, they'll not open the mill dam!' remarked Mrs Knox philosophically to Philippa, as she caught hold of Johnny's dirty ankles. 'Hold on to the tail, Johnny!'

She hauled, with, as might be expected, no appreciable result. 'Run, my dear, and look for somebody, and we'll have that fox yet!'

Philippa ran, whither she knew not, pursued by fearful visions of bursting mill-dams, and maddened foxes at bay. As she sped up the avenue, she heard voices, robust male voices, in a shrubbery, and made for them. Advancing along an embowered walk towards her was what she took for one wild instant to be a funeral; a second glance showed her that it was a party of clergymen of all ages, walking by twos and threes in the dappled shade of the over-arching trees. Obviously she had intruded her sacrilegious presence into a Clerical Meeting. She acknowledges that at this awe-inspiring spectacle she faltered, but the thought of Johnny, the hound, and the fox, suffocating, possibly drowning together in the culvert, nerved her. She does not remember what she said or how she said it, but I fancy she must have conveyed to them the impression that old Mrs Knox was being drowned, as she immediately found herself heading a charge of the Irish Church towards the scene of disaster.

Fate has not always used me well, but on this occasion it was mercifully decreed that I and the other members of the hunt should be privileged to arrive in time to see my wife and her rescue party precipitating themselves down the glen.

'Holy Biddy!' ejaculated Flurry, 'is she running a paper-chase with all the parsons? But look! For pity's sake will you look at my grandmother and my Uncle Eustace?'

Mrs Knox and her sworn enemy the old clergyman, whom I had met at dinner the night before, were standing, apparently in the stream, tugging at two bare legs that projected from a hole in the viaduct, and arguing at the top of their voices. The bath-chair lay on its side with the donkey grazing beside it, on the bank a stout Archdeacon was tendering advice, and the hounds danced and howled round the entire group.

'I tell you, Eliza, you had better let the Archdeacon try,' thundered Mr Hamilton.

'Then I tell you I will not!' vociferated Mrs Knox, with a tug at the end of the sentence that elicited a subterranean lament from Johnny. 'Now who was right about the second grating? I told you so twenty years ago!'

Exactly as Philippa and her rescue party arrived, the efforts of Mrs Knox and her brother-in-law triumphed. The struggling, sopping form of Johnny was slowly drawn from the hole, drenched, speechless, but clinging to the stern of a hound, who, in turn, had its jaws fast in the hindquarters of a limp, yellow cub.

'Oh, it's dead!' wailed Philippa, 'I *did* think I should have been in time to save it!'

'Well, if that doesn't beat all!' said Dr Hickey.

A Genuine Mexican Plug

MARK TWAIN

I RESOLVED to have a horse to ride. I had never seen such wild, free magnificent horsemanship outside of a circus as these picturesquely-clad Mexicans, Californians and Mexicanized Americans displayed in Carson streets every day. How they rode! Leaning just gently forward out of the perpendicular, easy and nonchalant, with broad slough-hat brim blown square up in front, and long *riata* swinging above the head, they swept through the town like the wind! The next minute they were only a sailing puff of dust on the far desert. If they trotted, they sat up gallantly and gracefully, and seemed part of the horse; did not go jiggering up and down after the silly Miss-Nancy fashion of the riding schools. I had quickly learned to tell a horse from a cow, and was full of anxiety to learn more. I was resolved to buy a horse.

While the thought was rankling in my mind, the auctioneer came scurrying through the plaza on a black beast that had as many humps and corners on him as a dromedary, and was necessarily uncomely; but he was 'going, going, at twenty two!—horse, saddle and bridle at twenty-two dollars, gentlemen!' and I could hardly resist.

A man whom I did not know (he turned out to be the auctioneer's brother) noticed the wistful look in my eye, and observed that that was a very remarkable horse to be going at such a price; and added that the saddle alone was worth the money. It was a Spanish saddle, with ponderous *tapidoros*, and furnished with the ungainly sole-leather covering with the unspellable name. I said I had half a notion to bid. Then this keen-eyed person appeared to me to be 'taking my measure'; but I dismissed the suspicion when he spoke, for his manner was full of guileless candor and truthfulness. Said he:

217

'I know that horse—know him well. You are a stranger, I take it, and so you might think he was an American horse, maybe, but I assure you he is not. He is nothing of the kind; but—excuse my speaking in a low voice, other people being near—he is, without the shadow of a doubt, a Genuine Mexican Plug!'

I did not know what a Genuine Mexican Plug was, but there was something about this man's way of saying it, that made me swear inwardly that I would own a Genuine Mexican Plug, or die.

'Has he any other—er—advantages? I inquired, suppressing what eagerness I could.

He hooked his forefinger in the pocket of my army-shirt, led me to one side, and breathed in my ear impressively these words:

'He can out-buck anything in America!'

'Going, going, going—at *twent-ty*-four dollars and a half, gen-'

'Twenty-seven!' I shouted, in a frenzy.

'And sold!' said the auctioneer, and passed over the Genuine Mexican Plug to me.

I could scarcely contain my exultation. I paid the money and put the animal in a neighboring livery-stable to dine and rest himself.

In the afternoon I brought the creature into the plaza, and certain citizens held him by the head, and others by the tail, while I mounted him. As soon as they let go, he placed all his feet in a bunch together, lowered his back, and then suddenly arched it upward, and shot me straight into the air a matter of three or four feet! I came straight down again, lit in the saddle, went instantly up again, came down almost on the high pommel, shot up again, and came down on the horse's neck—all in the space of three or four seconds. Then he rose and stood almost straight up on his hind feet, and I, clasping his lean neck desperately, slid back into the saddle, and held on. He came down, and immediately hoisted his heels into the air, delivering a vicious kick at the sky, and stood on his forefeet. And then down he came once more, and began the original exercise of shooting me straight up again. The third time I went up I heard a stranger say;

'Oh, *don't* he buck, though!'

While I was up, somebody struck the horse a sounding thwack with a leathern strap, and when I arrived again the Genuine Mexican Plug was not there. A Californian youth chased him up and caught him, and asked if he might have a ride. I granted him that luxury. He mounted the Genuine, got lifted into the air once, but sent his spurs home as he descended, and the horse darted away like a telegram. He soared over three fences like a bird, and disappeared down the road toward the Washoe Valley.

I sat down on a stone, with a sigh, and by a natural impulse one of my hands sought my forehead, and the other the base of my stomach. I believe I never appreciated, till then, the poverty of the human machinery—for I still needed a hand or two to place elsewhere. Pen cannot describe how I was jolted up. Imagination cannot conceive how disjointed I was—how internally, externally and universally I was unsettled, mixed up and ruptured. There was a sympathetic crowd around me, though.

One elderly-looking comforter said:

'Stranger, you've been taken in. Everybody in this camp knows that horse. Any child, any Injun, could have told you that he'd buck; his is the very worst devil to buck on the continent of America. You hear *me*. I'm old Curry. *Old* Curry. Old *Abe* Curry. And moreover, he is a simon-pure, out-and-out genuine d-d Mexican plug, and an uncommon mean one at that, too. Why, you turnip, if you had laid low and kept dark, there's chances to buy an *American* horse for mighty little more than you paid for that bloody old foreign relic.'

Lost in the Moors

DIANA PULLEIN-THOMPSON

THE ROAD that runs from Elvanfoot to Moffatt in the lowlands of Scotland, not far from the English border, was no place for a rider, even in the 'fifties, when, with a girl called Ailsa Ravencroft, I rode from John O'Groats to Land's End, so that we should know our own country from top to bottom. It wasn't very long since I had lain in bed for almost a year with tuberculosis, when it was a much-feared disease, for which rest was part of the cure, and I think I also wanted to prove to myself and my relations that I was now completely fit and well.

On that particular day when I was lost on the moors, Ailsa's horse, aptly named None The Wiser (for although pleasant-looking he never seemed to learn any sense), had lost his nerve, hating the foul-smelling lorries which pounded their way through the Scottish landscape, and I had gone on alone after arrangements had sadly been made for him to follow by horsebox. I didn't *feel* alone because I had the company of Favorita, and if I spoke to her she always put back one elegant flea-bitten grey ear to catch my words.

It wasn't agreeable for either of us as we made our way along the shining tarmac, regretting the absence of a verge and flinching at the noise and smell of the traffic. The drivers cared nothing for a solitary rider—many came so close that damp dust spattered us, and the motorbikes irritated us almost beyond endurance. And all the time to our left lay the great tempting moors of Moffatt, desolate, empty and quiet but for the call of the curlews and the distant baaing of sheep.

My map showed a Roman road, a track that ran almost all the way, it seemed, to Moffatt, which was a mile from the place where I had arranged to meet Ailsa at half-past six. No one had been able to tell me whether the way was still open, for no one but the shepherds walked the moors and none of them were to be found. But at Elvanfoot there had been people who were optimistic.

'Och, as likely as not it'll be open,' they told me. 'It's a grand ride when the weather's all right.' But I knew from experience that there were Scotsmen who, when in doubt, said what they thought you wanted to hear.

It wasn't long, however, before the contrast between the busy, exasperating road and the brown sweep of moorland was too much.

'Nothing venture, nothing win,' I told myself, turning up a track that led through a farmstead right to the Roman road.

As I went, my heart lifted and a new spring came into Favorita's long, swinging stride. It was lovely to escape the traffic at last, to canter across damp green fields, with the cool heather-scented breeze in my face and the wide clear sky above, streaked with soaring birds, touched by pale sunshine.

Soon I left the pasture and came to the bleaker moors that seemed to stretch for miles and miles, undulating like corrugated cardboard. Large trees gave way to stunted rowans and then to myrtle; the land grew browner, softer, the grass sparse. For a time the track was there, leading me onwards like a kind friend, and Favorita, my good grey mare, hurried on eagerly with pricked ears and bright eyes.

She had seen so much: a wild and angry sea at John O'Groats; the cold April sleet falling on the long straight road from Wick; Dunrobin Castle white as icing sugar, shuttered and turreted, a landmark for sailors. She had slept anxiously in its stables which she had believed haunted and in countless alien fields, stables and stalls. She had come through Drumochter Pass and stared wonderingly at the lofty Grampians and the naked hideousness of the hydro-electric developments. She had waited impatiently outside shops while we bought provisions, drunk deeply from burns and rushing rivers and buckets brought by well-wishers on the way. Now her Arab blood from the Royal Stud of Hungary which gave her courage, intelligence and a strong, impatient will, was to be tested in the wild, bog-ridden country that lay before us. But, although she could not be expected to have the native sense of an Exmoor or Fell pony, she had learned stoicism as a second whipper-in's horse, turning back into woods to bring out lost or lagging hounds while all her friends galloped on. As a brood mare she had gained a certain calmness and, in dressage tests, some self control.

Presently the Roman road narrowed, becoming, I thought, too winding and uncertain to be genuine, and, when we had covered about seven miles, it petered out. Now the shadows were lengthening with late afternoon. Round and beautiful, the sun was drifting behind clouds in the western sky. There were great gullies—the dips in the corrugated cardboard—which were to plague us all the way, and then, quite suddenly, quite horribly, a shining, glinting, brand new barbed wire fence stretching like a thin silver scar to right and left across the landscape as far as the eye could see.

I felt a sudden catch at the heart, as you can guess. Should I turn back and retrace the seven miles to that horrible road? No, I hate turning back. It goes against the very core of my nature. But if there was no path, how could I find my way across the moors? Supposing night came down and I rode in mad circles? Well then, I should come back here to the fence and perhaps pick up the track again and then the road, guided by the lights of the long-distance lorries making their way to England. A compass? I realised then, with a twinge of anger at myself, that I had left it with Ailsa. Determined to travel light, I had emptied a heap of belongings from my saddle bags for her to take in the horsebox. But I had a map, two miles to the inch; the sun was still visible in the changing sky, and my watch still ticked.

'When in doubt, go *on*,' I told myself. 'Never turn back.'

The posts rose eight inches above the wire, so I knew what to do, to lessen the chance of an accident. I fished Favorita's halter out of a saddle bag and tied it from one post to another where the ground seemed firmest. Then I unrolled my mackintosh and hung it over the halter, making that part of the fence into a formidable-looking jump. The top was now some six inches higher than the highest strand of wire and if Favorita made a mistake, which wasn't likely, she would probably hit the rope, which might cause her to fall but would not cut her. The obstacle had a solidness which would make her stand back and take care. She had never yet hit any jump hard enough to bring her to her knees. And she was no fool. She had jumped the timber waggon you can see in the photograph of Lorraine often without hesitation or fault. If anything, she was over-careful.

I mounted her again and, without waiting for any command, she swung round and took me over the jump (for had she not in her youth waited many a time while I made her obstacles out of petrol cans and rustic poles?). She landed heavily and the soil under her hoofs gave way with awful sucking noises, but she righted herself and with an effort pulled herself out and waited to be congratulated with a pat and a word of praise.

Halter and mackintosh back in their places, we continued on our way, stopping every now and then to consult the map, sun and watch. It was now ten minutes past five, so I presumed the sun would soon be due west and chose my direction according-ly, but the contours worried me, and I wished I had listened more carefully during geography lessons at school. Perhaps if I had grasped the nettle of longtitude and latitude more thoroughly I could have found the map more useful now that I was lost.

There only seemed to be crazy sheep paths that wound here and there and took us nowhere. The sheep who made them having been concerned with picking the best fodder and not with finding their way to Moffatt, or anywhere else for that matter, except perhaps to water when the hot August sun beat down on the shadeless acres. We were forced to make our way across untrodden land, where the ground grew softer the further we went until it squelched under us like a sponge being squeezed out of water.

Frightened of bogs, and already seeing Favorita sinking from sight before my very eyes, I dismounted and walked ahead, testing the ground as we went. But she was impatient to finish the journey and enjoy a feed of oats. She felt the first whispers of night in the soft air and heard it in the last eerie calls of the curlews. It was all I could do to keep her behind me and she made the most ridiculous suggestions about which directions we should take, not aware that we were heading for Moffatt— or so I hoped. It is amazing how small and solitary you feel when lost in open landscape, how wide the sky seems and how quickly dusk comes.

I wanted to keep the great curve of the highest hill to my left. I wanted to see another road, marked on the map as leading down into Moffatt, but there was nothing except the corrugated cardboard, and the sky, now empty of birds, and the golden glow of sunlight. Hues of grey and brown don't lighten the spirits and lift the heart. My thoughts became gloomy and Favorita only wanted to be off the moor and heading for— where? Home, I supposed, still hundreds of miles away.

The gullies grew deeper, sharper and more frequent, their steep sides made hazardous by boulders. Little streams of peaty brown water gurgled fitfully through their bowels. Myrtle grew on their banks.

I hated them, each one seemed worse than the last and the descent was always difficult with Favorita on my heels. Her patience was almost at an end. She wanted to go first, knowing she could manage the boulders without my guiding hand, and, after a while, I let her loose, to find that she always waited for me on the other side, taking the opportunity to pull at the heather and the sparse, nearly colourless grass.

I do not know how many miles we covered in this manner or whether I always kept in the direction I intended. When the ground was firmer I rode, and we made better time. Our side of the world passed the sun's rim, and the sky became blank and greyer still with the approach of night. The moors lay silent before me, hateful, treacherous and cruel, a place where people could die for lack of shade or shelter and sheep lay in winter deep in snowdrifts. With two sweaters under my coat I was warm, and, with spring far advanced, I was not much afraid of a night in the open, but I thought of Ailsa with None The Wiser dragging her around at the end of his halter rope on that little road beyond Moffatt. She would be waiting outside Oakridge Farm, just a name on the map to us and the point we had chosen as our meeting place, perhaps thinking of search parties. And how tiresome to be the cause of a search party, to be so inefficient that people had to forsake their leisure hours to comb the moors for someone who should have known better than to venture there alone without a compass. We had eaten digestive biscuits and cheese for lunch, but now, with my stomach rumbling, hunger added to the gloom.

My map reading was a failure. The road I wanted was not

even on the skyline. Even allowing for obstacles and a break of fifteen minutes to rest I should have crossed the moors by six o'clock. It was now half-past, and the moors seemed endless. The very sight and smell of them began to fill me with disgust. And the brown hill on my left was a traitor, not being where the map told me it should be.

My mother was fond of saying, 'Always darkest before dawn,' and it was this thought which consoled me as I rode down yet another gully, skirting the boulders, hitting angrily at an innocent twig or myrtle with my stick. As I came up the other side, I felt my heart lift again, for there, a few hundred yards away, was another road, black and stretched out across the landscape like a snake reaching to snatch its prey.

Never have I welcomed a road more ardently. Standing on my stirrups, I could see a few cars passing along it like insects on a curve of black earth, and, now and then, a lorry. I patted Favorita's firm freckled back.

'You'll soon be gobbling oats, and thank you for being so good,' I said.

She wouldn't wait for me to look at the map, or rather I could have *made* her, but I didn't. After all, she had suffered enough already on the long and tedious journey over terrain for which she had not been bred. I would still be late, but probably only an hour or so and I would reach Moffatt well before dark. The ground seemed firmer to my now optimistic eyes, and I pushed Favorita into a trot so that we soon reached the road, which was wide and curving with a white line down the middle. And then my heart went down again, for I saw my old enemy was there, older than the last one of its kind and rusty here and there, but firm—another barbed wire fence. And I couldn't jump Favorita over this one because there was no verge to the road and that meant we would have to land on the slippery tarmac.

Dismounted, I walked up and down, rocking posts to see if one was loose, but they were all strong and resisted me like rocks. I wished I was a huntsman with clippers attached to a dee on my saddle. I would have to follow the fence until I found a gap or a gate, but would I find one? And which road was it on the map, this or that? I felt bemused. Had I started to go in circles? Could it be the road I had left just after half past two, or the one I wanted? And which hill was that? All at once my self-confidence had gone. I waved to the motorists in the hope that one would stop and offer help, but although some waved back gaily, others ignored me and none stopped. Favorita dragged at the reins, then rubbed her head against me, nearly knocking me other. My legs began to feel like lead, and my heart scarcely lighter, when suddenly Favorita's head went up and I heard a welcome sound.

It was like hearing the bark of a lost dog and knowing that he is still alive, such was my relief. Looking into the brown distance, I saw a two-legged figure coming down a hillside, and on his left, pale dots which were the gathering sheep.

'Hi, Help! Hi, Help!'

The wind was against me, pushing back the sound.

'Holt, holt,' called the shepherd.

I turned Favorita round to face those specks in the distance. 'A grey horse is a wonderful landmark,' I said, as she stood like a statue, watching, her head very high, clean-cut in profile, with a wide cheek and a forehead so broad that a brow band had had to be made specially for her. Her face tapered sharply to a delicate muzzle the colour of the underside of field mushrooms, pinky grey, soft and plushy. Now her nostrils were wide and her breath came quickly as she sniffed the air and listened to the shepherd whistling to his dog.

I remounted, waved with both arms and gave a loud holloa, for suddenly the shadow of dusk had fallen over the hills, heralding the darkness which was soon to come. Should I ride down and meet the shepherd, or wait for him and rest my horse? Favorita, excited by the new hope she felt in me, the whistling and moving sheep, decided the matter by breaking into a brisk trot. And that was our undoing for, before I had even picked up the reins, I felt her sinking and heard the ominous squelch of ground sucking us downward.

In such moments I die a thousand deaths, and now in my imagination the treacherous peaty substance was in mouth, the liquid blinding my eyes and stifling my breath, and the sounds of life dimmed for ever in my ears.

But instinct always comes to the rescue. Without conscious though, I flung myself clear, landing on squelchy ground yet out of the bog. But what of Favorita? Her dismayed dark eyes

were looking straight into mine and there was no fight in them, only that pained surprise, as though she was saying, 'Where have you taken me *now*? What have you done?'

'Up, up, Favorita! Come on, up, up.'

In that wide expanse of land and sky my voice was a sad trickle of sound. 'Up, up!'

As I had flung myself clear I had at least had the sense to bring the reins with me, and now I pulled on these by way of encouragement, by heart hitting my ribs in hammer blows.

'Come on, up, up!'

But the sludge was rising higher on her flea-bitten grey sides, over the elbows it went and above her stifles. Was there no bottom? Were bogs without end?

Here, disappearing before my very eyes, was the horse I had bought as an iron-grey four-year-old, a mare sold cheap because she was going to be difficult to break, having an awkward temperament, it was said. And now she was more than a horse to me, because over the years we had shared so many adventures. She was a friend struggling for her life, far from home and those kinder Chilterns where she had spent the greater part of her life.

I loosened the reins, thinking she might wish to use her neck as a pivot, and said a silent prayer, and she sank further so that the sludge rose to the bottom of the saddle flaps.

'Up, up, Favorita! Come on, up!'

I made as though to hit her, and suddenly the light in her eyes changed, the heavy look of dismay vanished and was replaced by one of fear, then terror. She began to kick and to struggle as though she had come out of a dream into a terrible reality. She threw her head about. She floundered and heaved and puffed and panted, her nostrils wide, her sides heaving, and somewhere she must have hit firmer ground, for all at once I saw her chest again. She moved forward as well as upwards; her girth was visible, her elbows, dark with the liquid of the bog; her knees chocolate brown. Never have I been gladder to see knees, tendons, and a pair of fine fetlocks.

Then she was free. She was out, scrambling to firmer ground, her breath coming like air from a blacksmith's bellows, her eyes protruding like great marbles, glassy with fear.

'Oh, Favorita. Oh, Favorita!'

What does one say on such occasions? I patted her a score of times. I put my arm across her neck and cuddled her. And then I noted the dark blood like blackcurrant juice oozing from a puncture by a tendon. A punctured vein? How many more trials were to be sent to us? Had I a good strong handkerchief, a pencil or a stick to make a tourniquet? I put my thumb on the wound and pressed, and after a time the bleeding stopped. The puncture was deep, but the vein was uninjured as far as I could see.

Now the whistling of the shepherd was louder. Looking round, I saw he was a couple of hundred yards away and coming at last in our direction. I waved my arms and shouted. He left the dog looking after the sheep and came striding towards us with that spring in his step which belongs only to men who spend many hours on the hills walking across heather, and moss and myrtle. Handsome and aquiline, with a crook in his hand, he stood looking down on me as though I was a freak gone wilfully astray.

I was beginning to feel a little incoherent.

'She's cut her leg. We landed in a bog. Can you help? I want Moffatt. I have a friend to meet in Moffatt.'

His dark angular face showed no emotion, as though people like me were common and tiresome occurrences that interrupted an honest and hard-working man's work.

'Is it far—Moffatt, I mean?'

'It's a wee way to be sure, nine miles when you reach the road.'

'Nine miles!'

'Och, maybe a little less.'

'And how can I get on to the road? I mean—the fence — I want to be quick because of my horse's leg. You see it's swelling already.'

'I saw you earlier. I thought you knew the way.'

'So did I.'

He wasn't a horseman. He couldn't have been, because he didn't even glance at the wound. He waved a long arm.

'Go up that way, and at the top of yon hill there's a gate, which will take you out on the old Edinburgh road.'

'Like that, diagonally?' I pointed.

'Yes, and when you get through the gate, follow the fence

down to the road, and keep going down all the way to Moffatt.'

'How do I avoid bogs?'

'Keep to the sheep paths.'

'But they wind this way and that.'

'Och.' He gave a gesture of impatience, a frown lying like a ridge across his leather-tanned celtic brow. 'Keep to the dry land.'

'Thank you.'

'Avoid the brown patches,' he added, allowing the smallest of smiles.

'There was a brand new barbed wire fence across the right of way,' I said, encouraged.

'Put up a month back,' he replied.

'Well, goodbye then.'

We set off up the hill, which was steeper than it looked, and as we climbed the land grew firmer, but Favorita was lame so I would not ride. At the top there was no gate, only the same rusty fence.

I felt near to tears. Nine miles to go when we reached the road, and tomorrow sixteen miles to Lockerbie and then Gretna Green, and my horse was lame! The total journey to Land's End was to be between eight and nine hundred miles in all and we were not even half way and — and —

But what was the use of letting one's thoughts run in that vein? 'Deal with the matter in hand,' I told myself. And then I was lucky, for I spotted a broken strand of wire and saw that a slim verge ran along the road on the other side. The highest remaining strand was only about two feet nine inches off the ground, so I draped my mac across it and tried to make Favorita follow me over, but she jibbed. In exasperation I mounted, and then she jumped it at once, lame though she was.

At last we were on the road. Dusk was far advanced and passing cars had their lights on. My feet were blistered but I wasn't tired once I knew I was on my way to Moffatt. The sticking plaster was with Ailsa, but in a saddle bag I had a pair of socks with leather soles which someone had given me, and I quickly exchanged these for my jodphur boots. The air was fresh, the cars were few and, far away down in the valley, I could see lights coming on like the first stars, golden and twinkling. Favorita was limping but cheerful, and occasionally she stopped to snatch some grass. Eight o'clock came and I had a look at the map, to see that I had come down from Bog Hill and that on my left was the Devil's Beef Tub, a black abyss surrounded by four hills where the Annandale loons used to hide their stolen cattle. Here, too, in 1745, a Highlander had escaped capture and almost certain death by wrapping himself in his plaid and rolling like a hedgehog to the bottom of the Tub. I did not envy him the journey down.

Eight o'clock, nine o'clock, and there was a police car, climbing the hill towards me. It drew to a halt.

'Miss Ravencroft's companion?'

'Yes, I suppose you could call me that.'

'She said if we met you to say she was settled in at Oakridge Farm. Everything is arranged. You take the right turn the other side of the town.'

'Thank you. How far?'

'A mile and a half to the farm.'

'But to Moffatt?'

'Four or so.'

'Four!'

'Well, maybe a wee bit less, three and a half, perhaps.'

'I shall need a vet.'

'The farmer will help you.'

They drove away, and below me lay the valley, where I could now make out whitewashed cottages, dark firs, with the lights increasing as the curtain of darkness came down from the hills. I let Favorita graze for a time, taking the bit out of her mouth, and then we continued on our way.

Those last four miles seemed interminable, and my legs began to ache. But at last we were in the sleepy town and, catching sight of myself in a shop window, I realised how ridiculous and bedraggled I looked. Vanity make me put on the boots again, drag a comb through my hair and set my crash hat straight. I took the right turn and passed through kinder domesticated country with large trees, then I saw an old car approaching, and, besides the moustached driver, a familiar face.

'Found at last!'

Ailsa stepped out, blue-eyed, blonde, with her thick hair plaited into a pigtail. 'What happened?'

'My mother has everything ready for you,' said the man with the moustache. 'The beds are made up and tea is on the table.'

The man's name was Cameron Rankin, and he had a bull pen waiting for Favorita to share with None The Wiser, and, in no time, he was bathing her wound, while she was deep in a bucket of the best Scots oats.

So the long day ended by a warm fire with high tea at half-past ten at night, boiled eggs and scones, baps and cakes, and Cameron Rankin's father telling us tales of Nottingham where he had been brought up.

I learned that they had found Ailsa at the gate and offered hospitality, having read about our journey in the newspaper, and would accept no payment. In the morning, the vet came and packed Favorita's wound with penicillin, bandaged it, and injected her against tetanus, and by afternoon we were on our way, for I was told that walking would stop her leg stiffening. I led her the sixteen miles to Lockerbie, and we put up at a large hotel, a once-only extravagance, with a park in which the horses spent the next morning.

The following day Favorita was sound, and we rode on to Gretna Green—where not one of the famous blacksmiths knew how to shoe a horse.

It was summer when we reached Land's End on schedule, forty-two days after we left John O'Groats. While we admired the great white-crested waves of the Atlantic, an uninvited RSPCA Inspector looked at the horses and declared them very fit.

There had been many fearful, happy and moving experiences on the journey. But the most frightening still exists for me in those moments, when a dismayed Favorita sank down in the bog and I stood by utterly helpless, holding the reins.

Ballinasloe Buys
and Point-to-Points

MARJORIE QUARTON

O F ALL Ireland's fairs, Ballinasloe must surely be the most famous. It has a marvellous green, quite the best selling arena of any Irish fair. Only Limerick, before most of the green was built over, could compete with Ballinasloe.

The October horsefair is one which has survived against all odds, probably because there is a keen committee to keep it going, and it is in direct line from Dublin to tourist country in the west. A horse auction at Galway racecourse was tried, but flopped. Ballinasloe fair is still alive and kicking. There is a ring with practice jumps and, quite apart from the agricultural show across the road, generous prizes are offered for the best animal in the fair in each category.

It used to be possible to gallop a horse on the green, but I wouldn't advise it now. Movement is restricted by chip vans, sightseers, stray dogs, tiny and often unattended children, and hawkers. It is still possible to buy good horses there, but supplies are short, prices asked sometimes fanciful and competition strong.

I used to park my car out of harm's way, which was a long way off, and walk down the steep dirt path at the town end of the green. This was where lorries were loaded and unloaded. You could see from the steps up to the street how the fair was divided in two by the tarred road. Factory horses, tinkers' ponies and general flotsam to the right; better class animals to the left. Apart from being a good spot for viewing the fair at large, this was a great place for watching the horses arriving, and for picking up any useful bits of information that were

going. I have never known anywhere like Ballinasloe for the spreading of rumours.

Some of these were started deliberately for a joke. Unlike the street fairs, Ballinasloe attracts as many private buyers as dealers. On the rest of the circuit you saw the same faces again and again. Ballinasloe was full of strangers.

'That's the Duke of Beaufort; he's looking for six hunters. He's loaded!' I don't know how the rumour started, but the man in question, a visiting English hunting man having a look round, was almost mobbed. He looked about him in some alarm as he was surrounded on all sides by people riding or dragging horses which they hoped he would buy. Some blockers tugged at his arms, other shouted or whispered in his ears according to their preferred technique.

Freeing himself with difficulty, he hurried away, probably for a stiff drink in the hotel. He did not reappear.

Many will remember the day of the Russian Buyer. I was there myself at the outset, but didn't suspect where a simple remark would lead.

I was talking to a Galway man called Joe MacNamara. We were looking at a bunch of ponies which had all been sold together to one man. The man was checking his ponies' legs and teeth, putting halters on them and so on. Then he pulled out his wallet and counted out a large sum of money in notes. I think it was Joe who said to him, 'You rushed into that deal, didn't you? I never saw such a rushin' buyer.' Several other people were passing by. The remark was overheard.

I walked off, and thought no more about it. Then the rumours began to fly.

'Have you seen any Russians here? I heard there was one buying.'

'You won't get any troopers today, the Russian Buyer is after them.'

'Have you seen the Russian Buyer? He's looking for a hundred horses for the Russian Army.'

'There's the Russian Buyer—look!'

A tall pale-complexioned man in a fur hat was inspecting a horse, and at once a crowd collected. Somebody pushed forward and asked the fur-hatted one, 'Do you talk English?'

'What the hell are you raving about? Who do you think I am, the Russian Buyer?'

'Are you not from Russia then?'

'No, I'm from Mullingar,' said the man.

* * *

It was not a good idea to stay in Ballinasloe overnight on the Sunday. Not, that is, if you wanted to sleep. We were going to do so once and decided against it. I used to go home, forty miles, and return on Monday when my funds were severely limited. Later I stayed at Athlone or Banagher if I wanted to be on the move early on Monday.

As Monday progressed, the better-class horses thinned out, and droves of Clydesdale-type youngsters began to come in, mainly from the North Midlands. They ran loose, and I can remember when they fetched a pound a leg, or a fiver for a good one. These would be mostly yearlings. Older horses of the same type would make £15 to £40, but their value was dictated by their weight.

Later on Monday, preparations started for the great sheep fair on the Tuesday. The horses would gradually be edged out of the way as lorry loads of sheep pens arrived and were erected. (Riders schooled their horses over these, knocking them flat, and getting richly deserved abuse.) Soon after, the sheep began to stream in from all sides. By mid-afternoon, all the roads leading to the green were crammed with sheep travelling on foot, while lorry drivers inched their way along, carrying yet more sheep, and other lorries tried to get away with loads of horses.

Ballinasloe seemed to have the best and the worst to offer. The 'in-between horse', a category including Swiss troopers and average working hunters, were often scarce. You could see an unsurpassed show of high-class ridden hunters, show-ring winning three-year-olds and some of the best foals in the country. A few yards away, a mob of tired, ancient donkeys would be changing hands.

Talking of donkeys, I recall an incident a few years back which was the talk of the fair. A farmer took a donkey to the fair and sold him to a neighbour for £20 cash. The neighbour paid and the two went off and had a drink on the deal. Possibly two drinks. They were gone for some time, and left the donkey tied to the fence. After a while, another buyer noticed the donkey tied to the fence and a tinker standing near. 'What do you want for the ass?' he asked the tinker.

'£30,' said the tinker.

After some bargaining, a price of £20 was agreed on, and buyer number two paid the tinker, also in cash. The tinker then prudently vanished, and buyer number two led the donkey away. He was leaving the green when he was overtaken by buyer number one, returning from the pub.

'Where are you going with the ass?'

'He's my own. I bought him off a tinker for £20. I'm taking him home.'

'You are not. I bought him off this man here for the same money.' A noisy row developed; sides were taken, a crowd gathered.

The first buyer got the donkey. The second went home, sadder, wiser and poorer.

* * *

My first Ballinasloe buy was a thin bay three-year-old by Daunton which had been ridden twenty miles to the fair. All his four shoes, worn as thin as paper, were broken at the toe, hanging by the odd nail, clinking as he moved. I called him

Clinker, but it was changed to the finer-sounding Dauntless when I sold him. He won jumping competitions and carried a huntsman for many years.

It looked like a false economy, saving on the price of a set of shoes, and perhaps missing a sale. Clinker could easily have gashed his leg with his broken shoes. Other horses were brought long distances unshod, and arrived too footsore to show themselves off properly.

Saddlery was hardly the word for the assortment of tack sported by the horses for sale at the fairs. Strange bits were unearthed and polished up, long-cheeked Hanoverian pelhams, military reversables, and rubber snaffles with no rubber left on them. I have been asked to ride a horse with a round 'Chifney' bit in its mouth, an article only used for leading yearlings. I refused.

I have encountered strange saddles too. Great army saddles, more suited to pack animals, with wooden panels and blankets underneath; half-pound racing saddles whose stirrups I could barely get a toe into; even a battered Western saddle, only lacking a lariat.

At home, I rode on either an old Indian-made polo saddle or on one of two Whippys. All three were very flat, without knee rolls. You could mount and dismount with the minimum of fuss, a good thing with green horses. Also, you could lie across one of these saddles while your horse decided whether to accept the weight on his back or not. Lying across a modern saddle would be at best painful. I felt trapped on a hollow-seated saddle, unable to bale out neatly in an emergency. I wouldn't however go as far as a farmer who was showing his horse bare-backed, although it wore a double bridle and an obviously redundant martingale, tied in a knot.

'I never use a saddle,' he said. 'They're treacherous old things. They could trap you and kill you in a minute.'

At the other extreme was an anxious young man in Thurles fair, whose evident fear was communicating itself to his horse which curvetted about, chewing its bit and snorting. I noticed with horror that the young man had tied his feet into his stirrup irons by his shoelaces. I might never have bought that horse, but I was so anxious that the young man should be untied before it threw him, that I asked for a ride on it. He agreed eagerly, and his friends untied him. The horse, named Blarney Stone, was a successful showjumper after I sold him.

This reminds me of a gallant hunting farmer who thought he'd ride his hunter in the half-bred race at our point-to-point. He was a poor horseman who used to slide off over his horse's tail quite often when it was jumping onto banks. Provided with a seven-pound saddle, weight cloth and surcingle by the jockey's valet, he saddled up his horse. He then got somebody to give him a leg up, and asked his supporters to put the surcingle round his legs as well as round the saddle—tie him on in fact. The surcingle wasn't long enough; his friends went in search of some rope. The stewards were alerted and stopped his caper. He fell off at the first fence and walked back complaining that, but for the stewards' interference, he might have won.

*   *   *

These point-to-points of ours were terrifying affairs. I can scarcely remember the old course, when the horses raced across the public road. My mother vividly remembered watching her first race there—won by the nurse from the workhouse, riding the priest's horse. The new course, alongside a main road for much of its length, was used for many years. The fences included trappy single banks, a stone wall and an appalling water jump. This last was a deep trench, lined on the landing side with sleepers, with the flimsiest of take-off fences. It divided two ploughed fields, where we raced on the muddy headlands.

One lady used to sit in her car with a rug over her head when her son was riding, only coming out when the cheers told her that the race was over.

My first appearance on this course was in a half-bred event, officially named 'The Sportsman's Race'. The title was not well chosen. The race became the centre of some sort of conspiracy which went on for weeks beforehand. Nine of us took part in the race, in icy rain and mud (it was a February fixture). There were five fallers, and one horse was killed. My Matilda was a close third, far from disgraced as she was less than half bred, the first two almost thoroughbred.

All the horses involved in the conspiracy were fallers.

Our hunting correspondent had plenty to say. After a mention of an earlier event when he referred to 'the returning sportsmen, covered with blood and foam', we went on to describe 'the Dianas and the boys, so plastered with mud as to be unrecognisable'.

The following year, the Sportsman's Race was a calmer affair, no betting *coups* were planned, and there was less mud. I managed to finish second, but have never won a race. By degrees, some of the more dangerous obstacles were eliminated, others were faced with birch, but our natural course remained pretty hazardous. The Sportsman's Race, the sixth or seventh on the card, was sometimes run in the dusk.

The riders wore 'hunting attire' which could mean anything. One or two sported colours. There was a time when the jockeys' valet had only one cap to offer, and two riders came to blows over who should have it. The winner wore the crash skull, the loser put on the silk cover like a sun-bonnet, with the strings died under his chin. Neither was concerned with the finish. The horse of the bonneted one galloped off the course and plunged into the Nenagh river. I don't remember how they were got out, as I had my own survival to consider.

* * *

Horses are great swimmers—any cowboy movie will show this. As a small child I was taken to Whitegate in Co. Clare to see some cattle and a horse being swum across Lough Derg to Islandmore. This lake island covers two hundred acres. In recent years, grain was grown there, and it has any amount of game. At the time I'm talking of, it was all grazing except for the potatoes and vegetables grown by the people who live there. The lived by eel-fishing and farming, and retired to a house on the mainland some years ago.

They had a heavy rowing boat, and a swimming cow tied to the back of it to lead the other cattle and the horse. The cow was red and white, with great spreading horns, and swam unconcernedly behind the boat.

My father had a polo pony in Malta which made a determined effort to swim back to his native Egypt when the men and horses were bathing together: an attempt which nearly drowned them both.

I have only once been on a swimming horse. I am well aware that one should not remain on its back for fear of drowning it—cowboys swim alongside, offering encouragement. My swim was unintentional; I don't like cold baths. My horse Matilda's head and my own were just above the water as we, or rather she, struck out across the flooded Ballinahenry River, one day out hunting. An animal called Snowball rolled down the bank, lost his rider in several feet of water, and drifted downstream. There he became entangled in the top of a submerged willow tree.

When the rider surfaced, some eager helpers who'd pulled him out asked, 'How are you going to rescue Snowball?' The answer was, 'I don't think I'll bother.'

This unwelcome bath on a cold January day made several of us reckless foxhunters a lot more careful. After that, I almost always managed at least to keep my head above water.

My only other ducking occurred during one of those hair-raising point-to-points I mentioned earlier. Mind you, I didn't deserve to get round in one piece. My horse was the little showjumper Sugar Bush, fifteen hands high and three years old. She could gallop for her size, and I had no doubt of her stamina, but she was a shocking ride over banks. If she could see over them she flew them, landing in the ditch on the landing side if there was one. If she couldn't see over, she kicked back at them. This is all right in theory, but her kick usually missed. An accurate kick-back lifts a horse yards away from the fence, a missed one drops him as if he'd fallen out of a tree.

Sugar Bush was feeling the effects of a fortnight of concentrated schooling. She had jumped every fence perfectly when we reached that deadly water jump, and was just behind the leader, with an animal called Upper Ormond slightly behind and beside her. Upper Ormond cannoned into my mare's back end when she was in mid-air, sending us crashing through the wing, and into the river of which the water jump was a tributary. I landed first, at the bottom of four feet of muddy water. Sugar Bush sat on me briefly, and fortunately decided to move away. Yes, I know I said I'd only once been on a swimming horse—this one was more of a sinker.

When I struggled gasping out of the water, I saw my cap (borrowed for the occasion, my own wasn't fit to be seen). It was bobbing its way downstream, and I had to go after it and rescue it.

As I squelched my way back to the paddock, a number of people asked me, 'Did you fall off?' 'Where's your horse?' and even 'Did you get a wetting?' Luckily, my teeth were chattering too much for me to answer.

A Happy Ending

ANNA SEWELL

I WAS SOLD to a corn dealer and baker whom Jerry knew, and with him he thought I should have good food and fair work. In the first he was quite right, and if my master had always been on the premises, I do not think I should have been overloaded, but there was a foreman who was always hurrying and driving everyone, and frequently when I had quite a full load, he would order something else to be taken on. My carter, whose name was Jakes, often said it was more than I ought to take, but the other always overruled him: ' 'Twas no use going twice when once would do, and he chose to get business forward.'

Jakes, like the other carters, always had the bearing rein up, which prevented me from drawing easily, and by the time I had been there three or four months, I found the work telling very much on my strength.

One day, I was loaded more than usual, and part of the road was a steep uphill. I used all my strength, but I could not get on, and was obliged continually to stop. This did not please my driver, and he laid his whip on badly. 'Get on, you lazy fellow,' he said, 'or I'll make you.'

Again I started the heavy load, and struggled on a few yards: again the whip came down, and again I struggled forward. The pain of that great cart whip was sharp, but my mind was hurt quite as much as my poor sides. To be punished and abused when I was doing my best was so hard, it took the heart out of me. A third time he was flogging me cruelly, when a lady stepped quickly up to him, and said in a sweet, earnest voice:

'Oh! pray do not whip your good horse any more; I am sure he is doing all he can, and the road is very steep, I am sure he is doing his best.'

'If doing his best won't get this load up, he must do something more than his best; that's all I know, ma'am,' said Jakes.

'But is it not a very heavy load?' she said.

'Yes, yes, too heavy,' he said, 'but that's not my fault. The foreman came just as we were starting, and would have three hundredweight more put on to save him trouble, and I must get on with it as well as I can.'

He was raising his whip again, when the lady said:

'Pray, stop. I think I can help if you will let me.'

The man laughed.

'You see,' she said, 'you do not give him a fair chance; he cannot use all his power with his head held back as it is with that bearing rein; if you would take it off, I am sure he would do better—*do* try it,' she said persuasively. 'I should be very glad if you would.'

'Well, well,' said Jakes, with a short laugh, 'anything to please a lady, of course. How far would you wish it down, ma'am?'

'Quite down, give him his head altogether.'

The rein was taken off, and in a moment I put my head down to my knees. What a comfort it was. Then I tossed it up and down several times to get the aching stiffness out of my neck.

'Poor fellow! That is what you wanted,' said she, patting and stroking me with her gentle hand; 'and now if you will speak kindly to him and lead him on, I believe he will be able to do better.'

Jakes took the rein—'Come on, Blackie.' I put down my head, and threw my weight against the collar; I spared no strength. The load moved on, and I pulled it steadily up the hill, and then stopped to take breath.

The lady had walked along the footpath, and now came across into the road. She stroked and patted my neck, as I had not been patted for many a long day.

'You see he was quite willing when you gave him the chance; I am sure he is a fine-tempered creature, and I dare say has known better days. You won't put that rein on again, will you?' for he was just going to hitch it up on the old plan.

'Well, ma'am, I can't deny that having his head has helped him up the hill, and I'll remember it another time, and thank you, ma'am; but if he went without a bearing-rein, I should be the laughing-stock of all the carters; it is the fashion, you see.'

'Is it not better,' she said, 'to lead a good fashion, than to follow a bad one? A great many gentlemen do not use bearing reins now; our carriage horses have not worn them for fifteen years, and work with much less fatigue than those who have them. Besides,' she added in a very serious voice, 'we have no right to distress any of God's creatures without a very good

245

reason; we call them dumb animals, and so they are, for they cannot tell us how they feel, but they do not suffer less because they have no words. But I must not detain you now; I thank you for trying my plan with your good horse, and I am sure you will find it far better than the whip. Good day,' and with another soft pat on my neck she stepped lightly across the path, and I saw her no more.

'That was a real lady, I'll be bound for it,' said Jakes to himself; 'she spoke just as polite as if I was a gentleman, and I'll try her plan, uphill, at any rate;' and I must do him the justice to say, that he let my rein out several holes, and going uphill after that, he always gave me my head; but the heavy loads went on. Good feed and fair rest will keep up one's strength under full work, but no horse can stand against overloading; and I was getting so thoroughly pulled down from this cause, that a younger horse was bought in my place. I may as well mention here what I suffered at this time from another cause. I had heard horses speak of it, but had never myself had experience of the evil; this was a badly-lighted stable; there was only one very small window at the end, and the consequence was that the stalls were almost dark.

Besides the depressing effect this had on my spirits, it very much weakened my sight, and when I was suddenly brought out of the darkness into the glare of daylight, it was very painful to my eyes. Several times I stumbled over the threshold, and could scarcely see where I was going.

I believe, had I stayed there very long, I should have become purblind, and that would have been a great misfortune, for I have heard men say that a stone-blind horse was safer to drive than one which had imperfect sight, as it generally makes them very timid. However, I escaped without any permanent injury to my sight, and was sold to a large cab owner.

* * *

I shall never forget my new master; he had black eyes and a hook nose, his mouth was as full of teeth as a bulldog's, and his voice was as harsh as the grinding of cart wheels over gravel stones. His name was Nicholas Skinner, and I believe he was the same man that poor Seedy Sam drove for.

I have heard men say that seeing is believing; but I should say that *feeling* is believing; for much as I had seen before, I never knew till now the utter misery of a cab-horse's life.

Skinner had a low set of cabs and a low set of drivers; he was hard on the men, and the men were hard on the horses. In this place we had no Sunday rest, and it was in the heat of summer.

Sometimes on a Sunday morning, a party of fast men would hire the cab for the day; four of them inside and another with the driver, and I had to take them ten or fifteen miles out into the country, and back again: never would any of them get down to walk up a hill, let it be ever so steep, or the day ever so hot—unless, indeed, when the driver was afraid I could not manage it, and sometimes I was so fevered and worn that I could hardly touch my food. How I used to long for the nice bran mash with nitre in it that Jerry used to give us on Saturday nights in hot weather, that used to cool us down and make us so comfortable. Then we had two nights and a whole day for unbroken rest, and on Monday morning we were as fresh as young horses again; but here, there was no rest, and my driver was just as hard as his master. He had a cruel whip with something so sharp at the end that it sometimes drew blood, and he would even whip me under the belly, and flip the lash out at my head. Indignities like these took the heart out of me terribly, but still I did my best and never hung back; for, as poor Ginger said, it was no use; men are the strongest.

My life was now so utterly wretched, that I wished I might, like Ginger, drop down dead at work, and be out of my misery; and one day my wish very nearly came to pass.

I went on the stand at eight in the morning, and had done a good share of work, when we had to take a fare to the railway. A long train was just expected in, so my driver pulled up at the back of some of the outside cabs, to take the chance of a return fare. It was a very heavy train, and as all the cabs were soon engaged, ours was called for. There was a party of four; a noisy, blustering man with a lady, a little boy, and a little girl, and a great deal of luggage. The lady and the boy got into the cab, and while the man ordered about the luggage, the young girl came and looked at me.

'Papa,' she said, 'I am sure this poor horse cannot take us

and all our luggage so far, he is so weak and worn up. Do look at him.'

'Oh, he's all right, miss,' said my driver. 'He's strong enough.'

The porter, who was pulling about some heavy boxes, suggested to the gentleman, as there was so much luggage, whether he would not take a second cab.

'Can your horse do it, or can't he?' said the blustering man.

'Oh, he can do it all right, sir. Send up the boxes, porter; he could take more than that,' and he helped to haul up a box so heavy that I could feel the springs go down.

'Papa, papa, do take a second cab,' said the young girl in a beseeching tone; 'I am sure we are wrong, I am sure it is very cruel.'

'Nonsense, Grace, get in at once, and don't make all this fuss; a pretty thing it would be if a man of business had to examine every cab-horse before he hired it—the man knows his own business, of course. There, get in and hold your tongue!'

My gentle friend had to obey; and box after box was dragged up and lodged on the top of the cab, or settled by the side of the driver. At last all was ready, and with his usual jerk at the rein, and slash of the whip, he drove out of the station.

The load was very heavy, and I had had neither food nor rest since the morning; but I did my best, as I always had done, in spite of cruelty and injustice.

I got along fairly till we came to Ludgate Hill, but there the heavy load and my own exhaustion were too much. I was struggling to keep on, goaded by constant chucks of the rein and use of the whip, when, in a single moment—I cannot tell how—my feet flipped from under me, and I fell heavily to the ground on my side; the suddenness and the force with which I fell seemed to beat all the breath out of my body. I lay perfectly still; indeed, I had no power to move, and I thought now I was going to die. I heard a sort of confusion round me, loud angry voices, and the getting down of the luggage, but it was all like a dream. I though I heard that sweet pitiful voice saying, 'Oh, that poor horse! It is all our fault.' Someone came and loosened the throat strap of my bridle, and undid the traces which kept the collar so tight upon me. Someone said, 'He's dead, he'll never get up again.' Then I could hear a policeman giving orders, but I did not even open my eyes, I could only draw a grasping breath now and then. Some cold water was thrown over my head, and some cordial was poured into my mouth, and something was covered over me. I cannot tell how long I lay there, but I found my life coming back, and a kind-voiced man was patting me and encouraging me to rise. After some more cordial had been given me, and after one or two attempts, I staggered to my feet, and was gently led to some stables close by. Here I was put into a well-littered stall, and some warm gruel was brought to me, which I drank thankfully.

In the evening I was sufficiently recovered to be led back to Skinner's stables, where I think they did the best for me they could. In the morning Skinner came with a farrier to look at me. He examined me very closely, and said:

'This is a case of overwork more than disease, and if you could give him a run off for six months, he would be able to work again; but now there is not an ounce of strength in him.'

'Then he must just go to the dogs,' said Skinner; 'I have no meadows to nurse sick horses in—he might get well or he might not; that sort of thing don't suit my business, my plan is to work 'em as long as they'll go, and then sell 'em for what they'll fetch, at the knacker's or elsewhere.'

'If he was broken-winded,' said the farrier, 'you had better have him killed out of hand, but he is not. There is a sale of horses coming off in about ten days; if you rest him and feed him up, he may pick up, and you may get more than his skin is worth, at any rate.'

Upon this advice, Skinner, rather unwillingly, I think, gave orders that I should be well fed and cared for, and the stable man, happily for me, carried out the orders with a much better will than his master had in giving them. Ten days of perfect rest, plenty of good oats, hay, bran mashes, with boiled linseed mixed in them, did more to get my condition than anything else could have done; those linseed mashes were delicious, and I began to think, after all, it might be better to live than go to the dogs. When the twelfth day after the accident came, I was taken to the sale, a few miles out of London. I felt that any change from my present place must be an improvement, so I held up my head, and hoped for the best.

*　　*　　*

At this sale, of course, I found myself in company with the old broken-down horses—some lame, some broken-winded, some old, and some that I am sure it would have been merciful to shoot.

The buyers and sellers too, many of them, looked not much better off than the poor beasts they were bargaining about. There were poor old men, trying to get a horse or pony for a few pounds, that might drag about some little wood or coal cart. There were poor men trying to sell a worn-out beast for two or three pounds, rather than have the greater loss of killing him. Some of them looked as if poverty and hard times had hardened them all over; but there were others that I would have willingly used the last of my strength in serving; poor and shabby, but kind and human, with voices that I could trust. There was one tottering old man that took a great fancy to me, and I to him, but I was not strong enough—it was an anxious time! Coming from the better part of the fair, I noticed a man who looked like a gentleman farmer, with a young boy by his side; he had a broad back and round shoulders, a kind, ruddy face, and he wore a broad-brimmed hat. When he came up to me and my companions, he stood still, and gave a pitiful look round upon us. I saw his eye rest on me; I had still a good mane and tail, which did something for my appearance. I pricked my ears and looked at him.

'There's a horse, Willie, that has known better days.'

'Poor old fellow!' said the boy. 'Do you think, grandpapa, he was ever a carriage horse?'

'Oh yes, my boy,' said the farmer, coming closer. 'He might have been anything when he was young; look at his nostrils and his ears, the shape of his neck and shoulder; there's a deal of breeding about that horse.' He put out his hand and gave me a kind pat on the neck. I put out my nose in answer to his kindness; the boy stroked my face.

'Poor old fellow! See, grandpapa, how well he understands kindness. Could not you buy him and make him young again, as you did with Ladybird?'

'My dear boy, I can't make all old horses young; besides, Ladybird was not so very old, as she was run down and badly used.'

'Well, grandpapa, I don't believe that this one is old; look at

his main and tail. I wish you would look into his mouth, and then you could tell; though he is so very thin, his eyes are not sunk like some old horses'.'

The old gentleman laughed. 'Bless the boy! He is as horsey as his old grandfather.'

'But do look at his mouth, grandpapa, and ask the price; I am sure he would grow young in our meadows.'

The man who had brought me for sale now put in his word.

'The young gentleman's a real knowing one, sir: now the fact is, this 'ere hoss is just pulled down with overwork in the cabs; he's not an old one, and I heerd as how the vetenary should say, that a six months' run off would set him right up, being as how his wind was not broken. I've had the tending of him these ten days past, and a gratefuller, pleasanter animal I never met with, and 'twould be worth a gentleman's while to give a five-pound note for him, and let him have a chance. I'll be bound he'd be worth twenty pounds next spring.'

The old gentleman laughed, and the little boy looked up eagerly.

'Oh! grandpapa, did you not say the colt sold for five pounds more than you expected? You would not be poorer if you did buy this one.'

The farmer slowly felt my legs, which were much swelled and strained; then he looked at my mouth—'Thirteen or fourteen, I should say; just trot him out, will you?'

I arched my poor thin neck, raised my tail a little, and threw out my legs as well as I could, for they were very stiff.

'What is the lowest you will take for him?' said the farmer as I came back.

'Five pounds, sir; that was the lowest price my master set.'

''Tis a speculation,' said the old gentleman, shaking his head, but at the same time slowly drawing out his purse—'quite a speculation! Have you any more business here?' he said, counting the sovereigns into his hand.

'No sir. I can take him for you to the inn, if you please.'

'Do so. I am now going there.'

They walked forward, and I was led behind. The boy could hardly control his delight, and the old gentleman seemed to enjoy his pleasure. I had a good feed at the inn, and was then gently ridden home by a servant of my new master's, and turned into a large meadow with a shed in one corner of it.

Mr Thoroughgood, for that was the name of my benefactor, gave orders that I should have hay and oats every night and morning, and the run of the meadow during the day, and 'you, Willie,' said he, 'must take the oversight of him; I give him in charge to you.'

The boy was proud of his charge, and undertook it in all seriousness. There was not a day when he did not pay me a visit; sometimes picking me out from amongst the other horses and giving me a bit of carrot, or something good, or sometimes standing by me whilst I ate my oats. He always came with kind words and caresses, and of course I grew very fond of him. He called me Old Crony, as I used to come to him in the field and follow him about. Sometimes he brought his grandfather, who always looked closely at my legs:

'This is our point, Willie,' he would say; 'but he is improving so steadily that I think we shall see a change for the better in the spring.'

The perfect rest, the good food, the soft turf, and gentle exercise soon began to tell on my condition and my spirits. I had a good constitution from my mother, and I was never strained when I was young, so that I had a better chance than many horses who have been worked before they came to their strength. During the winter my legs improved so much, that I began to feel quite young again. The spring came round, and one day in March Mr Thoroughgood determined that he would try me in the phaeton. I was well pleased, and he and Willie drove me a few miles. My legs were not stiff now, and I did the work with perfect ease.

'He's growing young, Willie; we must give him a little gentle work now, and by midsummer he will be as good as Ladybird: he has a beautiful mouth, and good paces; they can't be better.

'Oh, grandpapa, how glad I am that you bought him!'

'So am I, my boy, but he has to thank you more than me; we must now be looking for a quiet, genteel place for him, where he will be valued.'

*　　*　　*

One day during this summer, the groom cleaned and dressed me with such extraordinary care, that I thought some new change must be at hand; he trimmed my fetlocks and legs, passed the tarbrush over my hoofs, and even parted my forelock. I think the harness had an extra polish. Willie seemed half anxious, half merry, as he got into the chaise with his grandfather.

'If the ladies take to him,' said the old gentleman, 'they'll be suited, and he'll be suited: we can but try.'

At the distance of a mile or two from the village, we came to a pretty, low house, with a lawn and shrubbery at the front and a drive up to the door. Willie rang the bell, and asked if Miss Blomefield or Miss Ellen was at home. Yes, they were. So, whilst Willie stayed with me, Mr Thoroughgood went into the house. In about ten minutes he returned, followed by three ladies; one tall, pale lady, wrapped in a white shawl, leaned on a younger, with dark eyes and a merry face; the other, a very stately-looking person, was Miss Blomefield. They all came and looked at me and asked questions. The younger lady—that was Miss Ellen—took to me very much; she said she was sure she should like me, I had such a good face. The tall, pale lady said that she should always be nervous in riding behind a horse that had once been down, as I might come down again, and if I did, she should never get over the fright.

'You see, ladies,' said Mr Thoroughgood, 'many first-rate horses have had their knees broken through the carelessness of their drivers, without any fault of their own, and from what I see of this horse, I should say that is his case; but of course I do not wish to influence you. If you incline, you can have him on trial, and then your coachman will see what he thinks of him.'

'You have always been such a good adviser to us about our horses,' said the stately lady, 'that your recommendation would go a long way with me, and if my sister Lavinia sees no objection, we will accept your offer of a trial, with thanks.'

It was then arranged that I should be sent for the next day.

In the morning a smart-looking young man came for me. At first, he looked pleased, but when he saw my knees, he said in a disappointed voice:

'I didn't think, sir, you would have recommended my ladies a blemished horse like that.'

' "Handsome is—that handsome does," ' said my master; 'you are only taking him on trial, and I am sure you will do fairly by him, young man, and if he is not as safe as any horse you ever drove, send him back.'

I was led home, placed in a comfortable stable, fed, and left to myself. The next day, when my groom was cleaning my face, he said:

'That is just like the star that Black Beauty had, he is much the same height too. I wonder where he is now.'

A little farther on, he came to the place in my neck where I was bled, and where a little knot was left in the skin. He almost started, and began to look me over carefully, talking to himself.

'White star in the forehead, one white foot on the off side, this little knot just in that place.' Then, looking at the middle of my back—'and as I am alive, there is that little patch of white hair that John used to call "Beauty's threepenny bit". It *must* be Black Beauty! Why, Beauty! Beauty! Do you know me? Little Joe Green, that almost killed you?' And he began patting and patting me as if he was quite overjoyed.

I could not say that I remembered him, for now he was a fine grown young fellow, with black whiskers and a man's voice, but I was sure he knew me, and that he was Joe Green, and I was very glad. I put my nose up to him, and tried to say we were friends. I never saw a man so pleased.

'Give you a fair trial! I should think so indeed! I wonder who the rascal was that broke your knees, my old Beauty! You must have been badly served out somewhere. Well, well, it won't be my fault if you haven't good times of it now. I wish John Manly was here to see you.'

In the afternoon I was put into a low Park chair and brought to the door. Miss Ellen was going to try me, and Green went with her. I soon found that she was a good driver, and she seemed pleased with my paces. I heard Joe telling her about me, and that he was sure I was Squire Gordon's old Black Beauty.

When we returned, the other sisters came out to hear how I had behaved myself. She told them what she had just heard, and said:

'I shall certainly write to Mrs Gordon, and tell her that her favourite horse has come to us. How pleased she will be!'

After this I was driven every day for a week or so, and as I appeared to be quite safe, Miss Lavinia at last ventured out in the small close carriage. After this it was quite decided to keep me and call me by my old name of 'Black Beauty'.

I have now lived in this happy place a whole year. Joe is the best and kindest of grooms. My work is easy and pleasant, and I feel my strength and spirits all coming back again. Mr Thoroughgood said to Joe the other day:

'In your place he will last till he is twenty years old—perhaps more.'

Willie always speaks to me when he can, and treats me as his special friend. My ladies have promised that I shall never be sold, and so I have nothing to fear; and here my story ends. My troubles are all over, and I am at home; and often before I am quite awake, I fancy I am still in the orchard at Birtwick, standing with my old friends under the apple trees.